LIBERALISM AND THE NEW EUROPE

Liberalism and the New Europe

Edited by
BOB BRECHER
School of Historical and Critical Studies
University of Brighton

OTAKAR FLEISCHMANN
Faculty of Education
J.E. Purkyně University

Avebury

Aldershot · Brookfield USA · Hong Kong · Singapore · Sydney

© Bob Brecher & O. Fleischmann 1993

All rights reserved. No part of this publication may be reproduced, stored in a retrieval system, or transmitted in any form or by any means, electronic, mechanical, photocopying or otherwise without the prior permission of the publisher.

Published by
Avebury
Ashgate Publishing Limited
Gower House
Croft Road
Aldershot
Hants GU11 3HR
England

Ashgate Publishing Company
Old Post Road
Brookfield
Vermont 05036
USA

British Library Cataloguing in Publication Data

Liberalism in the New Europe. - (Avebury
Series in Philosophy)
    I. Brecher, Robert II. Fleischmann,
    Otakar III. Series
    148

ISBN 1 85628 538 3

Typeset by
Just Your Type
7 Adur Court
Shoreham-by-Sea
West Sussex BN43 6LY

Printed and Bound in Great Britain by
Athenaeum Press Ltd, Newcastle upon Tyne.

Contents

Acknowledgements vii

Preface viii

Introduction 1

1. The shortcomings of liberal rationality: a Kantian suggestion 7
   Carol Jones

2. The liberal individual 23
   Bob Brecher

3. From liberal democracy to democratic liberalism 37
   Richard Bellamy

4. Are we facing the triumph of liberalism and the end of history? 49
   Miroslav Kryl

5. 'They are not tigers' – myth and myopia in the quest for a liberal economic order 59
   Tom Hickey

6. The poverty of affluence? The consumer society, its discontents and its malcontents 89
   Marcus Roberts

7. Liberalism and welfare: the limits of compensation 107
   Phillip Cole

8.	Can liberals be feminists? *Pat FitzGerald*	121
9.	Liberalism on the bolshevik model: the status of women in Lithuania *Alina Zvinkliene*	135
10.	Liberalism, Europe and the environment *Avner de-Shalit*	149
11.	Maoist liberalism? Higher education in contemporary Britain *Jo Halliday*	163
12.	Liberalism after communism: the Czech civil service *Ludek Kolman*	181
Contributors		195

Acknowledgements

The editors and contributors acknowledge with thanks the generous financial support of the undermentioned, who made possible the attendance at the conference which gave rise to this book of, among others, several of their own number:

AGET Language Services, UK;
Collet's, UK;
J. E. Purkyně University, Czech Republic;
Plettac GMBH, Germany; and
The University of Brighton, UK.

Preface

In July 1992 J.E. Purkyně University was pleased to host, as part of its inaugural celebrations, an international conference organized jointly with the University of Brighton, one of an increasing number of ventures between the two institutions. Its theme – the bases and implications of liberalism – was especially timely. For, revisions of Fukuyama's 'end of history' thesis notwithstanding, the assumptions and ideals of at least a certain variety of liberalism have since 1989 set the intellectual and political agenda, and may be expected to continue to do so for some time to come. These were the ideas debated by some seventy conference delegates, among them students as well as established academics, from a dozen countries. The articles collected here arose out of those debates: they represent a range both of evaluations of this development and of specific themes. What they have in common is an analysis which looks beyond the present: a concern with and for the Europe of the future. Whatever its precise shape, and whether or not a liberal – or, indeed, any other – consensus begins to emerge in Europe, we may at least hope that it will be marked by increasing international and cross-cultural cooperation: of which this volume is perhaps only an early example.

It is in this context that I look forward to what I hope may become a tradition of exchange and joint work between Brighton and Ústí.

Jan Kopka
Rector
J.E. Purkyně University
Ústí nad Labem

Introduction

Whether or not the course of events which culminated in the downfall of the variously bankrupt regimes of central and eastern Europe in 1989 was inevitable, as some of the contributors to this book claim, the production of the book as a result was fortuitous. Perhaps that is why the former is part of history, but the latter not. However that may be, the editors first met early in 1990 as a result of one happening to be a colleague of the other's cousin. A year later our two editors met again – not surprisingly, perhaps, over several pints of excellent beer – and, as the company turned to more serious conversation, we started to recognize, despite our academic, intellectual and political differences, a common interest. One of us, beginning to recover from a totalitarian past, saw the liberalization of the then Czechoslovakia in an unashamedly rosy light; the other's picture, while perhaps not hopelessly pessimistic, was nevertheless a dark, though reddish, grey. So started a long – though hardly dry – debate about the delights and horrors of 'the triumph of liberalism'; and as our nerve increased in proportion to our consumption, so a conference was proposed, for the ethical, political and economic issues were too important to limit to that particular setting. A year later, then, in July 1992, about seventy people from all over, and beyond, Europe, and from a wide variety of backgrounds, met in Ústí to continue that debate at a conference which was the first of its sort in (the then) Czechoslovakia. What would have been unthinkable three years earlier – free-ranging discussions and disagreements across political divides, encompassing more questions than answers and involving students as well as established academics – might perhaps be regarded as liberal practice at its best: critique both hospitable and tolerant, but nonetheless sharp. Not surprisingly, perhaps, the desirability of a wider audience was mooted, and, equally unsurprisingly, in circumstances not unlike those of a year previously. This book is the result.

Its theme is the nature of the liberalism which is said to have triumphed;

and at least a partial evaluation of it, an evaluation which, it must be said, is largely pessimistic. Since its concern is with the practice of liberalism as much as with its theoretical foundations, it is multidisciplinary, and includes contributions from economics, history, management and sociology as well as philosophy; and since its aim is to discuss issues which cannot but concern everyone – justice, freedom, the relation of the individual to society and the interaction between ideology and practice – they are written at least with the intention that they should be accessible across and beyond such specialisms.

The first two articles deal with central theoretical issues about liberalism, namely its understanding and use of rationality and its conception of the individual; there follow three which, from their different perspectives, challenge modish claims about its alleged triumph; and the remaining seven focus on specific areas of liberalism's practice and/or effect in relation to issues which are current across Europe – consumerism, welfare, feminism and the position of women, the environment, higher education and the experience of change and transition.

Carol Jones' article on liberal rationality asks whether or not the common feminist and postmodernist critiques of liberal, or Enlightenment, reason as being far from impartial are justified. Feminists are right to insist that it often fails in its aspirations to neutrality, she argues: but those who attribute such failure to Enlightenment reason itself may well be mistaken. For Kant's claims about 'formal' reason at least suggest that Enlightenment reason need not fail, after all, to be disinterested – just because it is empty of any particular content. Bob Brecher, in 'The Liberal Individual', argues that the atomic individual which is the bedrock of liberal thinking is far from an empty construct: rather, liberal thinkers from Hobbes onwards have assumed, and whether or not this has been explicitly recognized, that human beings are fundamentally 'wanting things'. That conception of our identity – as in an important sense consisting in our desires – crucially, and inescapably, informs the liberal tradition.

Richard Bellamy's contribution distinguishes democratic liberalism from liberal democracy, to the detriment of the latter. For what Fukuyama takes as a triumph is actually the dead end of ethical liberalism and its civic humanist foundations. The Absolute Justice to which such liberalism aspires needs to be replaced by a more Nietzschean understanding – in which conflict rather than consensus is central – and, harking back to classical republicanism, with an emphasis on equitability in political structures, which are today characterized by particularist pluralism. Miroslav Kryl offers, like Bellamy, a sceptical view of liberalism's alleged triumph, focussing on Václav Bělohradský's critique of Fukuyama as the purveyor of the very western intellectual tradition whose end his own thesis proclaims. For, Bělohradský argues, the end of history in fact betokens only an end of the History of the western tradition; with that, it heralds the uncertainties, intellectual as well as political, of postmodern times. Kryl's own scepticism, however, extends to Bělohradský as well as Fukuyama. Tom Hickey's following article, adapted from his Plenary Address, seeks to demolish economic liberalism's pretensions to coherence as well as to any sort of victory: the free market trumpeted across Europe as the salvation of the East is failing to deliver the goods even in the West. Seeking to expose the central myths on which it is based, Hickey argues that liberal economics has brought, and will continue to bring, only decline; that it does not at all constitute the objective science which its supporters claim it to be; and that the experience of Stalinism – that is, of a version of capitalism itself – is not to be confused or conflated with any sort of socialism. This thus remains as an alternative.

Marcus Roberts' concern is to puncture yet another myth, that of 'consumer sovereignty': but, he argues, many of the standard objections to consumerism fail, since it will not do merely to assume that increased consumption must be less satisfying than the toil necessary to make it possible. In particular, Gerry Cohen underestimates the lures of private consumption, wrongly conflating 'work' with 'toil': if consumerism is to be put in its proper place, a more subtle and far less 'purist' critique will be required. Citing the notion of compensation as the means whereby liberalism seeks to instantiate its theoretical commitment to the equal moral worth of people, Phillip Cole argues in 'Liberalism and welfare' that its theoretical inadequacies – in all its extant versions – let alone the shortcomings of actual policies based upon it, are insurmountable. For liberalism cannot recognize that the exclusion of individuals from active participation in the market is a structural weakness, rather than some sort of failing on the part of the individuals concerned. What is needed, therefore, is to replace that structure, rather than relying on compensation to ameliorate its effects. Pat FitzGerald's concerns are also with the internal contradictions of liberalism: but this time in relation to feminism. Her article seeks to demonstrate how liberalism and feminism must be antithetical. To act in the real world on any feminist agenda, she argues, demands illiberal policies; while liberalism's necessary individualism precludes any possible answer to the question of the origins of the oppression of women; any understanding of women as a class; or any questioning of its intellectual assumptions as patriarchal. The very idea of a liberal feminist is thus a contradiction. Examining the roots of Lithuania's liberal policies in its immediate communist past, Alina Zvinkliene argues that practices and institutions such as abortion, contraception and the family – which affect women in particular – run deeper than either liberalism or communism. Emphasizing the ambiguities of 'liberalism' as understood in the west and in Lithuania, together with the apparent paradox of an alliance about the rôle of women between a conservative traditionalism and the soviet tradition, she again raises the issue of the true nature of Stalinism – part of the legacy of which, she insists, is the current imposition of an economic 'liberalism on the bolshevik model', from which women especially have nothing to gain. In 'Liberalism, Europe and the environment', Avner de-Shalit urges that what he terms the European, as opposed to the strictly non-interventionist American, tradition of liberalism – to be found in the works of Hobhouse, de Ruggiero and others – affords a far more amenable framework for the resolution of environmental concerns. For such concerns require some 'democratically agreed notion of the good', something which much contemporary liberalism eschews, but which, on the contrary, it actually requires – and which the environmental crisis urgently demands. Understood in this way, liberalism has much to offer. Jo Halliday's 'Maoist liberalism' asks how it is that the traditional liberal ideals of higher education should so readily have been subverted in Britain. Citing 'vocationalism' as a pragmatic means of achieving ideological aims, she locates the problem as lying in liberalism's 'neutrality', inasmuch as this permits an educational system which is inevitably elitist – the Left's opposition to which the Right has used to gain control of higher education as a vehicle for wider, ideological, policies. Rather as in the case of economic liberalism in Lithuania, so the latter's methods may best be understood as a quasi-Maoist 'cultural revolution'. Ludek Kolman, on the contrary, using aspects of the Czech civil service as a case-study, proposes that the idea of myth is the key to understanding the limitations of liberalization and that liberalism's conception of reason and of its function might dispel the myths prevalent in contemporary Czech society. For liberalism, he maintains in 'Liberalism after communism: the Czech Civil Service', is to be distinguished from both communism and other, traditional, social systems as, uniquely, not any variety of myth: its commitment to rational procedure and to 'the facts' is what thus distinguishes it – a view with which we might return to the opening argument of the book.

What unites these disparate contributions then, is a common theme: a concern about liberalism's idea of rationality and its epistemological and ethical foundations, and about its concomitant understanding of human beings and their relations to society. From abstract to concrete examples; from Lithuania, via the Czech Republic, to Britain; from feminism through education, the environment, etc., to liberalism's own self-understanding; and from contributors of widely differing political and philosophical persuasion, a central issue emerges – whether or not a political philosophy based on what people want can succeed.

The translations, where necessary, of articles originally in Czech are by Bob Brecher: bibliographical references, however, have been left in the original.

Our thanks are of course due to all the contributors, not least for working to a very tight schedule: and they are due also to all those others who helped to make the conference on which the book is based the success that it was – not least Karel Klimeš and Stanislav Navrátil, who helped organize it; Ilona Hofbauerová and the students of the English Department at J.E. Purkyně University who helped run it and whose hospitality and real concern for all the delegates made the five days such a pleasure; and Irmgard Kolinská and her staff for their superb interpreting. Finally, we offer sincere thanks to Pat FitzGerald and Marcus Roberts, without whose editorial assistance, advice and encouragement the unclarities and inadequacies which doubtless remain would have been far greater; and, again to Pat FitzGerald, for preparing a camera-ready copy with an efficiency, speed and good humour which can only be described as remarkable.

Bob Brecher, Brighton
and
Otakar Fleischmann, Ústí nad Labem
August 1993

1 The shortcomings of liberal rationality: A Kantian suggestion

Carol Jones

Critics of liberalism, identifying the ideological interests underlying the liberal conception of rationality, commonly proceed to the rejection tout court of such a rationality, or deny the neutrality which would allow its special rôle in the assessment of truth claims. Opponents of postmodernism, on the other hand, reluctant to take the former view, are increasingly inclined to the latter, in the light of arguments which reveal the context-dependency of this putatively 'abstract' faculty. I shall argue here that the liberal ideal of rationality is indeed ideologically saturated, but that to identify the interests underlying it need not lead to an abandonment of rationality: rather it reveals an incoherence within liberalism. For the liberal view of human nature, I shall demonstrate, is quite at odds with its ideology of the autonomous, rational agent; and the notions of both rationality and of the self which bolster that ideology should not be confused with the Enlightenment understanding of those concepts. Liberalism and its critics alike, in conflating what I take to be distinct uses of reason and rationality, illegitimately reduce the concept of reason to a single application which is belied by the complexity of the very Enlightenment – and in particular Kantian – treatment of reason in which its roots are to be found. The problem is, I shall argue, that liberalism's values – the source of its 'abstract rationality' – are incommensurable with its solipsistic individualism.

I

What is it about rationality, then, that seems to tie it to liberalism and its interests? The liberal view of human nature is supposedly dependent on a notion of the unified self as a rational choosing agent; a self which, by virtue of its freedom from a bodily, causally determined nature, transcends the biological, material and cultural specificities which determine our animal instincts and culturally determined behaviour. Just as the Cartesian compromise to solve the inconsistencies engendered by, on the one hand, the newly scientific view of nature which made human beings subject to causal laws, and, on the other, the belief in the immortality of uniquely created souls, was a mind/body dualism; so liberalism's separation of public and private spheres was able to feed off this metaphysical solution. Thus the labourer could be exploited as a machine-body from Monday to Saturday and on Sundays take his soul to church. The affiliation, then, between a view of rationality as an abstract faculty which empowers man with tools which transcend nature, and the liberal separation of private and public spheres which values that faculty as distinctly human, cultural and mental, seems obvious. Furthermore, with the freedom thus gained come responsibility and opportunity. The agent has a responsibility to develop the faculty for rationality which allows him to transcend his emotions, his senses, and the **opportunity** to alter his merely contingent position in the meritocracy.

This view, then – that rationality is what allows us freedom **from our animal nature**, and the capacity to transcend our social position – is challenged on the grounds that it ignores the function that rationality plays in serving the interests of privileged groups and classes, thus disguising the systematic inequality of opportunity operating in a patriarchal, class society: factors which delimit the potential of each individual within society to develop that rationality to an equal degree. Real human beings, it is objected (by Alison Jaggar, 1988, for example) are not abstract individuals with an identical facility to reason: they are embodied; culturally and historically embedded; and have different histories, capacities, class interests, wants and needs. This 'universal' capacity to reason is no social leveller. The abstraction of the mental from the material both ignores the material conditions of our mental life and places responsibility at an individual level for developing the rational side of the will. On this account those engaged in non-rational pursuits – in the private sphere of domesticity and reproduction, as opposed to the cultural domain of mental work – are bound to be less valued and considered less ideally human, and will be accorded fewer rewards and privileges in consequence.

That those members of society (women in particular) who, in reality, do not engage in those public, abstractly rational pursuits are **manual** as opposed to **mental**, the producers rather than the owners of the means of production, is – for the liberal – a consequence of an inferior rationality or an inadequate education, rather than an effect of the inequality of power and advantage which structures a capitalist market economy. Liberal ideology claims that removable inequalities and a neutrally administered system of formal justice ensure the regulation of a social contract which allows identical rights and opportunities to competing individuals: no-one is barred from the market on grounds of sex, class, race or any accident of birth; and by the same token, no special privileges are accorded them on such accounts. Some liberals – particularly feminist liberals – will argue that positive discrimination must be demanded as a means of bringing competitors to a position from which they are able to remove a handicap of birth – their gender for example. But if such allowances are to be made they comprise a merely temporary and tactical intervention in order to correct a former bias: once equality is achieved, we're on our own.

Critics of the use of reason in liberal ideology, then, identify it as normative. Such privileging of the abstract smacks of a Platonic idealization of forms, of 'Ideas' soaring – independently of matter – above the confusion of the senses, a view of abstract reason which allows those with most access to its use to dictate 'The Truth' to those more bound by their material embodiment. The liberal valorization of abstract reason initially seems consistent with the Enlightenment ideals of a gradual but inexorable progress towards a goal of truth, guided by the light of a unifying principle of reason; a clear light which allows us to cut away the heterogeneity and confusion of irrationality, prejudice, mysticism, error and confusion, revealing the path of right, truth and the good. Kant's disavowal of such quasi-Platonic formalism has nonetheless been interpreted by some as an attempt to free reason from the matter which would muddy the pure form of an a priori faculty. Although he tied transcendental ideas of reason to the **search** for the unconditioned, denying that ideas of reason were 'the archetype of all copies in the field of appearance' (Kant, 1929, B 596), the transcendental application of reason was, nevertheless, the method by which we might attempt to **exceed** the bounds of sense.

II

Reason is embodied, protest its critics: the binary oppositions of western philosophy falsely detach the mental from the material; ideas are shaped out of historical conditions and social practices. Reason is neither extricable from the bodies which house it, nor transcendent of the culture which shapes its ends. Ideals of reason as pure, neutral and objective are misplaced or ideologically generated by interests which, in a liberal culture, seek to perpetuate the continuation of the 'free' market by encouraging the myth of a disinterested reason able to arbitrate between competing interests. Reason, some claim, is merely a means to an end, a deductive faculty whose conclusions depend on a covert initial premise which supports the values of the dominant ideology. Thus, in a liberal society, reason is tied instrumentally to an **implicit** notion of the good, 'the continued sustenance of the liberal social and political order', as MacIntyre puts it (1988, p. 345). With the loss of a teleological view of human nature which is the foundation of an Aristotelian ethics (in which 'the good' for human beings is functional, namely to act in accordance with the potential open to us as possessors of rationality) there can now be no universally applicable ends which rationality must pursue, no end inseparable from its means which could be grounded in an essential claim about human nature. For the modern individual, it seems (as J.S. Mill is purported to think) that that, and only that, is good which is perceived as good. [1] Thus, as MacIntyre argues, [2] the notion of rationality as a tool of morality – one which allows us to identify and achieve value in accordance with our purpose – is one which has outlived the culture in which it is now deployed. The rejection of a teleological view of human nature must certainly limit reason's rôle to a negative one: a merely calculative tool for assessing relations and making logical inferences.

MacIntyre argues, furthermore, that detaching the form of that deductive process from the values implicit within the ends is not possible, for means and ends cannot be clearly separated. Not only is reason not neutral with regard to the good: but forms of reasoning themselves are not ahistoric; they have changed with the development of a liberal-individualist culture. The transformation of first person expressions of desire 'into statements of a reason for action, into premises for practical reasoning', results, he argues, in a 'restructuring of thought and action in a way which accords with the procedures of ... liberal individualist politics' (MacIntyre, 1988, pp. 338-9). A heterogeneous range of desired goods, with no objective means of ordering the preferences for those goods beyond the subjective desires of the individual, results in a change in the method by which the reasoner deduces consequences from premises. The modern individual in a pluralist society, faced with an array of available goods and assessing them from a merely subjective standpoint, can clearly apply no rational universal principle to such a dilemma. While for the Aristotelian reasoner, MacIntyre argues, failure to act on the conclusion entailed by the practical syllogism would consist in irrationality, if essentialist and teleological claims about human nature are unavailable, then no such necessity can apply. Failure to act in a consistent manner to achieve an end is not necessarily irrational, but rather is explicable, in a pluralist value system, by individuals changing their minds about the ranking of the many preferences or values in operation: and this, as it were, in mid-syllogism.

How we reason then, as well as what we consider to be rational, is perhaps not a universal matter, and the content of what our rationality tells us to be morally correct is certain to be historically specific. MacIntyre's point is that both the content and the form of rationality have a Hegelian-style historical development: the achievements of the current morality over against past values can only be assessed in relation to the type of society to which they are applicable, and can only be valued in relation to the rejected or transformed values whence they emerged; there is no history-free moment for morality or rationality – they are relative to their culture. The Enlightenment project which presupposed universalizable aims, if not a universalizable content, of morality, lends its claims to objectivity quite illegitimately to a society whose value system is predicated on the celebration of difference and the subjectivity of assessing the individual's good.

Further, and critical, challenges to reason's neutrality come from the rejection of the liberal-humanist notion of the self: the view that the individual is an autonomous agent – whose search for truth involves transcendence of cognitive distortion – is dependent on a conception of the self as a potentially integrated whole which reason alone can command. Again, the Enlightenment ideals of progress towards a potentially perfect moral being seem at first glance to fit nicely with the liberal individual: the autonomous sovereign of his own good, to be defended from the impositions of others and the interference of the state. [3] Liberty, as Mill argued, is the necessary condition of morality: only by allowing individuals to choose their own lives and values can both totalitarian regimes and superstitious impositions be avoided. It is only in the practice of choosing that the capacity to discern the good will be learned, that the highest ends will be set by individuals, ends autonomously chosen through the exercise of rationality. As long as they are deemed to be responsible agents, as long as other persons within the public sphere are unharmed by their actions, individuals are given maximum liberty to develop those faculties of rationality which are implied by the exercise of choice. [4] This conception of the self as author of one's own destiny, in the most favourable position to choose one's own good, has been criticised on grounds of ahistoricity and of class- and sex-blindness. Who is deemed to **be** a subject capable of moral choice has, for one thing, been dependent on other than objective criteria. Women, the mad, the culturally underdeveloped and those deemed racially 'inferior' are among the groups sometimes considered outside the realm of moral agency. For what a 'person' is has never been a question of pure philosophy: rather, it has a history. The notion that the self has an essential core, furthermore, is claimed to be false: the self merely **is** its thoughts, feelings and so on. On Hume's 'bundle of sensations' account it is the flux of impressions which constructs the illusion of permanence and creates the fiction of continuing identity. Thus Nietzsche considered the self to be constructed out of the fear of fragmentation, produced by the 'desire to remain stationary in front of the actual, the factum brutum ...' (Nietzsche, 1969, p. 151): the self is placed against that terrifying chaos which threatens to engulf us, now that the god who used to keep it all in place is dead. The poststructuralist version of this is a **linguistic** mapping onto Hume's empiricism. The misrecognition of self is an illusion of authorship created by the interpellation of language. The development of the modern individual, then, sets up tensions between the anxiety of loss and dispersal, and the desire to remain separate from others in order to retain sovereignty over one's own unique interests.

If this invention may be shown to be the fiction of a bourgeois individualistic modernity, whose ideals (themselves borrowed from an earlier conceptual schema) have been dragged into a postmodern era, then the implications for rationality are plain. Not only is rationality interested and/or plural; not only must we reject any view of rationality as an essential characteristic of human nature which teleologically informs our moral reasoning: but rationality is not even an instrumental calculating faculty operating within a particular paradigm of values and perceived ends. Rather, it merely performs its part in the **illusion** that there is a distinct and integrated self, free to make autonomous judgements about its own experiences, wants and interests.

III

Rationality, then, is either rejected altogether or at any rate relativized on a number of possible counts. I have indicated, however, that the liberal conception of human nature is not actually consistent with its notion of the self as an autonomous rational agent; and further that the ideal of rationality employed in liberal ideology is a simplification of a far richer conception of reason from the eighteenth century. The Enlightenment project was, I have suggested, justified by certain universalistic claims about human beings, despite the denial of any essentialist descriptions of a fixed **content** to anything that might be deemed human nature. Kant, for example, certainly based his categorical ethical imperatives on the presupposition that although causally determined on a phenomenal level, we must act **as if** (a part of) the will were free, and thus that the acknowledgement of this freedom will obligate us to treat others as if they too were moral agents. The modern individual, however, has nothing which attaches its moral imperatives to those of others and hence no **objective** moral imperatives: we have seen that the egoistic, subjective interests perceived by the individual are all that can guide its reasoning. Liberal conceptions of human nature may purport to be based in a view of an integrated self as a rational agent, but for rationality to be other than a culturally relative, discursive device, some **necessary** principle must apply to its application which is not to be observed from an atomistic, empiricist view of human nature. Liberalism is predicated on the Hobbesian notion of the selfish individual competing in a state of natural anarchy against others in a conflictual universe, which necessitates a social contract in order to protect each atom from the others. Consistent with this political atomism is a parallel psychological egoism which behaviourial psychologists such as Skinner – liberalism's inevitable allies – have posited. Judgements, according to this theory, are learned responses to a complex system of reinforcements which reward or punish the behaviour in question: reasons for actions, then, are neither freely chosen nor rationally grounded. The end goal of an individual whose nature is essentially self-interested can only be the elimination of pain and the increase of pleasure. Socially constructed as the majority of the individual's wants and desires may be (and this is conceded by most liberals – hence the stress on education as a means of reforming individual wants to fit the society chosen by its dominant members) the subject nonetheless remains merely a 'wanting thing'. [5]

It seems clear then that rationality, for the liberal, can have only two possible functions. It may be taken to be simply a **process** by which the reasoner achieves self-determined ends, the grounds for which consist solely in the subjective assessment by the individual, qua individual, of his or her own good: reason is substantively detached from those ends and is thus merely instrumental. On this account, reason is ultimately motivated by the passions: for no objective properties attach to reason which would allow it transcendence from the specificity of that individual's particular wants and the cultural determinants which influence them. Alternatively, if a behaviourist explanation of human action is given credence, then rationality must be reducible to a biologically or socially evolved function: for, on this view, rationality is explicable as a set of adaptations to a social equivalent of Darwinian evolutionary change. Adaptive processes, like Adam Smith's 'invisible hand' in the market, select – metaphorically speaking – the fittest social behaviour; just as biologically, evolution 'selects' the fittest organisms for the continuation of the species. No teleological sense need be assumed in this notion of 'continuation' however – the tendency to survive is just the contingent effect of a causal chain. Even when extrapolated to the social sphere, human history is purposeless. For as Richard Rorty, the liberal pragmatist, puts it: 'evolution has no purpose and humanity no nature. So the moral world does not divide into the intrinsically decent and the intrinsically abominable, but rather into the goods of different groups and different epochs ... the enslavement of one human tribe ... by another... is not an intrinsic evil. The latter is a rejected good ...' (Rorty, 1991, p. 4).

The liberal model of the morally free agent, in possession of the 'reality tracking' tools (as Rorty terms them) with which to integrate concepts and reality, to discover universal truths and achieve personal autonomy by a progressive transcendence of inadequate cognitive structures, appears on either account to be mere ideology. Liberalism, a political theory which sees social groups built on the independently existing characteristics of abstract individuals, a view which conceives of the agent's interest in terms of the individual as an isolable entity, permits no conceivably objective criteria on which to judge those interests. The individual, a site of conflicting, competitive desires, whose interests are attached to others only incidentally, and by means of a contractual relationship, has no standard against which to measure the good. Reason cannot, on this sort of account, transcend the subjectivism of the particular contingent desires perceived by the self. Enlightenment ideals persist only as myth: and the totalizing discourses of modernity, postmodernists contend, are no longer tenable even as ideology. For we live now in an era of amorality and the sooner we accept that the fiction of the rational autonomous self which propped up bourgeois morality is an illusion, the better for the satisfaction of those individual desires it will be. Postmodernism's valorization of difference, assertion of the pluralism of desires, rejection of 'political correctness' and notions of false consciousness, all seem the logical inheritors of the liberal conception of self-interested individuals, their competing interests mediated, as in the market, by an invisible hand. For although 'pluralism' at first sight seems opposed to 'individualism', it is of course the pluralism of wants and interests as experienced by individual atoms (or even by the same individual) which are in competition. Postmodernism demonstrates the self-legitimizing character of the liberal ideology of a neutral rationality; unmasks liberalism's utilization of the Enlightenment notion of reason as incoherent; and then rejects the ideology of the autonomous rational self – while yet retaining many of liberalism's values.

I have tried to suggest here that postmodernism rightly unmasks the tendency within liberalism to smuggle in Enlightenment reason as an ideal, while failing to include the accompanying values which went with that view of reason. Justified though I take such a critique of liberalism's understanding and use of reason to be, however, I take issue with the postmodernist rejection of rationality on these grounds alone. For such a rejection is predicated at least in part on a – differently – mistaken understanding of what it is to be a self. One may reject, I think, the notion of the self as an autonomous whole, ontologically prior to the society in which it is situated, and to the language which constitutes it as a subject, while nonetheless retaining a concept of the self which is not a mere illusion. It is crucial here to distinguish the concept of a self from any autonomous liberal individual: for while allowing the post-structuralist insights into the rôle that language plays in constituting the subject, this does not deny the concept of an abiding self – over and above the empirical self – a self which is subject, not object, of thought. In other words, of course, I wish to reinstate Kant's transcendental self. In order that the self be known in relation to something other than itself, Kant claims, a **necessary**, and not merely contingent, relation is required: a relation which must occur in order that my world does not fragment, in order that I can organize the flux of empirical impressions and thoughts under concepts, through a priori categories, in a causally necessary, spatially permanent, temporally continuous framework. This is no psychological device of an imagination seeking to centre identity, to remain stationary in the midst of an undifferentiated flux, but an ontological a priori without which any experience at all would be impossible. The self, Kant suggests, may well be a sort of fiction, but, unlike Hume's, it is a necessary fiction with an **active** rôle in the synthesis of experience; it is not an **effect** of experience which leaves an impression – of a continuing self – in the mind.

Now, Kant considers the self/other relation to be an oppositional one, an atomistic self known **against** an object: thus the boundaries of inner and outer, of self and other, are quite distinct. In this respect, liberal individualism inherited a Newtonian view of an object-centred world composed of ontological atoms, and this conception of the nature of reality is of course historically explicable, both politically and scientifically. But it need not be accepted. Both Kant and Nietzsche, interestingly, seem to take this same – atomistic – starting point, while yet drawing diametrically opposite conclusions (and both quite different from those of liberalism) about morality. Nietzsche, for example, says that when morality reveals what it has 'simply been the means to (then) we discover that the ripest fruit is the *sovereign individual*, like only to himself, liberated again from morality of custom, autonomous and supramoral (for "autonomous" and "moral" are mutually exclusive)' (Nietzsche, 1969, p. 59). Nietzsche, I would contend, is right to note the incommensurability of autonomy and morality, but wrong to draw the conclusion that **morality** is what must be abandoned as 'a social straitjacket'. Kant's 'real' self, by contrast, is not the 'bourgeois fallacy' of the essential self to which Nietzsche takes exception, a being with privileged insight into its own cognitive states, particular interests and subjective desires. Instead, Kant's is a conception of the self as a process, not a substance: a synthesizing faculty which entails that the mind – in making judgments that the manifold of experience which it organizes in accordance with rules is its own – **presupposes** that transcendental continuing self, the self that **must** be thought. If, however, this self/other relation is regarded as being one of interdependence – not opposition – between individuals, then, epistemologically, the self need not cut itself off from that against which it is constructed, as in Kant's own version, but may be seen in a relation of contiguity with the other which is not itself, with no clear boundaries between those selves. Politically, the individual in society exists not first and foremost as an atomistic being, but as an individual in a whole which is greater than the sum of its parts, and which is not in opposition to the individuals within it, but which **is** those individuals. These then are possible only by virtue of there existing a set of social relations within which they are constituted. To demonstrate that the individual's interests are part of a web of social meaning does not imply that the self cannot be individuated from others in any but linguistic terms, or that it is an illusion. [6] Self-consciousness is a feature of human beings which distinguishes us from the ordinary empirical consciousness of other animals, and is what makes us knowing and experiencing animals: for Kant, the capacity to make the judgement that my experiences are my own is one which requires for its possibility that highest principle, the faculty of reason.

This, furthermore, is no mind/body dualism. The capacity to reason is not isolated or abstracted from the social and material conditions of being. The recognition that our own interests are inextricably bound to one another's, that to be a self is dependent on there being other selves like me, is of course dependent on our capacity to distinguish ourselves from others – with their different capacities, histories, gender and so on – in order that those differences may be accommodated and not suppressed. Equality, then, is not about starting with the assumption that we are all equal, or that we all should be equal – as though 'equal' required that we be treated identically, as if we were all white middle-class males for example. Neither does this merely valorize difference, for the recognition that there is a commonality of interests means that we **must** treat our differences as if they were part of an interconnected whole, as if they belonged to other selves who are like us in some essentially universal respect.

IV

If some relationship such as this of the self to society is taken seriously, and extended to more than a merely rhetorical objection to self-interested individualism, then it may be argued that the interests of individuals are discernible in terms of the social good and not reducible to those of 'ontologically prior' individuals. 'Good' thus need not designate merely subjective matters, serving simply as another term for 'want'. Rationality's rôle returns in something like its earlier form, the objective means by which we may judge the interests of society; and this by determining and assessing the grounds for reasons by means of a principle which – by virtue of its formality – must provide a **disinterested** guide to the interests to which it is applied. If rationality is not tied to a liberal atomism which makes ends dependent on personal opinion and internally related motivations, then to charge rationality with being 'merely' instrumental may in fact be a far from perjorative observation.

Now this certainly pushes rationality in the direction of that negative, logical form which may allow it that abstraction from the cultural and empirical specificities in light of which it was charged with being interested. If the relationship between individuals and society takes the form which I have sketched here, however, as opposed to the atomistic liberal model, then such abstraction would not appear necessarily to constitute a problem. It is the case that, like liberalism's conception of rationality as a deductive tool, this conception retains an abstract formalism: but unlike the liberal view of human nature which makes rationality the individual application of a psychological law of thought to a subjectively chosen end, this conception is of an a priori, transcendentally grounded principle without which society would fragment – into liberal atoms! Just as Kant shows that our experience would fragment without the transcendental synthesizing self, so rationality occupies a similarly necessary rôle for the coherence of society. Rationality on this model – as contrasted with that of a Platonic formalism – is not supposed to be abstract in order to **transcend** the empirical, but rather so that its formality may allow us to **make sense** of the empirical, the sensible, in a systematic and objective format. This is certainly problematic: and Kant warned that such a use of pure, general logic must be confined to the form of truth alone; for if the certainty of such a distinction between form and content could not, finally, be maintained, the implications for truth are clear.

My argument, then, does not show rationality to possess that objectivity and universality which would allow it a central rôle in morality. Whether a pure, universal logical form may be established transhistorically is not an argument I can engage in here. This would certainly require to be established for such a claim about rationality's rôle in morality to hold, otherwise logic could always be shown to be in the service of a normative rationality, a faculty which justifies morality *ex post facto*: **this** is the good; **this** is how we justify it; therefore, since we can show the route taken and show that the conclusion follows in a logical sequence from a hidden, value-laden initial premise, it is rational. If rationality is to escape this charge, we must be able to show that its logical form is universal; that the law of non-contradiction is absolute; and that particulars must be placed under universals, in accordance with an a priori principle. We would have to show that all human beings must represent an objective reality in accordance with a pattern which exists, prior to experience, in the mind, as Kant seeks to prove in the *First Critique*. If he is right, if this model is universal, then the principles of practical rationality will be similarly universal.

I am not sure whether Kant's ahistoric universals can in the end be defended. Nonetheless, if **restricted** universals are allowed, we may, as Sabina Lovibond points out, certainly assert that while being 'impressed by the perspectival character of knowledge claims', we may yet 'still see enquiry as necessarily seeking to bring all "perspectives" on reality into communication as the Kantian postulate of a "special interest of reason" in picturing reality as a single unified system does' (Lovibond, 1989, p. 14). Because Kant's metaphor involves an imaginary point – located beyond the limits of possible experience, upon which all lines of rational activity appear to converge – the objections levelled against a transcendent reason which is supposed to be a 'reality tracking' tool, as Rorty complains, is misplaced. 'Closure' can never actually be reached; concepts are not supposed to correspond to a material reality.

This, then, does not impute an absolute content to morality, even of the most general sort, for there must always be particular circumstances in which specific actions may or may not be justifiable, and there have to be ways in which hitherto unconceptualized values may be able to emerge. For practices such as slavery and marital rape, for example, cannot be condemned as immoral until the principles of rationality have identified the recipients of those actions as moral subjects whom it would be inconsistent to treat as property, rather than as persons.

But nevertheless, does this view of rationality not sound a trifle mechanistic and limited? Some objections to such a view of rationality ask questions such as these. How, if rationality is purely formal and analytic, would it be possible ever to create new imaginative possibilities, to expand the bounds of human conceptual schemes, to identify moral atrocities which had been hitherto unidentifiable in the limited conceptual schema available to our predecessors? How would ideological shifts be possible if reason were the calculative test of correctness, analytic and formal, and thus historically static? If all appeals to reason were tried by the same methodological process, how would we be able to change our ideas of what we took to be the good? If we are reasoning about reasoning, where can we find room to loosen the certainties within that reasoning? If analytic philosophy envisages reason as a house-cleaning device, we should presumably have perfected its practice long since and would have something to show for its application, i.e. a nice clean world with no moral error. Curiously, however, it seems that the process of preparing the tools and organizing the cleaning cupboard continues to occupy philosophers long after the identification and scope of the tools had supposedly been made.

Here it seems salient to point to Kant's distinctions between the employment of reason 'in a merely formal, that is, logical manner, wherein it abstracts from all content of knowledge' and reason's capacity for 'a real use, since it contains within itself the source of certain concepts and principles' (Kant, 1929, B 355). Kant calls the former – the pure, logical use of reason – the 'negative touchstone of truth' (ibid., B 84) for it belongs to the 'logic of truth', that is, to the 'Analytic' (ibid., B 170). The transcendental employment of reason, however, is not objectively valid, but 'gives birth to concepts' (ibid., B 355). This is the necessary illusion of reason which provides the natural and inevitable dialectic of pure reason, and thus plays a **constitutive** rôle in the expansion of imaginative possibilities, projecting the imagination beyond the limits of possible experience: it is not, therefore, abstracted from the empirical as is the mere form of thought. The **regulative** application of pure reason, however, can never be dialectical, yet neither is it confined to empirical understanding or logical inference: rather it is a heuristic device which enables us to conceive of the world **as if** the parts were completable, **as**

if there were a ground of our existence beyond experience, a principle which provides a systematic unity to the empirical and logical employment of reason.

I have used the terms 'rationality' and 'reason' more or less interdependently: but it would perhaps be useful to distinguish rationality from reason, to attach the former to a logic of truth; to make a distinction within reason (between pure, practical, dialectical and speculative reason); and to acknowledge the culturally and empirically embedded features of the imaginative use of reason, rather as it was understood in the eighteenth century. I am inclined to think that while freedom and the 'idea' of morality may well be a matter for transcendental reason, the application of morality should nevertheless **not** be seen as anything further than a negative means of eliminating error – a task well suited to an objective, mechanistic faculty – leaving for the necessary **illusion** of reason the more exciting rôle of forcing the mind to attempt to exceed the bounds of the possible to which the logical principles of rationality confines our **knowledge**. Together, these expand dialectically the conceptually possible content to which the **principles** of rationality must apply, and thereby prevent the conceit of pure, dialectical reason from straying into the field of empirically possible knowledge. Liberalism has fashioned 'rationality' after its atomistic conception of the rational agent; it is the latter which we should reject; and this might clear the way for renewed distinctions and a more positive re-evaluation of rationality's 'negative' rôle.

Notes

1. Mill actually said that 'the sole evidence it is possible to produce that anything is desirable is that people do actually desire it' (Mill, 1973, p. 438), a view which does not, I think, identify the good with the individual's wants; nonetheless, it is generally a characteristic of liberal thinking.
2. MacIntyre (1981) notes too the shift in theological attitudes to reason in the eighteenth century which ceased to envisage reason's capacity to supply comprehension of man's true end; the power of reason was now conceptualized as having been **destroyed** by the fall of man.
3. One might, of course, consider Kant to be asking questions about how it is that the human being is **not** rational, in contrast to the postulation of what a perfectly rational being (God) would be like. Rather than seeing how it is that we **become** rational, then, Kant demonstrates how it is that we are not rational **as against** that idea of complete rationality; and this is an altogether different approach from that progressive teleological advance generally considered to constitute the Enlightenment project.

4. Mill's view is perhaps not typical of liberals, associating as it does the **practice** of rationality with the **setting** of ends: his individualism nonetheless debars his interesting conception of rationality from the necessary objectivity which is a prerequisite of a disinterested neutrality.
5. To use Bob Brecher's term: see 'The Liberal Individual'.
6. On the subject of webs: Bataille's metaphor for the transcendental self as a sort of spider, spinning a web around itself which subsequently dissolves, is particularly fruitful, and very different from Nietzsche's 'self', a fly trapped in the fly bottle of language and unable to escape the imprisonment of grammar.

References

Grimshaw, J. (1986), *Feminist Philosophers,* Wheatsheaf, Brighton.
Jaggar, A. (1983), *Feminist Politics and Human Nature*, Rowman & Littlefield, New Jersey.
Kant, I. (1929), *Critique of Pure Reason*, Kemp Smith, Norman (trans.), Macmillan, London.
Lovibond, S. (1989), 'Feminism and Postmodernism', *New Left Review,* 178, pp. 5–28.
MacIntyre, A. (1981), *After Virtue*, Duckworth, London.
MacIntyre, A. (1988), *Whose Justice? Which Rationality?*, Duckworth, London.
Mill, J.S. (1929), *On Liberty*, Watts & Co., London.
Mill, J.S. (1973), *Utilitarianism* in *The Utilitarians*, Anchor Books, London.
Nietzsche, F. (1969), *On The Genealogy of Morals*, Kaufmann, Walter (trans.), Random House, New York.
Rorty, R. (1991), 'Feminism and Pragmatism', *Radical Philosophy*, 59, pp. 3–14.

2 The liberal individual

Bob Brecher

If, as Hume put it, 'reason is, and ought only to be, the slave of the passions' (1969, p. 462), then the answer Socrates gave to Thrasymachus (Plato, 1955, pp. 64–99 [bks. I and II, 337–367]), the figure who haunts western philosophy with his questions about why he should not simply do whatever he can get away with, remains unconvincing. For

> 'tis evident our passions, volitions, and actions, are not susceptible of any (such) agreement or disagreement; being original facts and realities, compleat in themselves, and implying no reference to other passions, volitions, and actions. 'Tis impossible, therefore, they can be pronounced either true or false, and be either contrary or conformable to reason. (Hume, op. cit., p. 510)

The fundamental irrationality of unjust or purely self-interested behaviour may constitute an accurate description of it: but not a moral judgement upon it. But if this dismissal of morality is unacceptable, and few think it is not, apart from philosophers of a particular hue and undergraduates imbued with the cynicism of the day, then what is there to say to Thrasymachus? The answer generally given, or at least generally implied in however roundabout a fashion, is that he must be shown to be mistaken about the nature, or character, or direction of what he **wants**: that is to say, he would not really want to behave unjustly if he thought about it harder, if he considered what he wanted in the context of his longer-term interests, the social framework necessary for the realization of any wants at all, and so on. But if after all he did still want to behave unjustly, then that would be that. Hume's word is the last. Hence the concern, from neo-Aristotelians to utilitarians, to ground morality either in what people actually want, or in what they would 'really' want if they thought about it or if others did so on their behalf. Wants, it has been assumed, must have a central rôle in morality.

It is Aristotle who – despite his teleological and functional approach to morality – nevertheless lays the foundations for the subsequent stress on wants, with his insistence that

> the origin of action – its efficient, not its final cause – is choice, and that of choice is desire and reasoning with a view to an end ... **Intellect itself, however, moves nothing**, but only the intellect which aims at an end and is practical ... for good action is an end, and desire aims at this. (1984, pp. 1798–9, my emphasis)

It is this view of rationality's impotence in respect of the will, a position well summarized by Stuart Hampshire as the assumption 'that my answer to the question "Why are you doing that?" **must** be of the form "I want so-and-so and I calculate that so-and-so"' (Hampshire, 1982, p. 166), that lies at the root of the tradition with which I am concerned. Whether or not Aristotle was right – whether, for example, reason can directly 'move' the will; or whether it can do so, if at all, only indirectly, via wants or desires; or whether this is even the right conceptual framework within which to think about the notion of rational action – is another matter. My purpose with regard to that question is here merely exploratory, insofar as I aim simply to suggest how wants have come, within the liberal tradition, to establish a dictatorship over morality; and to indicate something of what is at stake as a result. Hume, characteristically, and although hardly an obvious ally of Aristotle, goes straight to this point, which he recognizes as fundamental for the empiricist enterprise as a whole, and one which had underlain earlier locations of desire as the root of morality. The reason why 'reason is, and ought only to be, the slave of the passions' is this:

> ... reason alone can never be a motive to any action of the will ... The understanding exerts itself after two different ways, as it judges from demonstration or probability ... I believe it scarce will be asserted, that the first species of reasoning alone is ever the cause of any action. As its proper province is the world of ideas, and as the will always places us in the realm of realities, demonstration and volition seem, upon that account, to be totally remov'd, from each other ... But 'tis evident in this case (the second, concerning probability) that the impulse ('to discover the relation of cause and effect') arises not from reason, but is only directed by it. (Hume, 1969, pp. 460–1)

All of this, I think, is relatively well-known, even if relatively rarely the focus of explicit attention. What receives even less attention, partly because it is overlaid by the sheer scale of the Aristotle–Hume view of the relation of reason to action, is the (partly resultant, partly independent) epistemological role of wants in the empiricist, and thus, liberal,

construction and constitution of the individual: a rational being the liberal individual may be, but nevertheless a rational being crucially constituted by its wants. Any possible challenge to the Aristotle–Hume view of the impotence of reason with respect to action is ruled out by this view of the individual rational agent, a view which acts as a sort of protective 'outer fence' for the former. Empiricism's 'individual' being what it is, the Aristotle–Hume view is just assumed to be obvious.

I

The rise of empiricism saw the assumption that wants are central to morality firmly entrenched. Thus Hobbes:

> But whatsoever is the object of any man's Appetite or Desire; that is it, which he for his part calleth *Good*: And the object of his Hate, and Aversion, *Evill*. (1968, p. 264) [1]

Or, to go on to Locke:

> Things then are Good or Evil, only in reference to Pleasure or Pain. That we call *Good*, which *is apt to cause or increase Pleasure, or diminish Pain in us* ... Pleasure and Pain, and that which causes them, Good and Evil, are the hinges on which our *Passions* turn ... (1979, p. 229) [2]

Mill of course continued the tradition of Hobbes, Locke and Hume. For all his differences with Bentham, he grounded his utilitarianism in a similar assumption that it is what people desire which must be the basis of a moral theory and practice:

> pleasure, and freedom from pain, are the only things desirable as ends (1962, p. 257) ... [and, since] ... the sole evidence it is possible to produce that anything is desirable, is that people do actually desire it ... No reason can be given why the general happiness is desirable, except that each person, so far as he believes it to be attainable, desires his own happiness. (ibid., p. 288) [3]

Rawls is perhaps the pre-eminent theoretician of contemporary liberalism. Here is the foundation of his emphasis on primary goods as the object of discussion in his 'original position':

> ... given human nature, wanting them is part of being rational ... [so that] By assuming certain general desires, such as the desire for primary social goods, and by taking as a basis the agreements that

would be made in a suitably defined situation, we can achieve the requisite independence from existing circumstances. (1972, pp. 262–3)

I shall close this brief historical foray by drawing attention to an especially insidious outcome of the conviction that morality must be founded in people's wants, namely the abandonment of rationality under pressure of the latter. Thus, for example, Philippa Foot, a sensitive critic of the various mid-century versions of empiricist (mis-)understandings of morality, writes during the course of reflecting on her work that:

... It is not that I have given up thinking that there is a close connexion between the two, but that I no longer have to say that justice and advantage coincide, because I no longer think that each man, [sic] whatever his desires and whatever his situation, necessarily has reason to be just. (1978, p. xiv) [4]

Thrasymachus wins.

Now this whole way of thinking is in my view an error, the consequences of which have ramifications across the entire spectrum of moral and political philosophy, an error deeply rooted in the history of (at least) western empiricism from its Hobbesian to its postmodern versions. But it is not my intention here to pursue the moral arguments themselves. Rather, I aim to ask a question about the ubiquity and apparently commonsensical status of the view adumbrated above, a question about its origins which, I shall argue, both exposes its intellectual roots and constitutes grounds for at the very least re-examining the liberal conception of the individual which informs, and indeed necessitates, it. How is it, then, that what an individual wants should have come to occupy a central position in western moral and political philosophy, and, all too obviously, in so much of our everyday lives now that objections to the conceptual framework of the market seem at best naive, at worst unacceptably 'socialist'? Or, what is the same question at a higher level of generality, how does liberalism arise, as though by some natural necessity, out of an empiricist epistemology?

II

My suggestion is that it is the 'individual' of the empirio-liberal tradition which supplies the connection; and that its crucial feature is that it requires the individual to be 'a wanting thing'. What then is this individual? Certainly it is not something substantial, as Locke decisively argued:

Nothing but consciousness can unite remote Existences into the same

> Person, the Identity of Substance will not do it ... (1979, p. 341)

which is hardly surprising, since

> ...of *Substance* we have no *Idea* of what it is, but only a confused obscure one of what it does. (ibid., p. 95)

Nor, following on from this, is the individual even something continuous. For since experience is the basis of knowledge; and such experience of our selves which we have is ever discontinuous; any knowledge we have of our selves must be of a set of discontinuities. Palatable or not, Hume's rigour is unanswerable:

> If any impression gives rise to the idea of self, that impression must continue invariably the same, thro' the whole course of our lives; since self is suppos'd to exist after that manner. But there is no impression constant and invariable. Pain and pleasure, grief and joy, passions and sensations succeed each other, and never exist at the same time. It cannot, therefore, be from any of these impressions, or from any other, that the idea of self is deriv'd; and consequently there is no such idea. (1969, pp. 299–300) [5]

And yet – whatever exactly it is or is not – it remains nevertheless ontologically primary, from the early Protestants to latter-day Hayekians, whether it be vis-à-vis God, or nature or society. There is of course a great variety of difficulties with such a view, but for my present purposes I shall draw attention only to one, but one which I think is both decisively problematic and rarely addressed. If empirio-liberalism's 'individual' is both ontologically primary and substantially empty, then what **differentiates** one individual from another?

One, apparently obvious, answer may be given in terms of the empiricists' 'secondary qualities'. But how can such qualities be morally or politically relevant when it comes to making judgements as between individuals, to distinguish which must, after all, be at least one of their chief functions? How, for example, might hair colour, facial features, height, nationality, ancestry or parentage, be morally or politically relevant? In some actual instances, of course, such 'secondary qualities' are only too clearly held to be relevant: consider the Nazis' treatment of Gypsies, Jews and Slavs; some Slavs' treatment of other Slavs and of Gypsies; or Anglo-Saxons' treatment of blacks. But liberals are, rightly, concerned to avoid just this sort of **arbitrariness**: and it is this which crucially distinguishes the tradition from fascism and from some forms of conservatism. No qualities which could conceivably be understood as 'secondary' can serve as a basis for moral or political differentiation simply insofar as they must be accidental, changeable and thus more or less arbitrary: they might all have been other than they are and still the individual concerned would be the same human being. That is the very basis of liberalism's positive contribution to Enlightenment thought and to enlightened action. It is certainly a salutary state of affairs that liberalism does not have the logical resources to withstand the slide from a respect for difference – based on what is common – to the self-indulgent and self-congratulatory lauding of difference with which postmodern relativists cloak their inability and unwillingness to move beyond the exigencies of their own wants. This should not blind us, however, to liberalism's actual intellectual and political achievements, built as they are on the basis of a conception of a common rationality, a conception which, while perhaps deficient in terms of its rôle in action, and clearly deficient in respect at least of gender and culture, affords nevertheless a starting-point for an Enlightenment project which is not lightly to be jettisoned.

But if secondary qualities are of no use here, then neither are 'primary' qualities available to fill this or any comparable rôle for the empiricist, and hence the empiricist liberal. For either the 'individual' thus constituted is no individual at all (if 'primary' qualities are held to encompass simply mass, shape, etc.) since such qualities are purely abstract; or, taking Hume seriously, there really can be no substantial individual to have any qualities, whether primary or not. And yet a concern for equality of treatment demands – quite obviously – that there **be** things which can be treated equally or otherwise; and that there be **some** (relevant) differences between such things, since otherwise of course equality of treatment must perforce consist in an identity of treatment stemming from a literal identity of human beings. Aversion to postmodern over-emphases on differences notwithstanding, the salutary Spinoza is regrettably unavailable for any empirio-liberal enterprise. There has to be some reasonable means of identifying something or other as marking significant differences if the individual of what might be termed empirio-liberalism is not to collapse in on itself.

III

What might serve as such a means? What might hold together such an individual, if neither substantial nor secondary qualities can do so? It seems to me that, both logically and historically, it is but a short step, via Hobbes, Locke and Hume, from Descartes' claim that I am a thinking thing to the supposition that thinking things are, so to speak, 'Is', 'individuals' empty of content until filled with some. Thought itself will not do, of course, since that must await the presence of some content-filled individual before it can occur. My point is that while empirio-liberalism is inevitably committed to an ontological individualism, its 'individual', paradoxically perhaps, has no readily discernible content:

and wants come to fill the vacuum, as peculiarly, unmistakably, irreducibly our own. **They** are what we are, and what distinguishes us as individuals one from another, 'secondary' characteristics apart. However exactly 'I' might be understood, what essentially identifies me as the individual I am – as distinct from my accidental characteristics – is what I want. I want: therefore I am able to be who I am. For I am fundamentally a wanting thing, a bundle of desiring sensations.

Furthermore, and crucially, it is thus the peculiar configuration of my wants that distinguishes me from other bundles of desiring sensations, so that my individual identity comes to consist exactly therein. I am not you insofar as your wants are not mine. My wants are a part of me which cannot be removed by any 'outside' agency; like my thoughts, no one can take my wants away from me: 'an individual's thought and action,' as Lukes puts it, 'is his [sic] own' (1973, p. 52). [6] Rather as in the case of emotions, their source lies within the individual, so that, unlike my thoughts, they are peculiarly mine, rather than being mediated through some public and available framework which might serve as a means of evaluation and legitimation. In this, of course, they resemble my sensations: but again with the important difference that they do not simply happen to me; they do not 'arrive from outside', and thus constitute no threat to the autonomy which is central to liberalism's insistence on 'the freedom which consists in being one's own master [sic]' (Sandel, 1982, p. 23). For liberals there is no rôle for

> Platonic experts as masters, paternalistically prescribing needs by reference to their own judgment of what their subjects ideally ought to want. (Flew, 1977, pp. 213–28) [7]

No wonder that, for empiricism and for its political mirror, liberalism, what we want comes to constitute who we are: and that that is the form taken by the ontological primacy of its 'individual'.

Lest this be thought an exaggeration, consider one of your friends, one whom you have known for a long time. Now, you might well be familiar with the 'mad surgeon' problems which beset the traditional question of personal identity: how much of your friend's body can change without your becoming seriously worried that s/he is no longer the same person as you once knew? This may or may not be an interesting question, [8] but my point here is that any possible interest it might have is **intelligible** just insofar as any particular bits of the body (in contrast, perhaps, to some particular set or sets of bits of the body) constitute features inessential for determining the identity of the individual: hence their 'secondary' nature. But now suppose that your friend's familiar **wants** (and/or desires, likes, preferences, etc.) were radically to change. Yesterday s/he wanted lots of money, fame, beer, sausages, company and a holiday in California: today all that is different – s/he has no interest in money, wants to move to the local hills to live as a recluse, and is inclined to vomit at even the thought of beer and sausages, wanting only mineral water and raw vegetables. Would s/he have become someone else, a different individual from the one s/he was yesterday? It seems not, for even a radical transformation of an individual's desires fails to impinge on their identity. [9]

While Feuerbach argued that we are what we eat, the empirio-liberal tradition is committed to the view that we are what we want: and liberal morality would have us act upon it. Whether or not this is a matter for regret, however, empirio-liberalism's 'individual' is not entirely counter-intuitive – if only, perhaps, because it is formative of so much of our 'intuition'. Even though, I think, I am sometimes at least fairly sure that I do not know what I want; let alone, at other times, whether or not I do actually want what I suppose I want: nevertheless it is what I actually do want that makes me who I really am insofar as both subject and object of moral agency. It is not just – what liberals have always claimed – that 'each individual is their own best judge of ... their wants' (Flew, op. cit., p. 217), but that each individual is in an important sense constituted by what they want. That, at least, is the theory.

IV

For liberalism the individual differs significantly from other individuals in what s/he wants. Hence the tradition inescapably bases its moral and political systems, whether explicitly or implicitly, on what people want. Its central impasses are thus so-called fanatics, people who want things which most others think bizarre but who cannot be shown to be morally or politically mistaken. Indeed, the very idea of moral or political error can have no sense for liberals, since wants, desires or preferences cannot be erroneous: thus the 'fanatic' of R.M. Hare's *Freedom and Reason* (1963) is the tradition's epitome. Fanatics are people who cannot but give liberals, and utilitarian liberals in particular, a great deal of trouble. Being generally prepared to universalize **both** consistently **and** against what one would think was in their best interests, they would nevertheless appear, by their very fanaticism, their insistence on choosing and deciding, to be the very paragon of agency – a curious, not to say disconcerting, state of affairs. [10] Testimony to the importance of Hare's influence, fanatics, or at any rate their phantasms, lurked in every corner of the Anglo-Saxon philosophical world throughout the 1960s and early 70s: and it was in part due to their ubiquity that thinkers like Philippa Foot were to move on from Hare's positions.

It is worth pausing, then, to say just a little about two kinds of fanatic, endemic as they must be to liberalism, and product as they are of its obeisance to people's wants. Fanatics of the first kind, going back to

Plato's Thrasymachus, simply see no reason not to go after and get whatever they want, if they can get away with it: morality has no hold on them because they just do not recognize its constraints, on the simple grounds either that they do not want to, or that they want not to. And since morality is, fundamentally, only a matter of what people want, that is an end of it. Fanatics of the second kind are rather more complex. They accept morality, but suppose that their wants, or the wants of their class, sex, etc., outweigh the wants of others in their intensity, and that they are therefore justified in pursuing their fanatical course: troubled Nazis, perhaps, who lived with what they did by managing to get themselves to believe that their actions were for the greater good. Unhappily, and unlike unicorns, these are not just inhabitants of philosophical debate, but are all too real and all too ubiquitous, although it is only in the last decade or so that philosophers seem to have started to take these figures, and not just their phantasms, seriously. The Eichmann of Hannah Arendt's *Eichmann in Jerusalem* (1980), despite the central issues the book raises, seems until recently to have been largely ignored by moral and political philosophers; and Berel Lang in his recent and brilliant *Act and Idea in the Nazi Genocide* (1990) still has to struggle to persuade people to recognize the inadequacy of the 'sincerity' of the 'sincere Nazi' of Hare's *Freedom and Reason* (op. cit.).

Fanatics of this second kind, who, sincerely or otherwise, 'accept the universalized prescription that were they to become untouchables, women or blacks, they too could be discriminated against' (Lee, 1985, p. 62) are people who, universalizing their wants, simply accept that morality is, ultimately, an assertion, or perhaps confirmation, of the power of those who happen to be in a position to realize their wants: that morality is what the empiricist sceptics always thought it to be, and what their postmodern successors, in their mistaken assumption to be doing something radically new, still take it to be.

V

But such fanatics are no aberration, however problematic practically: they simply take to its logical conclusion the reliance of empirio-liberalism on the Aristotle–Hume view of the limits of reason in respect of action; and, arising from that, its conception of the individual, the bedrock of empirio-liberalism's epistemology and – therefore – of its understanding of morality.

What is important is that that tradition is not simply some sort of rationalization necessary for liberal economists to justify their 'market', or for liberal moralists (whether in classical or postmodern form) to justify their tolerance. It goes far deeper than that, to the nature of the individuals on which the empirio-liberal tradition is based, and who are crucially constituted by what they want. Whether or not it is right, the position arises ineluctably from empiricism's conception of what the individual is: a wanting thing.

Notes

1. C.B. Macpherson (1962, p. 264) describes a Hobbesian view of the individual 'as the sum of a man's [sic] power to get gratifications'.
2. While arguably not committed to the view that desire is the **source** of morality, he nevertheless cannot conceive of action without desire:

   'tis plain the meaning of the Question, *what determines the Will?* is this, What moves the mind, in every particular instance, to determine its general power of directing, to this or that particular Motion or Rest? And to this I answer, The motive ... to change is always uneasiness (ch. XXI, sec. 29, p. 249) [and so although] *desiring* and *willing* are two distinct Acts of the mind (ibid., sec. 30, p. 250) [nevertheless, since] *Uneasiness determines the Will* (ibid., sec. 31) ... [and] ... *Desire* is a state of uneasiness (ibid., sec. 32, p. 251) ... I am forced to conclude, that *good*, the *greater good*, though apprehended and acknowledged to be so, does not determine the *will*, until our desire, raised proportionably to it, makes us *uneasy* in the want of it. (ibid., sec. 35, p. 253)

3. See also the famous passage on higher and lower pleasures where Mill might have been – but was not – given pause:

   It is quite compatible with the principle of utility to recognize the fact, that some *kinds* of pleasure are more desirable and more valuable than others ... (ibid., p. 258) ... Of two pleasures, if there be one to which all or almost all who have experience of both give a decided preference, **irrespective of any feeling of moral obligation to prefer it**, that is the more desirable pleasure. (p. 259, my emphasis)

   But if 'moral obligation' might – logically – precede desire, and thus desirability, then neither 'desire' nor 'desirabilty' can constitute its basis. Cf. *On Liberty*, where Mill writes that 'the human faculties of perception, judgement, discriminative feeling, mental activity, and even moral preference, are exercised only in making a choice' (ibid., p. 187); since 'One whose desires and impulses are not his own, has no character, no more than a steam-engine has a character' (ibid., p. 189). The issues raised here about the rôle of sheer choosing – a bedrock of liberal theory – are of the first importance. In particular, their consideration might lead one to re-assess the alleged antithesis between the (liberal) empiricism of the 'Anglo-American' philosophical tradition and the existentially-oriented emphasis of the 'Continental' tradition.

4. Cf. Bernard Williams (1985): 'Looked at from the outside, this (the ethical) point of view belongs to someone in whom the ethical dispositions he [sic] has acquired lie deeper than other wants and preferences' (p. 51). Even Alasdair MacIntyre's (1985) observation that 'There seems to be no way of securing moral agreement in our culture' (p. 6) because we have 'no set of compelling reasons' (p. 8) on which to act, and his neo-Arisotelian critique stemming from it, seems to be based on an unargued conflation of grounds and motives. Charles Taylor's (1989) highly persuasive attempt to vindicate the Enlightenment's moral project is also somewhat vitiated by his emphasis on the latter's achievement in 'recognizing the goodness of ordinary desires ...' (p. 343) – a view he develops in his immediately subsequent critique of Rousseau's and Kant's rejection of the Enlightenment's impatience of 'good' and 'evil' as part of 'our normal make up' (p. 355) – despite his initial insistence that 'discriminations of right and wrong, better or worse, higher or lower, are not rendered valid by our own desires, inclinations, or choices, but rather stand independent of these and offer standards by which they can be judged' (p. 4).

5. This is the inevitable outcome of Locke's earlier insistence that ' ... self is not determined by Identity or Diversity of Substance, which it cannot be sure of, but only by Identity of consciousness' (op. cit., p. 345).

6. Cf. Ch. III of J.S. Mill's *On Liberty*, op. cit., passim.

7. Or at least, not in principle, even if Flew's description as a matter of fact puts me in mind of a good deal of liberal political practice: in particular, but by no means uniquely, of the recent separation of Czechoslovakia into the Czech Republic and Slovakia, insisted upon and accomplished by a free-market liberal government against the actual wishes of the majority of the population of both parts of the then country.

8. Derek Parfit (1984) deals with this once and for all (!) – and with much else besides.

9. A point brought to my attention by both Pat FitzGerald and Marcus Roberts, to whom thanks are due for helping me clarify this section of the article in particular.

10. But not unknown. Mill, for example, writes in *On Liberty* (op. cit., pp. 188–9):

> To say that one person's desires and feelings are stronger and more various than those of another, is merely to say that he has

more of the raw material of human nature, and is therefore more capable, perhaps of more evil, but certainly of more good. Strong impulses are but another name for energy ... A person whose desires and impulses are his own – are the expression of his own nature, as it has been developed and modified by his own culture – is said to have a character. If, and in addition to being his own, his impulses are strong, and are under the government of a strong will, he has an energetic character.

The brief reference to 'culture' notwithstanding, this passage is quite disconcerting, not only in its praise of 'the hero', but also in the extent to which Mill, usually a careful and measured writer, can be driven under the pressure of such a picture – to refer, for instance, to 'the raw material of human nature'.

References

Arendt, Hannah (1980), *Eichmann in Jerusalem*, (rev. ed.), Penguin, New York.
Aristotle (1984), *Nicomachean Ethics*, in Barnes, Jonathan (ed.), *The Complete Works of Aristotle*, Princeton University Press, Princeton.
Flew, Antony (1977), 'Wants or needs, choices or commands?', in Fitzgerald, Ross (ed.), *Human Needs and Politics,* Pergamon, Rushcutters Bay, NSW.
Foot, Philippa (1978), *Virtues and Vices,* Blackwell, Oxford.
Hampshire, Stuart (1982), *Thought and Action*, Chatto and Windus, London.
Hare, R.M. (1963), *Freedom and Reason*, Oxford University Press, Oxford.
Hobbes, Thomas (1968), *Leviathan*, McPherson, C.B. (ed.), Penguin, Harmondsworth.
Hume, David (1969), *A Treatise of Human Nature,* Penguin, Harmondsworth.
Lang, Berel (1990), *Act and Idea in the Nazi Genocide*, University of Chicago Press, Chicago.
Lee, Keekok (1985), *A New Basis for Moral Philosophy,* Routledge, London.
Locke, John (1979), *An Essay Concerning Human Understanding,* Oxford University Press, Oxford.
Lukes, Steven (1973), *Individualism,* Blackwell, Oxford.
MacIntyre, Alasdair (1985) *After Virtue,* (2nd. ed.), Duckworth, London.
McPherson, C.B. (1962), *The Political Theory of Possessive Individualism* , Oxford University Press, Oxford.
Mill, John Stuart (1962), *Utilitarianism, On Liberty and Essay on Bentham*, Warnock, Mary (ed.), Fontana, London.
Parfit, Derek (1984), *Reasons and Persons*, Clarendon Press, Oxford.

Plato (1955), *The Republic*, Lee, H.D.P, (trans.), Penguin, London.
Rawls, John (1972), *A Theory of Justice,* Harvard University Press, Cambridge, Mass.
Sandel, Michael J. (1982), *Liberalism and the Limits of Justice*, Cambridge University Press, Cambridge.
Taylor, Charles (1989), *Sources of the Self*, Cambridge University Press, Cambridge.
Williams, Bernard (1985), *Ethics and the Limits of Philosophy,* Fontana, London.

3 From liberal democracy to democratic liberalism

Richard Bellamy

Twentieth century liberalism has suffered the curious fate of steadily declining in most countries as an electoral force exclusive to a particular party, whilst prevailing and even growing as a background theory or set of presuppositions and sentiments of a supposedly neutral and universal kind which dominates political thinking across the ideological spectrum. Today all major groupings employ the liberal language of rights, freedom and equality to express and legitimize their views and demonstrate a corresponding general acceptance of liberal conceptions of democracy and the market. From New Right conservatives to democratic socialists, it seems we are all liberals now.

To some extent, this situation is unsurprising given that liberal ideals and politics fashioned the states and social and economic systems of the nineteenth century, creating the institutional framework and the values within which most of us in the West continue to live and to think. This circumstance, however, does not justify the widely accepted assertion that the apparent triumph of liberalism forms part of 'a universal human evolution in the direction of free societies' grounded in 'the empirically undeniable correlation between advancing industrialization and liberal democracy' (Fukuyama, 1990, p. 19). On the contrary, the empirical evidence suggests just the opposite – a fact of some concern for liberal thinkers in the past. If many earlier liberals shared the belief of their contemporary epigone in a guaranteed progress towards a bourgeois utopia, they also came to feel badly let down by the historical process as a number of their core assumptions were called into question by the further development of the very social order they had helped to create (Bellamy, 1992). Far from being a sign of its intellectual and practical ascendency, liberalism's recent mutation from ideology to meta-ideology is indicative of its current theoretical and political bankruptcy. No longer part of the dynamic of history, liberalism has simply been reduced to presenting itself as the culmination of the historical process in a desperate attempt to circumscribe and contain those social forces which threaten to undermine it.

Today the further evolution of advanced capitalist economies has undermined to an even greater extent the social environment that lent liberalism its coherence. Rather than reflecting and stabilizing the social relations of modern societies, as Durkheim for example believed (Durkheim, 1898), liberal morality has proved unable to cope with their growing differentiation and complexity. Outside of the historical context which gave them practical force, traditional liberal principles cease to be compelling. They cannot function as neutral presuppositions of universal validity. At best, they represent highly problematic goals to be achieved, and are as such in competition with other, equally valuable, forms of human well-being. The attempts by contemporary thinkers, such as Hayek (1960) and Rawls (1971), to revive the arguments of the liberal tradition within the totally different social context of the modern world is misconceived, therefore. In contemporary societies, what I have described elsewhere (Bellamy, 1992) as the 'ethical' liberalism of the past needs to be abandoned and replaced by a realist conception of liberalism far more suited to the complex political and moral issues currently confronting us.

Ethical and realist liberals offer two contrasting ways of conceiving the nature of social order. The former subscribe to a consensual model of society; the latter focus on conflict and on the rôle of power in holding a community together. Ethical liberals maintain that social stability rests on a set of shared norms, beliefs and values which are intrinsic to modern industrial societies. They identify this morality with a set of basic rights and entitlements capable of ensuring the maximum equal liberty for all. Earlier writers in this tradition, such as J.S. Mill and Durkheim, believed social progress itself was producing a growing convergence on these general principles. Recent ethical liberal philosophers, such as Rawls, have modified this position and merely claim that it offers the minimal morality required for any form of uncoerced social cooperation in the contemporary world. By contrast, realist liberals, like Weber, dispute the view of social relations underlying even the minimalist Rawlsian 'overlapping consensus' (Rawls, 1987), however. Influenced by Marx, Nietzsche and Machiavelli, they offer a very different picture of modernity. Drawing on Marx, they point to the sources of conflict between different classes and interests in modern economies, relating these to the clashes of values between groups and individuals. Observing the various collective and structural forces moulding and perverting the will of individuals, they question the ethical liberal assumption of an independent rational convergence of views. They regard such agreements as more often than not the product of socialization and various forms of covert and overt persuasion or coercion. Drawing on Nietzsche now to take this critique further, they identify all moralizing with the 'will to power' and the effort to stem the nihilism of a disenchanted world. Conflict does not just originate from differential access to scarce resources and the organs of authority – it is part of the existential condition of human beings possessed of free will and disabused of all metaphysical consolations. In the face of numerous equally plausible yet rationally irreconcilable attitudes to life, there can be no objective way of judging the legitimacy of different and competing claims to authority. The neutral Archimedian point desired by contemporary ethical liberal theorists is revealed as just one perspective amongst others. Drawing finally on Machiavelli, they examine the way the political system operates as a mechanism for the organization of coercion and consent by different ruling groups and individuals. Far from being an open forum for the expression of the popular will, they see mass democracy as an instrument of social control. From the perspective of realist liberalism, therefore, the ethical liberal tradition fails adequately to explore the connection between the distribution of power and the legitimation of values.

Ethical and realist liberalism give rise to two correspondingly different ways of conceiving the public sphere: liberal democracy and democratic liberalism. Whereas liberal democracy assumes (or seeks to create) a moral consensus which provides a framework for political deliberation, democratic liberalism gives central place to procedures that favour the expression and temporary conciliation of a plurality of ideals. Consequently, democratic liberalism responds to the complexity and particularist pluralism of modern life by regarding liberal constitutional principles and arrangements in terms of a modus vivendi. They arise out of the current circumstances of justice, rather than being the preconditions of all legitimate social coexistence. For the heterogeneity of rules generated by highly differentiated societies has rendered the notion of any pre-political 'overlapping consensus' suspect. Instead, consensus is an outcome of the political system, which seeks to reduce the complexity and conflicts of society to manageable proportions. Seen in this realist light, pragmatic rather than absolutist considerations apply. The important goal is to ensure that the making of agreements is equitable rather than that the outcomes are just in some absolute sense.

Democratic liberalism, therefore, disputes the liberal democratic aim to ground politics in a set of universal ethical principles. From a realist point of view, such an attempt merely reflects the desire of a particular group to legitimize its own position and restrict the actions of others. It forms a part of political debates and struggles rather than transcending them. Take for example, the liberal democratic argument for a constitutionally entrenched Bill of Rights. This proposal seeks to answer the realist's objections concerning the feasibility of liberal agency in the modern world by building the prerequisites for autonomous action into the political system. Unlike a number of earlier liberal thinkers, contemporary liberal theorists do not base their account of democratic rights on either theological foundations or perfectionist reasoning stemming from some contestable view of human nature. As we have seen, they try to construct rather than deduce the largest set of rights capable of being simultaneously held by a society of roughly free and equal but widely divergent individuals. David Held's model of democratic autonomy, which tries to synthesize the whole gamut of liberal theorizing on this issue, provides a fine example of the type of argument under discussion. He states the principle of autonomy as follows:

> Persons should enjoy equal rights (and, accordingly equal obligations) in the framework which generates and limits the opportunities available to them; that is they should be free and equal in the determination of the conditions of their own lives, so long as they do not deploy this framework to negate the rights of others. (Held, 1991, p. 228)

Constructions of rights along these lines fit most easily with physicalist theories of action and accounts of liberty which conceive freedom in terms of authority over a specific domain. On this view, each person must be accorded the maximal sphere of action compatible with an equivalent space for others. Setting the boundaries of these individual territories, however, is impossibly difficult once we leave the realm of metaphor and seek actually to apply this theory to the real world. The problem with this approach becomes clear when we consider the difficulty of making 'on-balance' judgements about freedom in the event of a clash of liberties (Gray, 1989, O'Neill, 1979/80). A negative interpretation of liberty, for example, yields a libertarian construction of rights against interference from others, whereas a positive conception of liberty gives rise to welfare rights requiring us to provide people with certain goods and services. These two views of liberty produce two sets of rights which are not only divergent, but also incompatible. If, for example, I have an unrestricted right to private property and to trade in the market, others cannot have rights to welfare, and vice versa. Socialists often seek to combine the two by claiming that social rights extend the traditional civil and political rights by enabling citizens to exercise them. However, such arguments – like those of the New Liberals and T.H. Marshall which inspire them – only make sense on the basis of some form of perfectionism. Reliance on such ethical naturalist assumptions undercuts the supposed pluralism of rights-based theories, though, and are in any case very hard to justify. For why should New Right theorists, who largely resist welfare rights on the grounds that they undermine individual and social morality, accept that these rights are more essential to human fulfilment than property rights? Moreover, the problems of identifying a basic set of compossible rights, common to all moralities, mirror those of constructing a maximal set. As the debate over abortion between those championing the right of the mother over her own body and those defending the right of the unborn foetus has shown, even the most basic of negative liberty rights can conflict at times. Indeed, the various parties have found it impossible even to agree on a common conception of what counts as life. Rights-based liberal moralities cannot provide the basic structure for all legitimate political systems, therefore, because rights only make sense as the coordinating principles of particular forms of life (Bellamy, 1990). Different communities fostering different kinds of human flourishing will give rise to different conceptions of rights. This communitarian aspect of rights comes to light most obviously when rights clash, as we have seen they inevitably do. For conflicts of rights can only be resolved, as the examples above illustrate, with reference to the common good or type of moral life valued by the community. This feature makes rights singularly ill-suited to providing the foundations of a political system in a disenchanted world such as our own, characterized by the fragmentation of our moral framework.

Once cut off from an agreed comprehensive conception of the good, assertions of basic human rights are liable to generate irreconcilable conflicts between rival ontological claims. Contemporary moral experience lacks the regularity that the advocates of a framework of absolute basic rights require. Even the most essential of civil and political rights come into conflict with each other at times. For example, it is correctly believed to be essential in a liberal democracy that everyone has a right to the fair procedures which guarantee an unprejudiced trial. However, suppose it is discovered that some of these rights lead to guilty persons getting off and committing crimes which infringe the equally important rights of innocent citizens? The present British government's decision to modify the right to silence reflects just such a perceived conflict of rights. In such instances we are faced with tragic choices in which doing right involves committing wrong. No ethical theory can adequately resolve such questions. If policy decisions are to be possible, then argument about the merits of different proposals has to be pitched at a less absolute level. The constitutional entrenchment of a given set of rights attempts to make a given conception of social life unalterable. Yet discussion of what sort of world we would like to live in and the kinds of collective goods the state ought to provide form a vital part of the subject matter of politics, and cannot be legitimately excluded from the political agenda. To do so has the effect of raising the temperature of political debate so that every challenge to the political system gets turned into a revolutionary demand. It places political disputes on a level where the opposing positions of the contesting parties cannot be discursively redeemed. This strategy could only succeed at the unacceptable price of a significant homogenization and simplification of modern societies.

The attempt to construct neutral principles of rights or justice fails because it inevitably rests on ungrounded and contentious idealizations of particular conceptions of human agency. Within the liberal tradition these typically involve notions of autonomy and of self-sufficiency, such as one finds in Rawls's 'Kantian ideal of the person' (Rawls, 1980). To avoid such a moralistic politics it must be kept separate from ethics. In the modern world, the distinctive function of the political system is to arrange compromises amongst a plurality of often conflicting views, rather than to achieve a rational consensus upon a non-existent common good.

To attack ethical liberal attempts to provide a moralistic foundation for politics is not to suggest that we do not require any notion of law, rights or justice. Some Marxists and anarchists have dreamed of the withering away of the state altogether. They have regarded the liberal legal framework as the product of a class divided society, to be replaced by a harmonious society in which 'the free development of each is the condition of the free development of all' (Marx and Engels, 1969, p. 127). Ironically, this utopia is in formal terms not very different from the ethical liberal ideal. However, this socialist idyll is only plausible on the basis of a number of highly unrealistic assumptions (Campbell, 1983, Lukes, 1985). For whereas one could reasonably expect that under socialism people might be better disposed towards each other, and their social relations more solidaristic, fraternal or sororial, it is unreasonable to suppose that the ordinary human weaknesses resulting from imperfect knowledge, carelessness, and our essential fallibility will have been transcended by a new race of superbeings. Similarly, whilst socialists can argue that wealth will be more equitably distributed and that people will be less materialist in their desires, to believe that there will be such superabundance that no constraints of resources exist stretches the bounds of credibility too far. Yet, if we remove the assumptions that human beings could be transformed into omniscient creatures possessing a saintly rectitude, and that the world could be made so bountiful as to satisfy each of our wildest desires, then the picture of a society without laws, rights or the need for politics ceases to be plausible. Even if citizens were to agree on which ends are to be pursued, the social processes within a society of any size and sophistication will be so complicated that people are liable to err owing either to insufficient information about their fellow citizens' needs, or to a lack of expertise about how best to meet them. The road to hell is paved with good intentions, and even the most altruistic individuals may be misguided as to what other people require. For all but the smallest groups, therefore, some formal framework establishing norms of conduct and the conditions for entering into agreements is unavoidable. However, if those Marxists who stigmatize all laws and rights as intrinsically bourgeois are mistaken, so are those of their critics who contend that the ethical liberal framework represents the only legitimate legal system capable of upholding individual freedom. As we have seen, it is fraught with contradictions and inadequacies.

A democratic liberalism overcomes the respective difficulties of both the ethical liberal and the Marxian view of justice by regarding the laws, rights, and distributive principles by which societies coordinate their affairs as mere rules of thumb. Far from reflecting universal ethical norms, they emerge from individual judgements in particular circumstances. As such, they have an ad hoc character which facilitates their revision when circumstances or needs alter. They serve to reduce the chaos and uncertainty of social life to manageable proportions, providing the regularity of expectations necessary for leading a reasonably stable life. From this perspective, the freedom of individuals and groups is not protected by written guarantees, however worthy, but by the existence of agencies which enable citizens to act in certain ways and which provide them with a means of defence against being hindered by others. Since the rights and liberties we enjoy depend on the structure of laws, the values and the priorities of the society we live in, we are only free when we have a rôle in determining the character of that society. This activity requires democratic institutions through which we can deliberate on our particular and collective interests. The laws and regulations emanating from such bodies create positive rights which have none of the drawbacks I have associated with various versions of ethical liberal pre-political human rights. Instead of representing inherent ontological attributes, they reflect socially determined purposes which are capable of reformulation to meet changing situations and attitudes. Legislation can be used to mediate between competing claims, granting rights which reflect the divergent requirements of different areas of social life, rather than conforming to some idealized image of the human subject which imposes a particular pattern of human agency upon society. Moreover, these political institutions not only allow us to define our freedom, they enable us to defend it. After all, even under Stalin the USSR boasted a written constitution guaranteeing certain fundamental human rights. Their denial stemmed from the concentration of power within the party apparatus. For the enjoyment of our rights and liberties depends to an important extent on a democratic institutional structure which distributes power amongst the citizen body. Without the possibility of widespread political participation, the state apparatus can fall into the hands of narrow cliques who seek to use it to further the particular interests of their class, group, religion, ideology or leader. The protection of minority groups, which plays a major part in the desire of rights theorists to limit the scope of democratic decisions, can best be served by having a variety of different loci of power and decision making which restrict the possibilities for any one agency or group to dominate all others. Without a differentiation of political functions which recognizes the plurality of society by preserving the autonomy of different spheres and levels of social life – separating, for example, judicial and executive functions, and local from central government –

constitutional rights will be worthless. Once disproportionate power falls into the hands of a restricted group or a single agency, individual freedom will soon be curtailed.

Thus, for liberalism to meet the challenge posed by the complexity and pluralism of modern societies, a complex plurality of political mechanisms must be devised to facilitate the influence and scrutiny of government policy by all relevant groups and individuals. This objective requires the distribution of decision making power throughout society and the designation of distinct areas of competence so as to limit the scope of central authority. Such a system replaces substantive 'moralistic' constitutional constraints on majority rule and government action with 'realistic' procedural democratic checks and controls. Procedures allowing a plurality of views to be expressed and which encourage their mediation take the place of pre-political notions of rights and justice. The preservation of pluralism in this manner constitutes a liberal as much as a democratic commitment. For only a pluralist society provides a sufficient range of worthwhile options for the equal exercise of liberty through choice to make sense. A system of democratic institutions, which reflects the diversity of values and interests within society and enables accommodations to be arranged between them, provides the framework for a genuinely political liberalism, therefore, adequate to 'the fact of pluralism'.

This way of thinking harks back to the classical republican tradition of thought (Skinner, 1986). Unlike the civic humanist tradition, classical republicanism sees politics as a means rather than an end in itself. A form of Aristotelianism, civic humanism regards human beings as essentially political animals for whom political participation is a necessary aspect of the good life. Classical republicanism, in contrast, originates with Machiavelli and treats civic involvement as merely the condition for retaining our liberty. Since it involves no special commitment to a particular conception of the good, it is compatible with a pluralist democratic liberalism. The virtues of political involvement are purely instrumental and prudential in character. The procedural norms of democratic liberalism, such as majority rule based on an equal vote, are simply functional components of the political system necessary for the peaceful resolution of social conflict. As such, their observance arises from a prudentially motivated political duty (i.e. if you do not uphold them, no one else will) rather than a moral right.

Libertarians argue that the main locus of individual choice and freedom is the market rather than the political sphere. So long as the market is free, then the price mechanism will reflect in an objective way the value people place on certain commodities. However, the market fails to provide an adequate mechanism for the neutral or fair mediation of a plurality of all human values and desires. Leaving aside the well known difficulties with the perfect competition model of the market (King, 1987,

Ch. 5) there are three basic objections to the extension of market principles to cover the whole range of social and political issues. First, as Brian Barry has pointed out, this version of liberalism assumes that all preferences reflect essentially material private wants (Barry, 1965, Ch. 4). Such preferences are entirely amenable to the market mechanism. Having no intrinsic worth, they may be traded off against each other, the only object being to achieve the greatest aggregate satisfaction of wants over all. Market operations prove unsatisfactory, however, when people hold ideal-regarding preferences. When I regard an object as intrinsically valuable I will not be satisfied with such trade-offs. Considering the relative merits of various educational policies, for example, is different to bargaining with various stall holders over the relative price of different items of food and clothing. In the second case, I can consider my wants and seek to maximize their satisfaction, sacrificing a banana here for an extra couple of apples there etc. The first case is not like that. I will have opinions about what a basic educational curriculum ought to include, say, and will expect those of opposing views to argue their case with me. If I believe children require a certain kind of teaching, I will not necessarily be satisfied just to be told that school productivity has been increased by doubling the number of pupils in each class and introducing rote learning. When evaluative as opposed to merely quantitative considerations apply, the market is no longer the appropriate decision making medium. By providing a forum for public discussion, politics enables ideal-regarding preferences to be transformed and not just aggregated, allowing opposed interests to find acceptable compromises or even agreement on common values. For political participation can educate citizens into a perception of the dependency of their social relations and group and individual autonomy upon collective rules and arrangements. This process discourages the free riding and other self-defeating forms of self-interest which bedevil markets. The need for collective decisions provides the second main objection to a totally market orientated liberalism. In the modern world, many of the goods which most concern us are not individualisable. The environment, peace, population control, information exchange – in sum, the most pressing policy issues of our time – all require concerted action for their solution. Indeed, the market is itself a collective good needing constant political regulation. Moreover, its very scope is a matter of political decision calling for constant discussion. For, my third and last point, markets do not avoid the problem of power within society. Unregulated markets based on private property rights in the means of production, distribution and exchange result not just in discrepancies in wealth but also in hierarchical relationships which create grave inequalities of power and influence that restrict the range of democratic control. The consequent private domination of the financial and industrial corporations may be better than that of a monolithic bureaucratic socialist state, but it is far from realizing the liberal ideas of freedom and equality which are often said to be synonymous with capitalism. Within a market system distorted by the concentration of capital and the power of organization, the average consumer's pull is severely limited. A socialist society composed of cooperatively owned and democratically self-managing enterprises arguably disperses economic power more effectively and equitably, and so proves more pluralist than capitalism. It is compatible with both democratic decision making in the area of public goods and the conciliation of ideal-regarding preferences, and the use of market and price mechanisms for the coordination of material preferences and ordinary consumption (Miller, 1989).

Liberalism remains important for anyone who takes the plurality and complexity of the modern world seriously. However, traditional liberal arguments, such as the importance of autonomy and diversity for human progress or mere scepticism about the existence of any objective values, fail to do so. For they are all based on recognizably liberal moral conceptions which do not do justice to alternative ethical systems (Larmore, 1987, pp. 51–2). Attempts to devise supposedly neutral legal frameworks which protect certain rights and liberties privilege particular points of view at the expense of others of equal importance. As a result, they become a source of conflict rather than of stability. Contemporary societies lack the convenient moral symmetry such theories require. In an increasingly functionally and ethically differentiated world, clashes between competing aspects of our lives and of our social system are inevitable. No overarching moral theory can resolve all the tensions within them. The compromises and rules required for peaceful co-existence can only emerge in an ad hoc manner. A democratic liberalism tries to perform this task by constructing a workable set of democratic institutions capable of providing the modus vivendi necessary to arrive at these agreements. It seeks to preserve individual and group freedom through the distribution of power. Unlike ethical liberalism, democratic liberalism does not aim at the construction of the just society *sub specie aeternitatis*. More modestly, it attempts to allow people in the here and now to articulate their needs and ideals and map out a basis for their present cooperation. A liberalism of this kind is not only necessary, it is the only way we can all be liberals now.

References

Barry, Brian (1965), *Political Argument*, Routledge, London.
Bellamy, Richard (1990), 'Liberal rights and socialist goals' in Maihofer, W. and Sprenger, G. (eds.), *Revolution and Human Rights, Archiv Für Rechts-und Sozialphilosophie*, Beiheft nr. 41, pp. 249–64.
Bellamy, Richard (1992), *Liberalism and Modern Society: An Historical Argument*, Polity Press, Cambridge.
Campbell, Tom (1983), *The Left and Rights*, Routledge, London.
Fukuyama, Francis (1990), 'The world against a family', *The Guardian*, 12 September.
Gray, John (1989), *Liberalisms: Essays in Political Philosophy*, Routledge, London.
Hayek, F.A. (1960), *The Constitution of Liberty*, Routledge, London.
Held, David (1991), 'Democracy, the national state and the global system' in idem, *Political Theory Today*, Polity Press, Cambridge.
King, Desmond (1987), *The New Right*, Macmillan, Basingstoke.
Larmore, Charles (1987), *Patterns of Moral Complexity*, Cambridge University Press, Cambridge.
Lukes, Steven (1985), *Marxism and Morality*, Oxford University Press, Oxford.
Marx, Karl and Engels, Friedrich (1969), 'The Communist Manifesto' in *Selected Works*, vol. I, Progress Press, Moscow.
Miller, David (1989), *Market, State and Community: Theoretical Foundations of Market Socialism*, Clarendon Press, Oxford.
O'Neill, Onora (1979/90), 'The most extensive liberty', *Proceedings of the Aristotelian Society*, 80, pp. 5–59.
Rawls, John (1971), *A Theory of Justice*, Clarendon Press, Oxford.
Rawls, John (1980), 'Kantian constructivism and moral theory', *Journal of Philosophy*, LXXVII, pp. 515–72.
Rawls, John (1987), 'The idea of an overlapping consensus', *Oxford Journal of Legal Studies*, 7, pp. 1–25.

Skinner, Quentin (1986), 'The paradoxes of political liberty' in McMurrin, S. (ed.), *The Tanner Lectures on Human Values*, vol. VII, Cambridge University Press, Cambridge, pp. 227–50.

4 Are we facing the triumph of liberalism and the end of history?

Miroslav Kryl

I

The majority of political scientists appear to agree that, with the demolition of the Berlin Wall and the end of communism, the current state of affairs in central and eastern Europe marks the triumph of liberal democracy. It seems that liberalism, in a variety of intellectual and political guises, is now the only ideology remaining which can claim legitimacy. That, at least, is certainly the view of Francis Fukuyama, who is persuaded that the revolutionary changes in central and eastern Europe and the adoption of market principles in Latin America are part of one and the same process, namely the victory of the free market over the political and economic forces of the Left. The latter are indeed in disarray throughout the world, having suffered just that crisis which Fukuyama forecast in 1989 in his now famous essay, 'The End of History' (Fukuyama, 1989a). [1]

Fukuyama has not been without his critics, of course, many of whom regard his thesis as unduly triumphalist and, especially in light of recent events such as those in Bosnia, unduly naive: but, as Gregory Elliott has recently pointed out (Elliott, 1993) such critics all too often overlook Fukuyama's very considerable pessimism about the sort of 'New World Order' to which liberalism's victory has given rise. On his own view, in fact, his conception of the end of history is one which beckons, not at all an era of peace, but rather an era of increasing local conflict in which no way forward can be found: with the end of a historical epoch which was characterized by at least the possibility of development comes stagnation, rather than any triumph in the traditional sense. Although the various local conflicts around the world which have followed the collapse of communism constitute for his critics testimony to the profound error of Fukuyama's thesis, his own view is that this is to misunderstand its real import – namely that there is a close affinity between the liberal democratic and the capitalist revolutions, and that liberal democracy is the inevitable accompaniment of advanced industrialisation. Fukuyama, that is to say, defends his thesis as one which concerns primarily a view of history as history of ideas – or, more accurately, history of 'correct' ideas, namely history of ideas about superior or better ordered societies. 'Liberal democracy', then, is the sole remaining universal ideology, the outcome of a long-drawn out historical process, and one which goes hand in hand with the economic victory of the market principles of capitalist organization. As such, Fukuyama is convinced, liberal democracy is simply – and for better or worse – the sole live option as a legitimate and rational political system. And this is no triumphalist triumph.

Nevertheless, it is a triumph of sorts: for although uncertainty, fear and aggression can always serve to motivate the practice of the political representatives of any state, the principles governing liberal democracy are the only **possible** means of avoiding such a state of affairs. Thus, for instance, and whether or not it **actually** does so, it is only liberal democracy which **could** lead to a new European order in any peaceful and even-handed manner. Furthermore, since there are no longer any fundamental ideological differences among the decisive powers – with the disappearance of the old stand-offs between liberalism on the one hand and fascism or communism on the other – there is an increasing common interest among them in remaining at peace with each other and in establishing such an order.

Now this might seem a fairly implausible view in the light of actual circumstances. If, however, one remembers that it is intended as a view about **possibilities**, a view of history as history of ideas; and if one recalls also the research of Michael Doyle upon which Fukuyama relies – research which claims that during the nearly two hundred years since the inception of modern liberal democracy, there is not a single instance of war between two liberal democracies – the implausibility diminishes (Fukuyama, 1990). For the world is now divided, not into 'East' and 'West', but rather into just these two groups: liberal democracies and the rest; or, in Fukuyama's words, 'post-historical' and 'historical' states. The former are the liberal democracies, marked by a free-market economy, political freedom and prosperity, to whom both war and interference with the rights, under international law, of other (liberal democratic, I would add) states is foreign. In the latter, however, military might or the rules of traditional geopolitics will continue to hold sway. Disagreements and clashes between these two groups and/or between members of the latter are not, of course, ruled out: just the opposite in fact. But such 'realism' in international relations, that is to say, in geopolitics, will inevitably fade into the background and give way to questions of democratic and popular rights, both internally and world-wide, as the idea of liberal democracy inexorably spreads.

What is certainly attractive about such a thesis is Fukuyama's insistence that it is no longer possible to deal with nations as though they were balls in a global billiards game: rather, it is now necessary for liberal democratic nations to render nascent liberal democracies every possible assistance (currently above all, perhaps, in central and eastern Europe) just because that is what they are. It is important to stress that Fukuyama's is no utopian vision, but rather is put forward as a matter of the objective laws of post-historical times. He treats the relevant factors governing international relations in what he takes to be a context of an inevitably all-conquering liberalism as something very close to obeying laws of future history. Again, this might, if true, seem considerably attractive, as though Rousseau's ideas had reached their apotheosis; but as a matter of historical necessity, rather than of contingent political fact. Fukuyama's forecast of ideological stagnation – the source for him of considerable pessimism, for others perhaps just the opposite – is, again, no speculation, but rather a claim about how history has to go. And that is to say that, to a far greater degree than hitherto, political activity will consist in internal and domestic politics; in the ability of the governments of nation-states to create decent living conditions and prosperity for their citizens; and to do so on the basis of freedom and equality – even though at the (arguable) cost of ideological stagnation.

Is Fukuyama right? The Czech philosopher and political theorist Bělohradský is one critic who denies both that the triumph of liberalism is a matter of the objective laws of history and that contemporary civilization finds itself at the sort of 'post-historical'/'historical' crossroads that Fukuyama describes. Furthermore, and Fukuyama's own denial of triumphalism notwithstanding, Bělohradský remains sceptical of the very idea of **any** sort of triumph of liberalism, citing the massive internal ruptures apparent in contemporary societies based on mass democracy and consumption, and emphasizing especially – as the greatest danger – the political powerlessness of democracies in the face of general ecological disaster. For Bělohradský, the sole real triumph of liberalism consists just in the end of communism (Castro's Cuba and Kim Il Sung's North Korea notwithstanding) a development which he interprets, however, as the triumph of critical over metaphysical reason; and which triumph, he argues, has in fact left Fukuyama behind as yet another in a long line of thinkers operating within the unreasonable confines of a long-standing western triumphalism of the intellect, let alone political triumphalism. Fukuyama's **conception of history**, he argues, belies the very liberalism which he takes to have triumphed. It is this response to Fukuyama's thesis that I wish to explore.

II

Bělohradský writes:

> The metaphysical conception of reason supposes that it is possible to put forward as **definitive** such of one's ideas as can be shown to have an indubitable basis and which every rational person must recognize as such. Those people are rational who seek **ultimate** grounds, from which they draw out an objective version of the world and before which all other versions of the world must give way as merely subjective. Metaphysical reason thus seeks some 'zero point of history' in which our version of the world – no longer in any way conditional – enables us to see the truth. The Soviet state was an incarnation of this metaphysical reason ... The triumph of liberalism consists in the collapse of this metaphysical conception of reason, a reason which seeks to become a political force and to plan everyone's lives on the basis of **objective necessity**. (Bělohradský 1991d, p. 3, my emphases) [2]

Let us investigate further Bělohradský's argument against 'metaphysical reason', which is how he identifies the principles which govern **both** the official communist philosophy and scientific method which were supposed to represent the sole scientifically correct view of the world **and** the western intellectual tradition as a whole (see p. 55) – from which he takes the contemporary liberal democratic practices of the postmodern world (that is to say, the exercise of 'critical reason') to be a departure.

> Liberal democracy is based on a critical understanding of reason, that is to say, on the conviction that nothing can be finally substantiated but that it is possible to criticize everything. Reason is not based in any absolute standpoint already in some way present and which we have to liberate from its dependence on particular contexts in order to attain the truth. On the contrary, that version of the world is rational which arises through the critique of other people and which passes the test of such criticism ... (ibid.)

The grounds on which the communist system was identified as the objective and thus only possible version of the world were presented as final. All other versions seemed to be subjective or relative. The experiences of those who grew up in this system underline, I think, Bělohradský's point: for despite all their unhappy experiences of this regime, an apparently considerable number of people – at least during certain periods of their lives – felt just this sort of 'objective certainty'. However, today's return to liberalism, or restoration of capitalism, also seems to be bringing along with it a somewhat too literal confirmation of

Bělohradský's view of the critical reason characteristic of liberal democracy: 'nothing can be finally substantiated but (that) it is possible to criticize everything'.

What solution does Bělohradský propose, then? He certainly does not regard the 'society of mass democracy and consumption ... [with its] terrible tensions, the greatest of which is the political powerlessness of democracy in the face of impending ecological disaster' (ibid.) as a triumph of liberalism. He is highly critical of the irresponsibility of the mass consumer society, with its diet of advertisements and mass-media bazaars: nor does he welcome what Fukuyama identifies in his essay as the final form of human consciousness, with which 'the history of the West' comes to a close. [3] Indeed, the only sense in which Bělohradský regards the triumph of liberalism as the end of history is a purely epistemological one: for since, 'on the liberal perspective, truth is not something that individuals possess, but which develops in those societies in which ideas are born readily but survive only with difficulty ... [it] ... has nothing to do with "objective laws of history"' (ibid.). He is, however, far from sceptical of the remorseless checks and criticisms to which a liberal society – with all its manifest problems – subjects all those who offer solutions to problems or who put forward their 'view of the world'. The medium is that of the market of goods. The consumer-producer relationship serves as a model for the 'market of ideas'; for open and independent opinion works in a similarly 'market' fashion, subjecting political representatives to the critical gaze of the voters. Most important of all is the general attitude to the individual person so typical of liberal societies. What Bělohradský has in mind here is the observation that only those can hold their ground in such a critical milieu who sincerely promote self-expression and who have no illusions about themselves, since the public is subject to the buffetings of such a heterogeneous range of influences – for example, the arts, sciences and a wide variety of cultural traditions and alternative ways of life. By referring to 'buffetings', he is trying to catch that sense of forever seeking and questioning which often results, he says, in credence being given to the statements of those who appear abnormal; to the unthinkable; and to the unforeseeable – all of which are put forward as cogent versions of the world, and which people may consider as possible answers to their questions. This openness is something for which the price of what might be termed 'postmodern anarchy' is worth paying, just because it rules out the false certainties of the Enlightenment.

Bělohradský thus regards Fukuyama's thesis as, in effect, yet another version of the grand narrative the end of which it in one sense purports to herald. According to Bělohradský, Fukuyama's view of history is thoroughly and unhappily Hegelian. On this understanding, history is taken to consist in just those events which resulted in clashes within certain social systems, including, among others, social formations and systems of government. These clashes are so violent that they cannot be resolved within the social systems in which they occur, with the result that people fight for their overthrow and replacement by some 'higher' form of system. On Bělohradský's interpretation, then, Fukuyama's thesis is understood as concerning, in fairly conventionally Hegelian manner, the Idea of History; and so only secondarily the actual events, both current and to come, which are the empirical consequences of that Idea – the actual formation of a world-wide consensus that liberal democracy is the only legitimate, viable and rational political system and thus the disappearance of any grounds on which people might look for radical alternatives to liberal democracy.

Now, this of course raises the extremely sensitive issue of what we might understand history to be (for after all, if we are to posit an **end** of history it is first necessary to say just what **history** is). And this is precisely the question that is raised by Bělohradský's objections to Fukuyama's thesis as itself part of the tradition of 'history' whose end it announces: Fukuyama, he insists, remains wedded to the 'metaphysical' conception of reason (and thus to a Hegelian conception of history) on the basis of which the west continues to attempt to (re-)create the rest of the world in its own image. He takes – as he himself agrees – his 'end of history' thesis to be an instantiation of that 'correct' history of ideas of which he thinks 'history' consists. What it actually amounts to, however, is an attempted imposition of such an understanding on the non-western world: the claim that liberalism has triumphed, Bělohradský argues, takes no cognisance of the realities and differences of the rest of the world. [4] Citing Husserl, he describes Fukuyama's work as part of that 'project of europeanising the rest of the world [which] is a symptom of absolute reason' (Bělohradský, 1991b, p. 209).

This verdict on Fukuyama – as simply offering yet another 'view from the west' – is to be understood in the context of Bělohradksý's antipathy to what he takes to be the traditional western view of the role of reason, and thus of the intellectual or the philosopher:

> At first I was still in thrall to the idea that the philosopher's job is to seek some authentic version of the world and to try to ensure that it remain unsullied. More recently, however, I have come to the conclusion that the job of the philosopher is quite different: it is systematically to criticize the claims of various versions of the world to authenticity ... This notion of philosophy is postmodern ... the term marks the fact that the version of the world in which enlightened human beings waged war against darkness, and in which to be modern was to overcome obstacles ... is exhausted. The postmodern sense of life does not consist just in understanding that modernity was not in fact an era beyond tradition, but in attempting to escape that era. The entire western tradition is metaphysical in the sense that it

assumes that there is some final end to which humanity is progressing. (ibid., pp. 9–10)

This postmodern view has appeared in Czech intellectual life like a bolt from the blue, all the more as our society is very considerably inward-looking and self-obsessed, both about its immediate and pressing problems and about the nature of the provenance of those of the recent past. It has therefore aroused considerable opposition from thinkers who object violently to its insistence that the communist system itself was the, or at least one, outcome of that very western Enlightenment tradition from which they argue that post-communist society should take its lead. The notion that liberalism is in **any** sense parallel to the communism which it has replaced – in this case inasmuch as both are or were put forward as 'final', as the apotheosis of progress – is in a very real sense shocking. [5] Yet this, as I indicated earlier (p. 52) is precisely what Bělohradský argues, that the communist state is **one** incarnation of western philosophy and its 'metaphysical' spirit (Bělohradský, 1991c, p. 3). No wonder, then, that his reading of Fukuyama as overly Hegelian and **therefore** overly and blindly triumphalist might seem more radical in the Czech Republic than in the west.

Nevertheless, and whatever one's view of the postmodern turn and its understanding both of the role of the intellectual and of the nature and function of reason, the gist of Bělohradský's critique seems to me well-founded, quite regardless of whether or not his reading of Fukuyama as 'traditionally' Hegelian is accurate. For the 'end of history' (however understood – see below) and the 'triumph of liberalism' (however shorn of triumphalism – that is to say, even on a reading of Fukuyama as 'pessimistic' rather than as offering a 'happy ending') need not be one and the same thing. To insist on equating the two is surely to offer something which, politically, is very much 'the view from the west', however one evaluates the merits or otherwise of the intellectual tradition which informs it. There is a sense, I think, in which Bělohradský is right to urge that philosophers should not be 'the bureaucrats of humanity, but rather its gypsies ... that they have no mission to look for absolute principles [which have] universal validity and are binding on the whole of humanity' (Bělohradský, 1991b, p. 218). [6] For insofar as Fukuyama insists that there is a 'final answer' – namely liberal democracy – it is difficult to see how his thesis might open up rather than close down debate. Bělohradský's 'critical reason' and his conception of the intellectual's task, however antithetical to the intellectual and, above all, academic, traditions of eastern and central Europe in particular, are, I think, well-taken. To agree with him on that count, however, does not entail agreeing with his own identification of such a view as uniquely characteristic of 'postphilosophical times'. Nor need one be committed to the association of his position that he himself makes with Solzhenytsin's objections to the western tradition (objections which, again, might strike an interesting chord with those familiar with Rorty's views) as dominated by 'an apocalyptic tone ... the legacy of Greek metaphysics and Jewish monotheism ...which was imported by philosophers and prophets into politics and infiltrated its institutions ...' (cited in Bělohradský 1991d, p. 3).

III

In the end, however, I am not entirely convinced that Fukuyama is in fact committed to such a thoroughly Hegelian conception of history as Bělohradský attributes to him. I am inclined to think, rather, that Fukuyama's thesis is itself just one of those 'cogent versions of the world' which Bělohradský regards as characteristic of liberal society in its postmodern state. In that sense, and although one may dispute his perhaps excessively simplistic or single-minded ideas, or the specific formulation of his conclusions, one has nevertheless to grant the accuracy of Fukuyama's characterisation of certain components of the global elements of European and world-wide developments. It may be a question of identifying future peaceful developments with an accelerating diminution of traditional geopolitics; or perhaps Fukuyama is offering us ideals to which the world of politics ought to aspire. (Neither recent conflicts such as the Gulf War, nor the current Balkan crisis and the other local ethnic wars doubtless to come around the world – especially in the ex-USSR – constitute a counter-example to Fukuyama. The current ethnic and civil conflict in Bosnia-Herzegovina, for example, does not in my view show him to have been mistaken: the fact that the surrounding liberal, or liberalizing, world can neither understand nor come to terms with the horrors of the situation – which are the result of highly specific historical conditions – does not affect his claim about the relations among liberal democracies; those – different – relations among other states; or relations between these two groups.) Fukuyama's views remain importantly stimulating insofar as they at least prompt thought about what, if anything, may have ended with the end of communism – and thus about how the world might go. Whether Fukuyama's is a thoroughly Hegelian conception of history, so that 'the end of history' thesis is a claim about ideology – to the effect that a Hegelian apogee has now been reached, albeit in liberal rather than in communist form; or one which is somewhat less rationalistic, so that the thesis is to be understood more as an empirical claim, or perhaps forecast, about the likely impact of liberalism's actual political victory on the course of political thinking and, via that, on the course of actual events; or whether Bělohradský's understanding of the claim – 'history' has been shown not to be an appropriate, let alone adequate, explanation of the course of events – is the more fruitful one: Fukuyama's work forces careful reconsideration not only of our understanding of 'history', but also of the nature of our political ideals and the sort of world we might actually be able to build. And that is no small achievement.

Notes

1. See also Fukuyama (1990).
2. Compare the well-known marxist definition of freedom as 'the recognition of necessity'.
3. See especially Bělohradský (1991c) for discussion of the politico-philosophical understandings of 'the West' and of the crises of democracy associated with specifically western interpretations of 'the West'. In particular, he locates the naive environmentalism of those advocating 'technical' solutions to the environmental crisis as central in obscuring what is really required, namely a radical change of lifestyle.
4. Bělohradský's conception of the task of philosophers and intellectuals generally is strongly reminiscent of Rorty's view of it as conversation and criticism rather than as metaphysical theorizing (Rorty, 1989): in his rejection of what might be described as the west's tendency to 'intellectual imperialism', however, he not only goes against Rorty's conception of such conversation as 'of the west', but, in doing so, exposes his inconsistency. Just why should conversation, of whatever sort, be thus parochial?
5. The storm first broke with his article on 'Post-communism even in the USSR' (in Bělohradský, 1991b) which was fiercely attacked by Ladislav Hejdánek (1991), who regards Bělohradský's postmodernism as a virus which society – trying to recover from years of totalitarianism – could well do without, as a sophistry which is an affront to a long democratic tradition stretching back to Jan Hus. Bělohradský's view of communism as stemming from the totalizing spirit of western philosophy, Hejdánek argues, is one which he is particularly ill-equipped to offer, having been abroad for twenty years and thus possessing little real understanding of the nature of communism – to which Bělohradský's response is that prophets are rarely welcomed in their own countries. This ill-tempered debate is not yet at an end.
6. Cf. Havel (1990).

References

Bělohradský, V. (1991a), *Myslet Zeleň Světa*, Mladá Fronta, Prague.
Bělohradský, V. (1991b), 'Přirozený svět jako politický problém', in Bělohradský, V., *Eseje o Člověku Pozdní Doby*, Mladá Fronta, Prague.
Bělohradský, V. (1991c), 'Přítomnost', *Přít*, 9, pp. 3–4.
Bělohradský, V. (1991d), 'Triumf liberalismu a konec dějin', *Mladá Fronta Dnes*, 25 April, p. 3.
Elliott, G. (1993), 'The cards of confusion: reflections on historical communism and the "end of history"', *Radical Philosophy*, 64, pp. 3–12.
Fukuyama, F. (1989a), 'The end of history?', *The National Interest*, 16, pp. 3–18.
Fukuyama, F. (1989b), 'Reply to my critics', *The National Interest*, 18, pp. 21–28.
Fukuyama, F. (1990), 'Forget Iraq – history is dead', *The Guardian*, 7 September.
Havel, V. (1990), *Disturbing the Peace: a Conversation with Karel Hvížďalka*, Hvížďalka, K. (ed.), Faber, London.
Heydánek, L. (1991), 'Musí demokracie rezignovat na pravdu?', *Literární Noviny*, vol. 2, 44, pp. 1–3.
Rorty, R. (1989), *Contingency, Irony and Solidarity*, Cambridge University Press, Cambridge.

5 'They are not tigers' — myth and myopia in the quest for a liberal economic order

Tom Hickey

Než bych já se dívala na vaší zaostalost – to se raději za živa pohřbim!
(Janáček, 1923) [1]

With the events of 1989 in central and eastern Europe, and of 1991 in the then Soviet Union, even if History has not reached some terminus, much less revealed its purpose, we may be assured that it has now overcome one anguished choice. But which choice? No consensus exists as to how best to characterize the route that has been rejected. Is it the abandonment of all collectivist or interventionist programmes, or only those associated with discredited egalitarian, or more comprehensively socialist, visions? If it is either of these, does it constitute a rejection contingent on the manifest failures and tyrannies of the Stalinist version of such programmes, or is it the outcome of a convincing, or even compelling, demonstration of their inherent flaws? Certainly, for established liberal opinion, East and West, the implications are taken to be self-evident, and theoretical generalizations supervene the events with indecent haste: free markets have not merely proven their superiority over economic planning, but have established their indispensability, given what is now generally perceived to be the irrationality of the latter; capitalism and the private property relations in the means of production which are taken to be its defining characteristic (but see section III below) have shown themselves to be preconditions for democracy; and individualism – economic, political and methodological – and its policy conclusions – economic liberalism and political pluralism – stand triumphant in the field. Empirical confirmation of such a view has apparently become all but quotidian as reform-minded politicians in industrialized countries abandon the surviving vestiges of Social Democracy (Elliott, 1993a), governments of less developed countries (LDCs) abandon interventionist development strategies in favour of further integration into the world market, and the meliorists of the academy, whose structuralist critiques seem increasingly like theoretical evanescences dissolving as the peculiarities of the postwar decades remove their temporary framework, cede even the concepts of the debate to the New Right. Life itself seems to be holding forth to individualism a relentlessly confirmatory mirror – or, at least, so it would seem from a reading of the literature and from the temporizing of most of those still sceptical of its deliquescent reduction of social theory. Liberalism, particularly economic liberalism, which since the late 1970s has been self-assured, is today apparently triumphant and undeniably triumphalist. Yet it is an inapposite jubilation.

Economic liberalism, as both theory and policy, aims to enhance the rôle of the market, and progressively to reduce the rôle of the state in the economic sphere, towards the latter's eventual elimination as an economic actor, other than as the sentinel for private property and as the provider of the effective constraint and opportunity of contract law. We are invited to view this corrective process not merely as the establishment of a superior allocative mechanism, but as the erection of an essential precondition of human freedom (Hayek, 1944 and 1960, Friedman, 1962). We are further invited to transcribe this conviction, whether as scholars or as economic actors, from high theory to all areas of human activity.

It is as if the evidence of liberalism's failures in the real world did not exist, and the intellectual history of economic liberalism's theoretical vagaries and vacuities had been successfully cauterized. It is as if the famines of sub-Saharan Africa, the floods of South Asia, the poverty, destitution and illiteracy of what was once called the Third World, and the current levels of mass unemployment of the industrialized world (in excess of thirty million in the OECD countries) were all vulgar irrelevancies with no pertinence to the argument. It is as if it were not true: that infant mortality rates in some areas of New York now exceed those of Malaysia, and that in the South Bronx 531 infants in every 1,000 require neo-natal hospitalization (Kozol, 1992); or that in East St. Louis, Illinois, USA, one finds not only few jobs, but also a city without a garbage collection service or an effective sewage system due to a combination of municipal indebtedness and the impact of institutionalized racism on the zoning of urban infrastructural investment (ibid.). It is as if environmental despoilation, homelessness, poverty, demoralization, and disillusion were not to be found within liberalism's orbit. It is as if the history of economics had been successfully rewritten to suppress the ways in which dissenting alternatives to mainstream thought have undermined the coherence of the notions of market perfectability, utility maximizing *homo economicus*, consumer sovereignty, Pareto-optimality, a golden age of laissez faire, prices as market clearing signals, and capital as a measurable object. Many economists, both professional and academic, have for long been critical of the theoretical narcissism and self-referentiality of the neo-classical model. Now, however, it is as if its schisms and contradictions no longer existed, or no longer mattered. Whatever the contrary evidence or the reasoned doubt, sceptics of the modish reductions of the social to the individual, and of the macro to the micro, can be safely ignored.

Those not innocent of the philosophical and methodological problems involved in such an enduring, almost atavistic, commitment to individualism may retreat behind an appeal to the inviolability of the 'hard core' of their 'research programme' (Lakatos, 1970 and 1978), but the norm today would seem to be simply to ignore discomfiting argument. Paradoxically, these elisions often serve as poignant reminders of the richness of the insights provided by the terrain outside the pristine severity of abstract theorizing; the severities of existence, in the form of unemployment and poverty and subjection, though offering no guarantee of acuity, accuracy or cogency, often supply both a spur to critical reflection, and a corrective to the greyness of esoteric model building. This does not mean that fascination with the artefacts of liberal economic doctrine is confined to the academy, or to the corridors of political display. In eastern Europe, at least, it has, in these heady early days of post-Stalinism, a widespread popular resonance.

This article is an attempt to redress the balance. I will argue that the quest for a liberal economic order is informed by a liberal ideology that both produces and feeds upon a series of identifiable myths and disingenuous blindnesses which allow and encourage the view that, whatever its failings, there is no alternative to the market as a method of effective and efficient economic organization. It is such a view that allows Fukuyama (1989) to see history as a process that has terminated – a perception facilitated by what Elliott (1993a) and McCarney (1989) have identified as a facile generalization from recent social and economic trends, and what Anderson (1991) locates as a pivotal misreading of Hegel.

I want to deal with three major myths of economic liberalism. By 'myth' in this context is not meant error, untruth, misrepresentation or illusion, but rather that system of communication which not only indicates a generality about our world but imposes its existence imperiously upon us. In this sense, a myth is not misleading, but rather is distortive and deformative of reality; its referent is not truth, but rather the value that it is propounding, its interpretive function and intention, and its despotic injunction to use its concepts in thinking about the world. As Barthes has put it: 'Neither a lie nor a confession, it is an inflection' (Barthes, 1993). The key mechanisms employed to this end in the case of the myths of economic liberalism are consistent with the general case: the emptying of reality of its history and the signified of its contingency; and the replacement of this history and the significance of meanings (and hence of human agency) with a naturalized image of reality in which intentions and interests have disappeared. Contingent circumstances and arrangements are presented as eternal, as natural necessities, whose fundamental justification is, therefore, ineffable. [2]

The first myth is that markets, and the policy outcomes of economic liberalism, work – i.e. that they produce social stability and economic growth. I shall argue that all the evidence points to the opposite conclusion. The second myth is that economic liberalism, as a form of economic analysis, provides the basis for an objective economic science. I shall argue that it is rather a dogmatic, and sometimes fanatical, ideology designed to serve specific and identifiable interests. Finally, I shall confront the view that, since the experience and collapse of Stalinism have shown that the socialist project was a snare and an illusion, there is no alternative economic and social system to free-market capitalism. I shall argue that with the re-emergence since the early 1970s of increasingly severe oscillations in the global economy, with desperate, and even life-threatening, consequences for millions, any presumption against the **possibility** of **some** systemic alternative can only reflect prejudice rather than critical reflection; that were capitalism to enjoy no instantiation other than the experience of 'actually existing capitalist economies' then as a vision of the future it is one that betokens little hope for free markets, and in the case of societies with underdeveloped economies (including those of eastern Europe) little hope for many other kinds of freedom either; and that, were an alternative to prove not only possible but necessary, there are good reasons why the experience of Stalinism cannot be taken as any kind of evidence against the socialist project.

I

> GROSS: I'm sorry, Mr Ballas, but the circumstances I've allowed myself to point out is simply a fact.
> BALLAS: What of it? We won't be bullied by facts!
>
> (Havel, 1966)

The most virulent of the myths, and the most evident myopia, are to be uncovered in the claim that the pursuit of liberal economic policies can achieve stable economies and rapid economic growth and development. And nowhere, it seems, has the virus taken a stronger hold than in eastern Europe. [3] Even the Hungarian economist, Janos Kornai – who was as famous for his penetrating critiques of the unrealism of market equilibrium (Kornai, 1975 and 1972) as for his advocacy of reform, and belief in the reformability of, the eastern economies (Kornai, 1959) – had abandoned any notion of change within the system by the mid-1980s (Kornai, 1986a and b). Today, he celebrates the 'minimal state' (Kornai, 1990). Among the rulers of the old regimes just such an ideological shift was already occurring, and for some well before 1989. While Gorbachev's early economic advisor Aganbegan was extolling a partial marketization under the Soviet restructuring programme (Aganbegan, 1988), sections of these regimes were evidently manoeuvering for their own political survival in the face of what was perceived by them as an unavoidable liberalization of both economy and polity. Market reform was the order of the day (UN, 1989, Solimano, 1990, Fischer and Gelb, 1990): not that it was assumed to be a painless process, but rather one to which, it was believed, there was no alternative.

The first problem with this scenario of rapid progress being seen as dependent on world economic growth is that even the optimistic growth targets for eastern Europe estimated by the IMF (1991) are only two per cent per annum. At that rate it would take between ten and fifteen years for pre-1989 levels of output to be attained – by which time the gap between East and West would have increased since other growth rates (even for LDCs) are forecast to be higher. There are, however, more pressing reasons to be sceptical of the fruits of liberalization and the integration of eastern Europe into the world trading system. The pattern of trade and specialization that developed in eastern Europe, under the tutelage of Stalinism and the auspices of the Council for Mutual Economic Assistance, was one that was underpinned by a dual protectionism: an insulation from world competition; and a subsidy from the import of raw materials from the USSR at less than world market prices, in exchange for manufactured exports to the USSR that were overpriced in world terms. The shift to world prices paid in convertible currencies has produced huge trade deficits for all the eastern European countries, and contributed to a process of deindustrialization. The expanding trade with the industrialized west has partially compensated for lost markets in the east, but the pattern of trade has altered with a significant decline in the industrial content of exports in favour of agricultural commodities, raw materials and semi-manufactures (Havrylyshyn and Pritchett, 1991). The OECD (1991a) predicts annual current account deficits of US$7 to US$8 billion during the 1990s. The prospects look grim not least because 25–30 per cent of exports to the West from Hungary, Poland, the Czech Republic and Slovakia are in commodity categories where significant trade barriers, tariff and non-tariff, exist. This is particularly the case in respect of agricultural commodities that might be targeted at the EC. In the face of a militant farming lobby, escalating protectionist pressure from manufacturers and trades unions, and in the context of an incipient trade war with the USA, Japan and the Newly Industrialized Countries (NICs), the EC is unlikely to be in any position to make significant trade concessions in agricultural commodities in the foreseeable future (CEPR, 1990, Bergeijk and Pritchett, 1991).

Effective protection for industry under the old regimes also created long-term structural problems for their economies should world competition ever have had to be faced. The permanent protection and automatic subsidies of the 'soft budget constraint' (Kornai, 1986a) ensured that industries, which in western economic literature would have been called the 'infants' of an industrial development strategy, never matured to competitive productivity levels. The experience of the eastern German economy after unification is instructive here. In contrast to the optimistic projections of the IMF for 'catch up', the economy of the east all but collapsed following unification in 1990: manufacturing output fell 30 per cent in one month, and by the end of 1990 total output had fallen 54.5 per cent. By July 1991, unemployment had reached 12.1 per cent, with short-time working affecting in excess of 20 per cent of the labour force.

In these circumstances, the aspiration for membership of the EC will remain a chimera. The 'new Europe' may today consist of more states than at any time in modern history, linked through a variety of frameworks (Nugent, 1992), but it is hard to see how these links with the EC could develop beyond trade and cooperation agreements, and association status in the medium term. As the process of economic and political integration of the EC member states and their economies accelerates, there can now be little doubt that it is accompanied by the internal development of a major political crisis. Part of that crisis is contingent and conjunctural in origin, but its genesis is also partly structural and systemic. The persistence of the recession in the EC economies is normally explained by reference to the impact of high German interest rates (consequent upon the budgetary effects of unification in tandem with the existence of an independent Bundesbank) on Community-wide monetary aggregates and instruments via the European Monetary System transmission mechanism. Yet it is not only a monetarily squeezed western Europe that faces prolonged recession. Economic stagnation is now a global phenomenon. Thus, even had German interest rates been dramatically reduced in 1992, it is hard to see how EC economic performance in that year could have exceeded one per cent growth – a performance it might well be proud of even in 1993. More striking still is the observation that, even with 1 per cent growth, unemployment in the EC would still have increased by as much as two million, and taken the total for the EC past seventeen million at the end of 1992. The phenomenon has come to be known as 'jobless growth'. It has now become a commonplace to accept that, with existing trends in productivity growth, an overall growth rate in excess of 2.5 per cent is necessary merely to check the rise in unemployment. In current conditions, such a target is unattainable.

Average growth performance for the Community as a whole is, in addition, a statistic that conceals the widening gulf separating those EC states whose economies are contracting from those whose consistently better than average performances ensure that the EC average remains a positive number. It is this reality that currently constitutes a severe threat to the future of European unification. While the process of global trade and production integration creates strong centripetal forces within the EC, the consequences of the associated geographical concentration of economic and political influence, and investment location, which are only partly offset by the emergence of 'footloose' industries using computer-integrated design, production and distribution systems, is the creation of potentially powerful, centrifugal political and social movements. The de facto, if not yet de jure, existence today of a 'two speed Europe' within the EC creates fertile conditions for the re-emergence of European nationalisms and sub-national regionalisms in various possible forms, and with a variety of possible aspirations. As each new initiative towards unification is launched it seems to provoke its alterity: homogenization of standards, a disdain of bureaucratic meddling; monetary union, a resurgence of national parochialism dressed as an imagined tradition of popular sovereignty; etc. Though Hegel might not be beguiled by the suggestion that contemporary events have rejuvenated his 'Philosophy of History', there can be little doubt that he would find manifest in the EC sufficient of that inner articulation requisite for him to claim some support for the arguments of his *Logic*. In these conditions, it is not just proposals to 'widen' the EC that will face increasingly trenchant criticism, but also the drive to 'deepen' its integration through economic, monetary and political union.

The second source of scepticism with respect to the benefits of a liberal economic order in eastern Europe is the shortage of funds for investment. The World Bank's estimate for eastern Europe (excluding the ex-Yugoslavia and the ex-USSR) is US$20 billion simply to keep the economies at their existing output; attaining competitiveness would require some US$300 billion over a reasonable period (Haynes, 1992b, Zloch-Christy, 1987). Such transfers are unlikely in the extreme given the current level of recession in the western economies (Zloch-Christy, 1990). Meanwhile, the insistence by western banks and governments that eastern European states should honour the debts of the old regimes reproduces the sick irony of the emerging relation between Third World and First World capital flows. With the net debt of eastern Europe (including the ex-USSR) at US$123 billion, interest payments to western banks and states totalled US$12 billion in 1990 (OECD, 1991c). Eastern Europe is about to join the 'Third World' in becoming a net exporter of capital, subsidizing economic activity in the richer, industrialized countries – the OECD (1991b) showed Poland, Hungary and the then Czechoslovakia paying 71 per cent, 65 per cent and 25 per cent of export earnings respectively in interest and in principal repayment. It is difficult to judge how long such strategically inept foreign policy paralysis will afflict western governments, or how much politically destabilizing social instability in eastern Europe it will take for short-term commercial considerations in the West to be relegated to second place. Even when enlightened self-interest does appear, however, and whether in the form of a rescheduling, a moratorium, new credits, swap arrangements, or some 'debt forgiveness', it will doubtless be portrayed as a beneficent, if benignant, largesse. What is equally certain is that even the maximum amount of grant that might be conceivable from a consortium of OECD or G7 countries will not be sufficient to make a significant impact on the total debt outstanding. To avoid the danger of 'moral hazard', as well as for reasons of monetary rectitude in the midst of a recession, neither individual governments, nor consortia thereof, are likely to underwrite any substantial commercial exposure, nor cancel more than a small proportion of sovereign loans. Concomitantly, the potential and actual political instability of the region has naturally reduced the willingness of western commercial banks to make further loans (Fairlamb, 1990).

It is at this stage of the argument that I would expect defenders of liberalization and the market to refer to the success stories of economic liberalism; to point to the economic performance of those western economies that have adopted the policies of neo-liberalism; to appeal to the example of the dramatically successful East Asian economies – South Korea, Taiwan, Singapore and Hong Kong – as models to be emulated.

In 1979, the first Thatcher administration was elected on a programme that was inspired by neo-liberalism, and which committed the Government to a key objective: the halting of the long-run, relative decline of the UK economy through faster growth, an increase in manufactured exports, the control of inflation, and an increase in labour productivity. The set of policies selected to achieve this objective were impressively representative of economic liberalism in modern guise (Rowthorn, 1992): monetarism – to control the nominal money supply, in the belief, following Friedman, that 'inflation is always and everywhere a monetary phenomenon'; cuts in government spending – to reduce the proportion of government activity in GDP and to stop the 'crowding out' of the private sector; cuts in direct taxation – to erode the 'dependency culture' and to encourage initiative and self-reliance by increasing incentives for individuals; privatization – to increase competition and the deregulation of industry and finance; and trade union legislation – to impose discipline on the labour force and to increase managerial flexibility. How have these policies performed?

There is, amongst economists in the UK, some disagreement on this question, but given that the successor Major administration has been managing the worst recession since the 1930s, and in the light of some key aspects of the Thatcher Government's record, those policies could not be said to have been a startling success. With the declared intention of defeating price inflation, that government commenced by managing, through the creation of high interest rates, an upward appreciation of the currency by 20 per cent against those of its trading partners, ostensibly to lower the price of imports, but, arguably, to discipline employers in the export sector into refusing high wage claims. The effect was to bankrupt in excess of 20 per cent of UK manufacturing during the 1979–81 recession (Keegan, 1986). The UK recession certainly contributed, in conjunction with the global recession, to a decline in inflation, but at the cost of levels of unemployment unprecedented since the 1930s (Johnson, 1991). The objective of controlling the money supply proved to be an impossible task since the private banking sector could always evade government controls, and the deregulation of financial services multiplied the sources of credit (Coakley and Harris, 1992). By 1985, the government had abandoned domestic monetarism. By 1987 inflation was accelerating, fuelled by a sharp rise in property values, and further stimulated, in 1988, by additional tax cuts introduced in the period immediately preceding the 1987 election (Keegan, 1989). By 1990, inflation, at 11 per cent, was back to the figure it had reached in 1979, but with much higher levels of unemployment. July 1990 saw the onset of the current recession, but British entry into the Exchange Rate Mechanism of the EC forced further rises in real interest rate differentials between the UK and Germany to defend the stipulated value of sterling, thereby further depressing both investment and consumption demand, and opening sharp divisions amongst the ranks of the governing party. The ignominious abandonment of the central tenets of economic policy with the UK withdrawal of sterling from the European Exchange Rate Mechanism was to follow, as were the emergence of record trade deficits, despite the impact of the recession on domestic demand.

Apart from the unemployment and loss of production consequent on government policy, the latter's record can also be assessed by reference to the efficiency impact of its industrial policy, and the equity effect of its fiscal and labour market policy (Johnson, 1991, Smith, 1987 and 1992). Industrial policy consisted almost exclusively of an extended programme of privatization, which has been successfully implemented: in one decade 50 per cent of the state industrial sector, involving 800,000 jobs, had been transferred to the private sector (Fine and Poletti, 1992), a success to which is credited the annual average rate of 5.4 per cent productivity growth in British manufacturing industry in the mid-1980s (Haskel and Kay, 1990). What is less frequently observed, however, is that, contra intention, this has not achieved any reduction in the share of government expenditure in GDP: Maddison (1989) shows that between 1973 and 1986 the state sector share of GDP increased for the UK from 41.5 per cent to 45.9 per cent (and that what was the case for the UK was replicated in all developed industrial economies). Furthermore, the bulk of this 'Thatcher miracle' in enhancing industrial productivity was achieved through labour-displacing investment and a reorganization of production, and thus was and remains a fast depleting productivity resource. In fact, the UK economy's capacity to manifest technological innovation has **weakened** during this period as research and development expenditure as a proportion of GDP has declined in relation to that of other OECD economies (Englander and Mittelstadt, 1988). Far from the privatization of public utilities having encouraged competitive markets, moreover, it has merely transformed public monopolies into private monopolies, whose shareholders and directors are among the few whose incomes have shown a significant real increase, while the rise in prices of their products to consumers has accelerated faster than the general rate of inflation. Simultaneously, the combination of regressive tax reform and the use of legislation to shift the bargaining balance against trade union organization, while failing in its core objective to de-unionize any significant sector, has led to a marked worsening of income distribution. Finally, between 1989 and 1991 there were 47,000 company liquidations in the UK, and in the eighteen months from the beginning of 1990 to mid-1991 an additional one million people had become unemployed.

A similar history of 1980s policy and performance could be written about most other EC member states, irrespective of the formal political identity of their governing parties – the French, Greek and Spanish socialist parties having followed the dictates of economic fashion even to the point of a potentially self-immolating erosion of their traditional electoral support. In the USA, the picture only differs by dint of the success of the Reagan and Bush administrations in having enabled, through the exercise of state power, a significant bout of wage cutting by employers so as to secure enhancements of industrial productivity.

If, however, the European and North American economies do not offer inspiring examples of economic liberalism in practice, is it not the case that those of the East Asian 'Gang of Four' do? Here, surely, are economic tigers. Between 1963 and 1984 all four dramatically increased the share of manufactures in exports; their export base broadened and deepened, moving progressively from labour intensive textiles and semiconductors, via capital-intensive steel and shipbuilding, to technology-intensive vehicles, business machines and telecommunications; they increased the share of high technology goods in their exports from 2.2 per cent to 25 per cent in the two decades to 1985; and, in the 1963–73 period, South Korea and Taiwan achieved astounding annual average growth rates of 10.7 per cent and 11.1 per cent respectively (Harris, 1986). Thus it is concluded that economic liberalism has a blueprint for the future, and that on the Pacific Rim it can be seen to be working.

The difficulty with this argument, however, is that most economic and political histories of the development process in these societies strongly suggest that an account of these economies' evolutions and trajectories as being characterized by free markets could only be described as obtuse and misleading (Wade, 1991, Ariff and Hill, 1987). Far from there being less state intervention, the development process has been heavily dependent on both extensive and insistent state direction, particularly in identifying key areas for expansion, given the stage attained in the process of industrialization and the identifiable trading opportunities, and in devising consistent and supportive policies for those areas. While industrialization in Singapore was heavily dependent on the attraction of foreign multinational capital investment, the South Korean and Taiwanese strategy focussed on the encouragement of indigenous industrial development through the manipulation of the urban-rural terms of trade, the strict and careful management of price relativities, and various forms of state subsidy for the favoured, strategic sectors (Harris, 1986, Ariff and Hill, 1987). It was neither free markets nor free market prices that achieved these outcomes, but appropriately **managed** prices, and carefully **administered** markets. What was also characteristic of those regimes, of course, was the relative independence of their states from the constraint of effective trade unionism, and, indeed, from the influence of a politically well organized capitalist class. Throughout this period, all four 'Asian Tigers' had repressive regimes that prevented, until the late 1970s, the spread of trade union organization or open political dissent. Whether such regimes are morally or politically favoured, or whether there has been an interested rewriting of the history of state intervention in some East Asian NICs, are, however, separate questions – if important ones – from that of whether the East Asian model is generalizable. Can such conditions be replicated in Latin America, in sub-Saharan Africa, or in eastern Europe? Where, for example, could the markets be found to absorb the exports of LDCs (and those of the economies of the post-Stalinist states by extension) were only some of them to have even a shadow of the export success of the East Asian NICs (Singer, 1988, Singer and Grey, 1988)?

Yet it remains the case that a trade-oriented, neo-liberal development strategy is thought to be based on sound and compelling empirical evidence. An extensive literature exists documenting the results of statistical investigations into the relationship between 'openness' and economic growth, responsibility for some of which the author himself must admit to (World Bank, 1983 and 1987, Argawala, 1983, Syrquin and Chenery, 1989, Michaely, 1977, Balassa, 1978, Hickey, 1979 and 1980). Evans (1991), citing joint work with Aghezedeh (Aghezedeh and Evans, 1988), submits some of this endeavour to devastating criticism, identifying the ways in which the outcomes of the investigations often pivot on the unavoidable adjudications of researchers in the absence of any clear cut, objective index for grading particular countries in terms of their degree of inward or outward orientation, and, hence, on the particular definition of 'outward orientation' used. Whereas South Korea and Singapore always appear in the literature as 'outward oriented', alternative definitions of the concept – which might reasonably be adopted on good economic grounds – would exclude them. Evans concludes that 'there is a real danger that the set of judgements which were made in classifying countries by trade orientation in the ... World Bank (1987) study was influenced by the **attribution** of a favourable growth performance of the countries in the sample to the degree of outward orientation' (emphasis added), and he adds that 'in terms of the growth of GDP, and of per capita GDP, domestic savings and inflation, the moderately inward oriented countries did better than the moderately outward oriented countries in the period 1973-85' (ibid.). Contrary to the received wisdom of neo-liberal discourse, therefore, there is no strong empirical evidence in favour of a shift to outward orientation in the interests of economic growth; and the evidence that is available, moreover, cannot support the notion that trade policy is the most important variable in determining rates of economic growth.

Part of the difficulty of the debate, however, is the unwillingness of many advocates of a liberal economic order to accept the persuasiveness, or even the relevance, of empirical evidence, whether it be in terms of the adoption of alternative trade regimes as outlined above, or in relation to the damaging impact more generally of economic policies inspired by economic liberalism (Parkin, 1983, Bacha, 1983, Killick, 1984, Edwards, 1985, Pastor, 1987, Taylor, 1988, Colclough and Green, 1988, Ramirez, 1991). As Colclough observes, the 'response ... to the evidence of failure is to blame insufficient commitment to reform or the strength of opposition to it' (Colclough, 1991). [4] This neo-liberal dismissal of evidence, however, strikes one as precisely the kind of ad hoc stratagem so corruscatingly dealt with by earlier advocates of liberalism working in the philosophy of science (Popper, 1972 and 1976). It is difficult to conclude, in the face of these retorts, that there exists any evidence, of any kind, that could count against the correctness of policy prescriptions in particular cases, much less against the theoretical grounding on the basis of which they are advocated. One need not be persuaded of the cogency of falsificationist criteria for the scientificity of propositions to notice the contradiction between the **principle** of falsifiability, forcefully urged by ardent liberals in the philosophy of science as a scourge of Marxism, and the **practice** of contemporary economic liberals.

II

> An individual here and there may score a point in secret, but no one hears it until afterwards, no one knows how it has been done. So there's no real community, people come across each other in the lobbies, but there's not much conversation. The superstitious beliefs are an old tradition and increase automatically.
>
> (Kafka, 1925)

The second myth I wish to deal with is the notion that economic liberalism, in both its philosophical and methodological forms on the one hand and its substantive theories on the other, is undogmatic, impartial and pragmatic: that it is a science that at once provides the concepts necessary for dispassionate inquiry and for the categorization and codification of the world; and that it also explains the relationships observed, thereby providing the necessary basis for effective policy intervention. These claims are made not only in relation to liberalism's still dominant neo-classical tradition in economic analysis, but also in relation to its Austrian School variant. They are false claims.

It was always the case that neo-classicism described the esoteric details of the operation of an imaginary market in which perfect knowledge and perfect competition reigned, in which the uncertainty that characterizes the future was of no theoretical significance – since the style of analysis was comparative statics rather than the dynamics of change – and in which all economic actors behaved as utility-maximizing individuals constrained by their budget, and by the dictates of a narrow definition of economic rationality. Neo-classicists never pretended that their model was other than this; nor did they claim it to be a representation of the real world. It was a model without distortions whether in the form of scale economies or diseconomies, externalities, trusts, or monopolies; in which there could, in principle, be no divergence between private net benefits and social welfare, the latter being merely the sum of the former; and in which prices, including wages, adjusted instantaneously to their market-clearing equilibrium level so as perfectly to reflect opportunity cost. It was precisely the difference between real markets and the markets of the model that furnished neo-classicism with the explanatory and predictive power that its advocates claimed. By identifying the divergences of the real markets from the imagined 'first best' alternative, the optimal policy mix might be devised that could, through corrective intervention, attempt an approximation of the outcomes that would have existed in the absence of market distortions. Economic analysis thus provided a technical 'tool-box', free of normative elements, and available, in principle, to any 'mechanic' minded to use it. When Friedman (1953) made his notorious and robust retreat to instrumentalism in defence of 'positive economics', it was an entirely consistent move, notwithstanding any scepticism with respect to the philosophical coherence of pragmatism that many in the discipline retained – though, in choosing to ignore the accumulation of counter-argument, in somewhat Nelsonian fashion. The demonstration by Lipsey and Lancaster (1956–7) that, in the presence of more than one market distortion, the appropriate policy response for moving closer to an optimum allocation of resources becomes indeterminate, ought to have induced a severe crisis of self-confidence amongst pragmatic 'positivists'. In the event, it appears to have had little impact on them, or on the nature of their work.

Today, economic liberalism presents itself in a variety of forms, as

Anderson's recent summatorial endeavour (1992) outlines: the neo-classical synthesis, which reconciled General Equilibrium marginalism with the destabilizing elements of time, expectations and money, has now been joined by Rational Expectations and Public Choice theories which share an inspiration in the Austrian School. What all possess in common is a profound esteem for the value of a consumer society, and for the 'consumer sovereignty' that it presumes. For Brittan (1988) it is the absence of any force constraining human agents to act or consume in any particular fashion that constitutes the great virtue of competitive capitalism, irrespective of what degree or type of inequality that it tolerates or engenders. That this feature of capitalism is reserved for praise derives, it is claimed, from the concern of the economic liberal with the aspirations of individuals rather than with the supposedly superior collective goods that are both the objectives and inspirations of paternalist thought and action. The selection of this feature for elevation results in liberalism designating itself, soi-disant, as the philosophy that 'attaches a special value to freedom' (ibid., p. 35). This emphasis also reflects the growth in influence, since the early 1970s, of the Austrian School variant of liberal economic thought, the progenitor of contemporary neo-liberalism. The notion of 'freedom' being here defended is, of course, Berlin's 'negative freedom' (Berlin, 1969) – the absence of compulsion. It is the nature of this celebration, then, that furnishes the Hayekian project (1960) of minimizing the ambit of the coercive state. This is not the same as extending democracy, however, as most contemporary liberal theorists make clear: Brittan, for example, qualifies this freedom as of a personal and economic kind (ibid. p. 36). It is, therefore, entirely consistent with the existence of dictatorship, which imposes specific injunctions, as opposed to 'totalitarianism', which enforces all-encompassing ideological constraints; and is, therefore, inconsistent with the freedom-seeking project as defined. The case is not infrequently made that most western European and North American societies are **over-provided** with democracy (Brittan, 1977); and the logic of this argument, in which democracy figures only as a means rather than as an end, leads inexorably to an insistence on the need to limit the power of democratic processes, to shackle the democratic beast because it is not Prometheus, but the Demogorgon. [5]

In the interests of freedom, narrowly and negatively construed, many of the powers exercised by government at the behest, and in the interests, of the majority must be relocated to the private sphere of transactions, where the real and appreciable opportunity costs of decision-making are made perceptible. That this transfer of power would, in conditions of a highly unequal income distribution, be towards a small minority is not deemed a democratic cost of the change since the change is unavoidable if **any** degree of democracy is to be viable. While the formal semblance of democracy is to be maintained, the imperative is to concentrate effective power in the hands of an oligarchic minority through the constitutional limitation of the purview of majoritarian voting. Many prominent advocates of neo-liberalism are not coy, moreover, about the political implications of their policy prescriptions. Manor (1991), surveying some neo-liberal writing on development theory, reveals the obscission of the political repression that is often the handmaiden, if not the universally necessary concomitant, of the economic strategy proposed. In some works he finds this fact discreetly neglected, while in others it is openly acknowledged, with a minimization of electoral activity (Baur, 1981), or a maximization of the dictatorial powers of ruthless, and ruthlessly undemocratic, governments being forcefully recommended. In the case of Pinochet's Chile, for example, the silence is thundering (Balassa, 1985). Note, then, a dual illusion that is reasonably widespread in eastern Europe: that market capitalism provides the economic foundation for democracy; and that western liberalism provides the social philosophy to capture conceptually such a happy divalence.

Nor is it the case that, in the Austrian School literature, the project is justified on the grounds that markets provide a superior allocative mechanism; but rather, because markets constitute the social contours and information reservoirs that facilitate the challenge in which free agents strive for information. Indeed, for Hayek (1960), freedom itself is not an end: following Mill (1982), it is defended instrumentally as a condition for the acquisition of knowledge, which itself is the basis for human progress. The economy is not perceived at all as a set of interlocking structures in stasis, but as a process that centrally concerns learning and the acquisition of knowledge. For the Austrian School liberals, therefore, in contrast to traditional neo-classicists, even evidence of the most widespread and distortive market failures and imperfections does not create a presumption in favour of political intervention – not only because of the comparable or greater failures that political solutions are evidently also subject to, but most crucially because such interference in the free transactions between economic agents threatens the basis of human progress. Thus, economic theory does not so much offer the conceptual basis for analysis and discovery, but rather provides a 'way of thinking' that is useful for hortatory purposes.

The coherence of economic liberalism's theoretical edifice – despite the modish accommodation to, or acquiescence in, it that is now fashionable – pivots on the viability of a series of conceptual nuclei: the notion of 'consumer sovereignty'; the accuracy of the claim that markets, via price signals, provide the best available sources of economic information; the defensibility of the definition of 'freedom' that is proposed; the cogency of the accounts of politics and political processes that are offered; the force of the methodological individualism on which the perspective is founded; and the denial of the relevance of a distinction between the private and the social in estimating costs and benefits. All are flawed.

If 'consumer sovereignty' plays a central, if differently inflected, rôle in both neo-classical and Austrian School versions of economic liberalism, it is no less fragile at the end of the century than it was earlier. No adequate riposte has been offered to Galbraith's observations (1970) on the consumer society and on the magisterial prerogatives and authority that its people are supposed to possess. What answer might there be to the claim that, contrary to any version of the liberal economic model of free market capitalism, modern capitalism is characterized by a high degree of monopolization, and a continuing tendency, through mergers and corporate acquisitions, for industrial concentration which, even by 1976, had allowed the largest fifty firms in the then EEC to be responsible for no less than 25 per cent of total output (Locksley and Ward, 1979)? In what manner might it be contested that these dominant firms, in conjunction with other influential corporate interests, are active agencies in the construction and promotion of new wants, and of the tastes on which they are fabricated? The implication here is not to doubt that human needs develop, change and expand historically, or that they do so, in large part, in response to the development of new products and processes; nor is it to reflect regretfully on this fact of human existence, to impose some ethereal moral 'ought' in place of a discovery about human nature, to be discomfited by the modern and the new, and to wish for a lapidescent stability as uncongenial as it would be impossible. It is, however, to provide strong grounds for scepticism in relation to the claims for the sovereignty of the consumer. How, moreover, could the consumer be expected to exercise such sovereignty, to judge how to cast her dollar vote, in the absence of sufficient knowledge about the complex products of advanced industrial capitalism, particularly in terms of their safety, longevity, efficiency, durability, unanticipated ramifications, etc.; and in terms of the availability, and/or the prices, of effective substitutes or comparable products? Those sceptical of the easy verities of economic liberalism believe themselves to be inhabiting a world in which the wants and needs of consumers do not, as a matter of fact, emerge independently of the activity of producers, and could not conceivably, as a matter of rational reflection, do so in any sophisticated industrial society; rather it is a world in which the pattern of commodity demand is a socially constructed phenomenon, subject to continual change and expansion. This belief rests both on the rational grounds that its possessors find themselves unable to conceive of a source for new consumer wants that is independent of the information and exhortation provided by advertising, and on the empirical grounds provided by observations of the behaviour of firms. I am unaware of any argument confounding the implications of these implicit interrogations for the notion of consumer sovereignty. A review of the history of economic thought would reveal grounds for an equivalent scepticism with respect to the cogency of the other foundational concepts of economic liberalism.

Economic liberalism, as both theory and policy, in both its neo-classical and Austrian School variants, and in its contemporary manifestation as neo-liberalism in free market, public choice and rational expectations theories, is, therefore, without evidential support; and it is flawed, probably fatally, as theory. Does it, nonetheless, retain its status as a contribution, however imperfect, to the **scientific** study of economic relationships and circumstances? Such a view might have been defensible were there no evidence of the systematic partiality of the outcomes of economic liberalism as policy. But there **is** such evidence (Bacha, 1983, Edwards, 1985, Parkin, 1983, Pastor, 1987, Pfeffermann, 1987, Ramirez, 1991, Shroff, 1990, Waagstein, 1989). The starkest, yet most contained, form in which economic liberalism manifests itself as a policy for stimulating individual initiative, and freeing the latter from casual or malevolent infractions by the state of its freedom to strive and prosper, is to be discovered in the structural adjustment programmes of the IMF and World Bank, the adoption of which by national governments is the condition for the extension of IMF loans and World Bank funds, and is normally the object of uncritical acclaim by economic liberals (Sachs, 1985). This 'conditionality' has already been brought to bear in negotiations with central and eastern European governments. Each programme, though tailored for the circumstances of the particular economy at which it is targeted, always contains key common ingredients (Killick, 1984): austerity measures that remove subsidies on basic consumer goods; deregulation; the removal of protectionist tariff and non-tariff barriers, and of industrial subsidies, to open the economy to international trade; the sharp reduction of the state budget as a proportion of GDP; and a devaluation of the currency. The effects of such drastic measures are always the same: a steep rise in unemployment and in the level of poverty with the – often extensive – collapse of indigenous industries and a partial collapse of agriculture; a deterioration in industrial output and of production generally; a sharp rise in food prices, and in food insecurity as domestic agriculture moves further towards the production of 'cash crops' for export; a rise in crime rates as desperation demoralizes increasingly marginalized sections of society; a very substantial increase in economic inequality in terms of both the size and the functional distribution of income; and worsening rates of, for example, infant mortality, longevity, and illiteracy. The consequences for the majority of the populations affected are dramatic: a reduction in living standards; increasing employment insecurity as the informal (black economy) sector grows to compensate for the 'freedoms' bestowed on those who lose their office and factory jobs; anxiety, anguish and despair in the face of daily sufferings that afflict the poor in poor countries in many ways as yet uninventoried by scholars or pundits.

One might be tempted to suggest that the advocacy or pursuit of such policies are either immoral or self-defeating, or both. If liberalization programmes destroy productive capacity rather than create it, is it not illogical to construct and impose them? The answer, I think, is 'No'. The imposition of a liberal economic order serves two important functions. Firstly, as Haynes argues (1992a and b), the restoration of the profitability of those economic activities that survive the rigours of unprotected markets enables the societies of which they are part to meet the debt burdens imposed by western banks and western states, and reintegrates these economies into the market of world capitalism. In comparison to this external function of liberal economic policy, the human cost of the reforms is secondary. Internally, the reforms reassert the political dominance and authority of those in control of the state even if that state's direct economic engagement shrinks. Once this authority is re-established, those sections of the population that will be affected most severely by the consequences of the reforms – and particularly the industrial working class – can be prevented by the strengthened state, through either political intimidation or repression, from resisting those consequences.

Far from economic liberalism being undogmatic, therefore, it is highly dogmatic, unconcerned with any evidence of its failure as policy. Far from it being an unpolitical, impartial science of economic life, it is a highly partial dogma that serves the interests of particular groups in any society, and in the world system of which those societies are components. The beneficiaries of its theories are those classes who own **or control** the non-human productive resources of these societies, and whose incomes and wealth depend upon securing that **effective** ownership. These characteristics are not normally those we associate with, or incorporate in the definition of, a science. They are rather the standard associations we make with, and elements we include in the definition of, an ideology.

The question of whether economic liberals who engage in the dissemination of this ideology are morally reprehensible (whether they are bad people) is not very important in this context. The most incisive response to this question was in fact provided by the British writer Thomas Carlyle in 1839. Arblaster (1983) recounts one of the practical consequences of liberal economic thought in the nineteenth century – the introduction of the New Poor Laws. In Adam Smith's optimistic liberalism free markets would lead, via the 'invisible hand', to the general good of all; in the subsequent one hundred years, industrialization, and the consequent poverty, degradation and unemployment that accompanied it, changed liberal thought. While Smith thought the individual pursuit of private vices, motivated by greed, small mindedness and childish vanity, would lead to public virtues, later liberals would need to explain away the poverty and degradation by blaming the poor themselves for their poverty. Malthusian population theory was the result – the conclusion of which being that if more aid were given to the poor there would be, through population growth, more poor to be aided. The policy implication was to make the poor suffer in return for any assistance offered, both to punish them for their laziness, and to give them an incentive to work. Poverty and unemployment were not seen as having any structural causes, but rather as being the individual responsibility of poor people. The reduction in assistance to the poor drove thousands to choose to remain in the most appalling squalor, and some to commit suicide, rather than voluntarily to enter the workhouse. When asked if the architects of this policy were evil men, Carlyle replied that they were not. 'They are not tigers ... they are men filled with the idea of a theory.' With the experience and record of economic liberalism over the past 150 years available to us, we might reasonably disagree with Carlyle, but only by cautioning against his excessive generosity. The dogmatism, ideological fanaticism, and partiality of liberal economic thought would seem to have changed little.

III

Is it not the case, however, that – whatever the failings of market capitalism – the experience of Stalinism, and the long struggle against the tyranny of planning and against the political terror exercised by the Party, proves that there is no alternative to the market? Communism is dead, buried by the revolutions of 1989 in Europe, and by the overthrow of the Soviet regime in 1991; capitalism is not just a superior economic and social system, but is the **only** viable system. Is it not also the case, moreover, that, with the triumph of free market capitalism, the ideological basis for international conflict and for civil wars has been removed? A dominant capitalism, world-wide, heralds a new dawn of peace and security. Even if capitalism cannot produce a universal prosperity, at least it can offer global peace.

The first part of this myth has developed on the basis of the assumption that the experience of Stalinism in the USSR from the mid-1920s was the experience of a socialist alternative. This is the popular wisdom that is shared both by the vast majority of those in the East and the West who were opposed to Stalinist tyranny, and by those, both today and in the past, who would want to be, or inadvertently became, apologists for Stalinism. There is, however, another view, according to which the societies of Eastern Europe had never been socialist in anything more than name; neither had the USSR been socialist since the final and complete victory of the Stalinist counter-revolution over the Left Opposition in 1928–9; and this counter-revolution constituted a reversal of everything that Marxism and Bolshevism stood for. According to this view, Stalin, the USSR, and the Stalinist regimes installed by the Red Army in central and eastern Europe between 1946 and 1948, shrouded themselves in the rhetoric and language of Marxism, and surrounded themselves with the icons of proletarian revolution, but this was no more nor less than the creation of a state ideology that could justify, and mobilize parts of the population in support of, the rapid industrialization of the 1930s, and secure a toleration, however resentful, of the sacrifice of consumer needs to the vast expenditure on military defence during the Cold War. It was an ideology that simultaneously justified the dominance of the monolithic Party, and the associated privileges with which it rewarded its members. [6] As such it was the counterpart to the ideology of liberalism in the West – an ideology that served and serves a similar function there. What connection could it be claimed to have had, however, with socialism or with Marxism? Callinicos (1990), in his book celebrating the popular revolutions of 1989, indicates the inconsistencies: a socialism supposed to produce for need rather than for profit – but which accumulates military power at the cost of living standards; a socialism which was, for Marx, as for Lenin, to be created by a revolutionary proletariat, and which was, for the first time in human history, to empower the direct producers of wealth – but which was forced on the populations of eastern Europe at the point of a bayonet, and which denied even a periodic vote for governments, much less organized the democratization of everyday life; a socialism that was intended to overcome the anarchic waste of a crisis-ridden capitalism by conscious democratic planning to satisfy human needs – but which, in fact, squandered vast resources in military competition, and imposed a centralized, undemocratic, administered economy. Callinicos concludes that, far from being socialist, those societies manifested all the key features of the capitalism that Marx both defined as a theoretical object, and analysed as an historical phenomenon: competition forcing the regimes to prioritize accumulation over consumption, irrespective of their wishes; and the exploitation of the working class to generate a surplus for investment, and to pay for the salaries and the privileges of the rulers. Whatever the apparent differences between the societies of the West and the East – substantial differences in economic organization, and in the ways in which the rulers secured their political dominance – both were, in fundamental terms, versions of capitalism: centrally administered, bureaucratic state capitalism in the East; and liberal democratic, mixed economy state capitalism in the West. Both were state capitalisms by virtue of the dominant rôle of the state in both. This analysis did not post-date the revolutions of 1989, in a form of ad hoc accommodation, but emerged first in the work of Cliff (1955 and 1988) in the 1940s. It has since been developed by Gluckstein (1952) and Harman (1976) in extension to all the Stalinist states of eastern Europe; by Harris (1979) to China; and by Binns and Gonzales (1983) to Cuba.

Notice then the conclusion that can be drawn. If Callinicos and others are correct, or even partly correct, then the argument that there is no alternative to market capitalism falls insofar as it is based on the Stalinist experience. It also follows that socialism was indeed overthrown in the USSR, but in 1928, not in 1991; and that, while the revolutions of 1989 certainly overthrew Stalinism, they overthrew in doing so one particularly inefficient form of administration of an industrially sophisticated capitalist economy, while leaving the economic system itself, and most of the individuals who made and make up its ruling class – as managers and administrators – intact and in place. Far from being tested by Stalinism, therefore, there is a strong argument that the socialist project has yet to be tried as an alternative to capitalism, East, West or South.

Finally, on peace, security and liberalism. The resurgence and triumph of liberalism over the last decade and a half, East and West, has been associated not with fraternity and peace, but with the resurgence of nationalism and regionalism, with the growth of fascism and zenophobia, with political and economic conflicts globally, and with a resurgent religious intolerance. Globally, the simmering conflict between the EC, the USA, Japan and the NICs of the Pacific Rim continues to threaten the emergence of trade wars as the USA – the foremost champion of free trade when its economic hegemony was secure – is now becoming the most prominent protectionist nation, as import penetration of the US market threatens the domestic industrial base of its ruling class, and as persistent, and apparently irreversible, increases in Japanese trade surpluses (despite an almost continual appreciation, and occasional inter-governmental revaluations, of the Yen) threaten the stability of the international trading system, and to tilt the latter towards global trade management. In Western Europe, the push towards unification of the EC faces centrifugal tendencies as the consequences for the populations of western, northern and southern Europe become clearer, and as nationalist politicians of the right see an opportunity to wave their flags. Simultaneously, the universal governmental response in western Europe to the increase in the East–West flow of migrants consequent upon recent political and economic upheavals is to engage in a dual hypocrisy. On the one hand, the 'Iron Curtain' is reconstructed, though this time to keep slavonic refugees **out** rather than fencing them in; and, on the other hand, full economic advantage is taken of the existing pool of illegal migrant labour (with its negligible social insurance cost) – while officially engaging in the reduction of rights to political asylum, and further restricting economic migration. This is evidently not a stable situation. It is a situation that is the consequence of the two dominant, if contradictory, tendencies that the world system has been subject to throughout the forty five years since the end of World War II (Harman, 1992, Callinicos, 1991a): the progressive integration and globalization of production, and economic inter-dependence reflected in the growth of world trade, on the one hand; and, on the other, the growth in the rôle of states as champions and defenders of their own particular geographical and political parts of that global system. There has always been a tension as well as an interdependence between these two trends, but there is no evidence that either of them is going to end, or that either could end. In a world of competing nation states, moreover, there is the ever-present threat of conflict; behind the diplomatic smile is always the less diplomatic but equally self-interested club (Harman, 1992, Callinicos, 1991b). It is the unavoidable continuance of the tension between these two tendencies that ought to preclude any sanguine vision of an harmonious future in international relations.

Even more disturbing are the incipient intra-state conflicts as economic crisis generates the search for scapegoats. Throughout western Europe, and now in the east, unscrupulous politicians seeking popular mandates are no longer waiting to play the card of nationalism and racism; the game is in full swing. The rise of racist and fascist organizations in Europe is a serious problem, often contributed to on a daily basis, usually unwittingly or unintentionally, by those uttering or condoning the prejudiced remark about minorities – whether it be about Asians in Britain, about Gypsies or Vietnamese in the Czech Republic or about Hungarians in Slovakia. When President Havel asked, in 1991, why the political climate was systematically being poisoned by demagogy, by political, ethnic and racial intolerance, he was asking a very important question. If the search for the answer starts by assuming that liberalism is the solution rather than part of the problem then the answer will not be found. In so far as the espousal of economic liberalism worsens the economic conditions of those subject to its consequences, it will contribute to, even if it is not the cause of, racism and nationalism. That would not portend well for the future of the New Europe, or for that of its peoples.

Acknowledgements

This is an extract from the plenary lecture delivered to the *Liberalism and the New Europe* conference held at J.E. Purkyně University, Ústí nad Labem, in July 1992. The author recognizes the financial and other support from the University of Brighton that made its preparation and delivery possible, particularly support from the funds of the Research Policy Committee, and those for staff development in the School of Historical and Critical Studies. The full version of the lecture appears in *Current Politics and Economics of Europe*, vol. 3, no. 4, 1993. The author, and the editors of this collection, would like to thank the editors and publishers of *CPEE* for permission to reproduce this extract. Bob Brecher, Gillian Scott, Peter McCullen and Gregory Elliott made helpful comments on earlier drafts.

Notes

1. Liška Bystrouská (the vixen Sharpears) in *The Cunning Little Vixen*: 'I can't stand the sight of your reactionary ways – so I'd rather bury myself alive!'
2. Compare 'myth' here with Ludek Kolman's Lévi-Straussian use in 'Liberalism after communism – the Czech civil service', p. 183 ff. of this volume.
3. The author records his debt to the recent work of Haynes (1992a, b and c) for much of the material on which the argument about the impact of marketization on eastern and central Europe is based.
4. In Britain during the 1980s a similarly messianic, Maoist spontanianism, laying emphasis on the subject factor, the will and determination to exact change, transfixed much conservative opinion in admiringly rapt attention as a lost language of inner-party struggle for the correct line was darkly rescued from the past, and suffused with new political meaning. For ministerial survival it was supremely important not to be thought a 'wet' by the Leader, to give no suggestion that one harboured any doubt whatsoever. Once so labelled the only hope was in self-criticism, rectification, and abasement, a neurotic parody of Stalinism in Tory guise. For the anti-Stalinists of the left in the UK, this new configuration for the political terror of inner-party authoritarianism, if not comparable to its historical forebear in its inhumanity, provided at least a rich irony. In the USA, the decade proved worse in these respects, with expertise, proficiency and probity, and even basic competence and sobriety, being subordinated to 'right thinking' and 'being one of us' as criteria for appointment to office pursuant to the crusades of defeating Communism abroad; an objective supplemented in the UK by the marginalization of what went by the name of 'socialism' at home. Miraculously, the villainous became venial. It will, presumably, be a small worry for both principals and dispensers that moral judgements are possessed of a somewhat cyclical character, and that history may yet discover them all to have been corrupt.
5. Shelley's 'people-monster' (Shelley, 1970), the antithesis of Godliness or omnipotence, was the repose of that power and potential whose mobilization was the condition for freedom and destiny to be realized; for personal deference and intellectual inspiration to become revolution, the power to overthrow Jupiter; it was the metaphor for a risen people the thought of which, in the aftermath of the French Revolution, struck cold terror into the hearts of the defenders and beneficiaries of the established order, and which earned from them the epithets, 'the mob' and 'the crowd': but it also provided hope and insight for at least some of those Enlightened revolutionaries

rendered impotent, and haunted, by the failure of the Revolution (Foot, 1984).
6. The well-appointed building of the University in which the Conference was held had been, prior to 1989, a regional training school for the Czechoslovak Communist Party.

References

Aganbegan, A. (1988), *The Challenge: the Economics of Perestroika*, Hutchinson, London.
Aghezedeh, E. and Evans, D. (1988), 'Price distortions, efficiency and growth', mimeo, *Institute of Development Studies*, University of Sussex, Brighton.
Anderson, P. (1991), 'The ends of history', in idem, *A Zone of Engagement*, Verso, London.
Anderson, P. (1992), 'Components of the national culture' and 'A culture in contraflow', in idem, *English Questions*, Verso, London.
Arblaster, A. (1983), *The Rise and Fall of Western Liberalism*, Allen & Unwin, London.
Argawala, R. (1983), 'Price distortions and growth in developing countries', *World Bank Staff Working Papers*, 575, (Management and Development), IBRD, Washington.
Ariff, M. and Hill, H. (1987), *Export-Oriented Industrialization: the ASEAN Experience*, Allen & Unwin, London.
Bacha, E. (1983), 'A critique of southern cone monetarism', *International Social Science Journal*, 97.
Balassa, B. (1978), 'Exports and economic growth: further evidence', *Journal of Development Economics*, 5.
Balassa, B. (1985), *Change and Challenge in the World Economy*, Macmillan, Basingstoke.
Barthes, R. (1993), *Mythologies*, Levers, A. (trans.),Vintage, London.
Baur, T. (1981), *Equality, the Third World and Economic Delusion*, Weidenfeld & Nicholson, London.
Bergeijk, P. and Pritchett, L. (1991), 'Detente, market oriented reform and German unification: potential consequences for the world trade system', *Kyklos*, 43, 4.
Berlin, I. (1969), *Four Essays on Liberty*, Oxford University Press, Oxford.

Binns, P. and Gonzales, M. (1983), *Cuba, Castro and Socialism*, Bookmarks, London.
Brittan, S. (1977), *The Economic Consequences of Democracy*, Temple-Smith, London.
Brittan, S. (1988), *A Restatement of Economic Liberalism*, Macmillan, Basingstoke.
Callinicos, A. (1990), *The Revenge of History: the Revolutions in Eastern Europe*, Polity Press, Oxford.
Callinicos, A. (1991a), 'Marxism and imperialism today', *International Socialism*, 50.
Callinicos, A. (1991b), 'The end of nationalism?', *International Socialism*, 51.
CEPR (1990), *Maintaining European Integration: The Impact of Eastern Europe*, CEPR, London.
Cliff, T. (1955), *Stalinist Russia: a Marxist Analysis*, n. p., London.
Cliff, T. (1988), *State Capitalism in Russia*, Bookmarks, London.
Coakley, J. and Harris, L. (1992), 'Financial globalization and deregulation', in Michie, J. (ed.), *The Economic Legacy 1979–1992*, Academic Press, London.
Colclough, C. (1991), 'Structuralism versus neo-liberalism: an introduction', in idem and Manor, J. (eds.), op. cit.
Colclough, C. & Green, H. (1988), 'Stabilization – for growth or decay?', *IDS Bulletin*, 19, 1, Institute of Development Studies, University of Sussex.
Colclough, C. and Manor, J. (eds.) (1991), *States or Markets? Neo-liberalism and the Development Policy Debate*, Clarendon Press, Oxford.
Edwards, S. (1985), 'Stabilization with liberalization: an evaluation of ten years of Chile's experiment with free market policies', *Economic Development and Cultural Change*, 33, 2.
Elliott, G. (1993a), 'The cards of confusion: reflections on historical communism and the "end of history"', *Radical Philosophy*, 64.
Elliott, G. (1993b), *Labourism and the English Genius: The Strange Death of Labour England?*, Verso, London.
Englander and Mittelstadt (1988), 'Total factor productivity: macro-economic and structural aspects of slowdown', *OECD Economic Studies*, 10.
Evans, D. (1991), 'Visible and invisible hands in trade policy reform', in Colclough and Manor, op. cit.
Fairlamb, D. (1990), 'Eastern Europe: opportunities for bankers', *Banking World*, April.
Fine, B. and Poletti, C. (1992), 'Industrial prospects in the light of privatisation', in Michie, J. (ed.), op. cit.
Fischer, S. and Gelb, A. (1990), 'Issues in socialist economic reform', *IBRD: Policy Research and External Affairs, Working Papers*, 565.

Foot, P. (1984), *Red Shelley*, Bookmarks, London.
Friedman, M. (1953), 'The methodology of positive economics', in idem, *Essays in Positive Economics*, University of Chicago Press, Chicago.
Friedman, M. (1962), *Capitalism and Freedom*, University of Chicago Press, Chicago.
Fukuyama, F. (1989), 'The end of history?', *The National Interest*, 16.
Galbraith, J. (1970), *The Affluent Society*, Penguin, London.
Gluckstein, Y. (1952), *Stalin's Satellites in Europe*, Allen & Unwin, London.
Harman, C. (1976), *Bureaucracy and Revolution in Eastern Europe*, Pluto Press, London.
Harman, C. (1992), 'The return of the national question', *International Socialism*, 56.
Harris, N. (1979), *The Mandate of Heaven: Marx and Mao in Modern China*, Quartet, London.
Harris, N. (1986), *The End of the Third World: Newly Industrializing Countries and the Decline of an Ideology*, Taurus, London.
Haskel, J. and Kay, J. (1990), 'Productivity in British industry under Mrs Thatcher', in Congdon, T. et al., (eds.), *The State of the Economy*, IEA, London.
Havel, V. (1966), *The Memorandum*, Paladin, London.
Havrylyshyn, O. and Pritchett, L. (1991), 'European trade patterns after the transition', *IBRD: Policy Research and External Affairs, Working Papers*, 748.
Hayek, F. (1944), *The Road to Serfdom*, Routledge and Kegan Paul, London.
Hayek, F. (1960), *The Constitution of Liberty*, Routledge and Kegan Paul, London.
Haynes, M. (1992a), 'Class and crisis: the transition in eastern Europe', *International Socialism*, 54.
Haynes, M. (1992b), 'The new market economies and the world economy – some briefing material', *ULU Seminar*, University of London.
Haynes, M. (1992c), 'State and market and the "transition" crisis in eastern Europe', *Realism and the Human Sciences Conference*, St. Catherine's College, Oxford.
Hickey, T. (1979), 'Export performance and economic growth in LDCs: a statistical investigation', *School of Oriental and African Studies, University of London*, Economic Development Seminar Working Paper, 52.
Hickey, T. (1980), 'Exports and economic development: reflections on some statistical evidence', University of Sussex, Economics Division Graduate/Faculty Seminar Paper.
IMF (1991), *IMF Survey*, July 29.
Janáček, L. (1923), *The Cunning Little Vixen*, Viney, D. (trans.), Universal, London.

Johnson, C. (1991), *The Economy Under Mrs Thatcher*, Penguin, London.
Kafka, F. (1956), *The Trial*, Muir, W. and E. (trans.), Secker & Warburg, London.
Keegan, W. (1986), *Mrs Thatcher's Economic Experiment*, Penguin, London.
Keegan, W. (1989), *Mr Lawson's Gamble*, Hodder & Stoughton, London.
Killick, T. (1984), *The IMF and Stabilization: Developing Country Experiences*, vol. I, Gower/Overseas Development Institute, London.
Kornai, J. (1959), *Overcentralization in Economic Administration*, Oxford University Press, Oxford.
Kornai, J. (1972), *Anti-equilibrium*, Elsevier, North Holland.
Kornai, J. (1975), *The Mathematical Planning of Structural Decisions*, Elsevier, North Holland.
Kornai, J. (1986a), 'The Hungarian reform process: visions, hopes and reality', *Journal of Economic Literature*, XXIV, 4.
Kornai, J. (1986b), 'Individual freedom and reform in the socialist economy', *European Economic Review*, 32, 2/3.
Kornai, J. (1990), *The Road to a Free Economy: Shifting from a Socialist System – the Example of Hungary*, Norton, New York.
Kozol, J. (1992), *Savage Inequalities – Children in American Schools*, Harper, New York.
Lakatos, I. (1970), 'Falsification and the methodology of scientific research programmes', in idem and Musgrave, A. (eds.), *Criticism and the Growth of Knowledge*, Cambridge University Press, Cambridge.
Lakatos, I. (1978), *The Methodology of Scientific Research Programmes*, Cambridge University Press, Cambridge.
Lipsey, R. and Lancaster, K. (1956–7), 'The general theory of second best', *Review of Economics and Statistics*, 6.
Locksley, G. and Ward, T. (1979), 'Concentration in manufacturing in the EEC', *Cambridge Journal of Economics*, 3.
Maddison, A. (1989), *The World Economy in the Twentieth Century*, OECD, Paris/New York.
Manor, J. (1991), 'Politics and the neo-liberals', in Colclough and Manor (1991), op. cit.
McCarney, J. (1989), 'History under the hammer', *Times Higher Education Supplement*, 1 December.
Michaely, M. (1977), 'Exports and growth: an empirical investigation', *Journal of Development Economics*, 4.
Michie, J. (ed.) (1992), *The Economic Legacy 1979–1992*, Academic Press, London.
Mill, J.S. (1982), *On Liberty*, Penguin, Harmondsworth.
Nugent, N. (1992), 'The deepening and widening of the European Community', *Journal of Common Market Studies*, xxx, 3.
OECD (1991a), *Economic Outlook*, 49.

OECD (1991b), *Economic Outlook*, 50.
OECD (1991c), *Financial Market Trends*, 48.
Parkin, V. (1983), 'Economic liberalism in Chile, 1973-82: a model for growth or a recipe for stagnation and impoverishment?', *Cambridge Journal of Economics*, 7.
Pastor, M. (1987), 'The effects of IMF programmes in the Third World: debate and evidence from Latin America', *World Development*, 15, 2.
Pfeffermann, G. (1987), 'Economic crisis and the poor in some Latin American countries', *Finance and Development*, June.
Popper, K. (1972), *Conjectures and Refutations: The Growth of Scientific Knowledge*, (4th edn.), Routledge and Kegan Paul, London.
Popper, K. (1976), *The Poverty of Historicism*, Routledge and Kegan Paul, London.
Ramirez, M.D. (1991), 'The impact of austerity on Latin America, 1983–89: a critical assessment', *Comparative Economic Studies*, xxxiii, 1.
Rowthorn, B. (1992), 'Government spending and taxation in the Thatcher era', in Michie, J., op. cit.
Sachs, J. (1985), 'External debt and macroeconomic performance in Latin America and East Asia', *Brookings Papers on Economic Activity*.
Shelley, P.B. (1970), *Prometheus Unbound*, in idem, *Poetical Works*, Hutchinson, T. (ed.), Oxford University Press, Oxford.
Shroff, M. (1990), 'Liberalization of the economy: the Indian experience', *South Asia*, xiii, 1.
Singer, H. (1988), 'World development report 1987 on the blessings of "outward orientation": a necessary correction', *Journal of Development Studies*, 24, 2.
Singer, H. and Grey, P. (1988), 'Trade policy and growth of developing countries: some new data', *World Development*, 16, 3.
Smith, D. (1987), *The Rise and Fall of Monetarism: the Theories and Politics of an Economic Experiment*, Penguin, London.
Smith, D. (1992), *From Boom to Bust: Trial and Error in British Economic Policy*, Penguin, London.
Solimano, A. (1990), 'Macroeconomic adjustment, stabilization and growth in reforming socialist economies: analytical and policy issues', *IBRD: Policy Research and External Affairs, Working Papers*, 399.
Syrquin, M. and Chenery, H. (1989), 'Patterns of development 1950 to 1983', *World Bank Discussion Paper*, no. 41.
Taylor, L. (1988), *Varieties of Stabilization Experience*, Clarendon, Oxford.
United Nations (1989), 'Economic reforms in the European centrally planned economies', *United Nations' Economic Commission for Europe: Economic Studies,* no. 1, New York.
Waagstein, T. (1989), 'Neoliberalism as a lever for structural change in the southern cone – from "miracle" to disaster', *Copenhagen University,*

Institute of Economics, Working Papers, 172.

Wade, R. (1991), *Governing the Market: Economic Theory and the Rôle of Government in East Asian Industrialization*, Princeton University Press, Princeton.

World Bank (1983), *World Development Report*, Oxford University Press, New York.

World Bank (1987), *World Development Report*, Oxford University Press, New York.

Zloch-Christy, I. (1987), *Debt Problems in Eastern Europe*, Cambridge University Press, Cambridge.

Zloch-Christy, I. (1990), 'Political risk assessment in lending to eastern Europe', *European Management Journal*, 8, 4.

6 The poverty of affluence? The consumer society, its discontents and its malcontents

Marcus Roberts

While critics of the 'consumer society' have seldom offered a systematic account of its salient characteristics, a number of central points can readily be identified. First, production in the 'post-industrial society' is increasingly geared towards the output of frivolous goods: and this is accompanied by huge investments in the marketing of new products – in particular, by the growth of the advertising industry. Second, consumption becomes an end in itself: thus Hannah Arendt writes that 'even Presidents, Kings and Prime Ministers think of their offices in terms of a job necessary for the life of society, and among the intellectuals, only solitary individuals are left who consider what they are doing in terms of work and not in terms of making a living' (Arendt, 1958, p. 5). Similarly, the pursuit of increased production becomes divorced from any considerations about its content. Third, the individual's self-esteem and social status come to depend upon relative consumption levels: what people earn becomes more important than what they do. Finally, as long as economic success is equated exclusively with securing ever-increasing levels of mass consumption, the space for social criticism is closed down: 'under the conditions of a rising standard of living, non-conformity with the system itself appears to be socially useless, and the more so when it entails tangible economic and political disadvantages and threatens the smooth operation of the whole' (Marcuse, 1964, p. 2).

I

One common response to these kinds of objection is to insist that the consumer society delivers the things that people want. Some liberal critics detect an unholy mixture of the Bare Bones Parliament and the Committee for Public Safety lurking behind all this withering professorial contempt for 'frivolous' and 'bizarre' products. If people want electric carving knives, or yet another brand of breakfast cereal, then why shouldn't they have them? It follows that the uncompromising agnosticism of economists concerning the content of production is entirely proper: it is not for them to decide what should be produced. This kind of response embraces a good deal of the mythology that has contributed to the beatification of the free market. We are to picture the individual consumer confronted with an array of products, and choosing to purchase the most alluring of them (within a feasible set determined by income). Firms which successfully anticipate and respond to changes in consumer tastes will flourish; those that fail to do so will be driven out of business. This mechanism, it is said, ensures that the market adjusts in such a way that the available technology is deployed to produce those things that people wish to consume. It is the sovereign consumer who determines the content of production: in the realm of the 'one-dimensional man' the shopping trolley is king.

This ignores what J.K. Galbraith has designated as The Myth of Consumer Sovereignty (Galbraith, 1984), a myth which thrives upon the economist's profound indifference to all questions concerning the **origins** of demand. The neoclassical economist – embracing the foundational assumptions of economic liberalism – pictures 'all wants emerging as if by virgin birth from the sovereign will of the consumer' (ibid., p. xvii); and the economist's function is 'sufficiently fulfilled by maximizing the goods that supply those wants' (ibid., p. 119). It might be responded that the economist adopts this position only qua economist, and need not be otherwise hostile to social criticism concerned with the manipulative generation of wants. But such a response misses the point that the defence of the free market economy, and of the ideology that surrounds it, is largely dependent upon its supposed ability to satisfy the autonomous demands of sovereign consumers. The market-place, it is implied, extends 'democracy' into the economic sphere. But if 'the people' are not sovereign over themselves, then neither are they sovereign over the content of production. The fact that people want the things that are being produced in the post-industrial society is as irrelevant as it is true. The central question becomes, 'Who is sovereign over the consumer?'

II

Attacks upon such a consumer society have, therefore, been concerned with the process of want-formation. The argument can be summarized as follows: (i) desires which arise as a result of 'manipulation' are not properly the agent's own; (ii) if a desire does not properly 'belong' to the agent, then its satisfaction does not contribute to the good of the agent;

(iii) the desire for the goods produced in the post-industrial society is itself a product of manipulation; therefore, (iv) the production of these goods is not justified by demonstrating that the agent does in fact want them. For example, Marcuse argues that, so long as their needs are manipulatively generated by 'vested interests', what people might happen to want is simply irrelevant. What then **do** people really want? He argues that this question can only be finally resolved by individuals themselves, when once the conditions exist which would allow for genuinely autonomous preference-formation (Marcuse, 1964, pp. 4–7). [1]

Point (iii) is fundamental. I shall consider first, then, the extent to which the demand for products in the 'post-industrial society' is dependent upon large investments in manipulative marketing and advertising: for if we assume that producers are rational, then it would follow from the fact that they sanction such vast expenditures that they are in the business of demand creation. Moreover, we might readily concede that we are inclined to prefer advertised brands to unadvertised ones. It is also the case that many products are not purchased for their intrinsic properties, but rather because their conspicuous consumption is a means to the enhancement of status. However, it is far more difficult to conjure wants up, simply out of thin air, than the critics of the consumer society sometimes imply. An advertising firm might be expected to have an easier time marketing a self-cleaning suit, for instance, than it would selling a self-destructing one. Certainly, it is because they are concerned to win markets that firms invest in product innovation, but this investment is guided by reasonable assumptions about what people might **conceivably want**. A prohibition on manipulative advertising would lead to significant, and no doubt desirable, modifications in investment and consumption patterns, but it is highly implausible to suggest that it would inhibit the impetus to product innovation, halting mass consumerism in its tracks. If manipulative advertising were outlawed, and marketing were entirely restricted to the provision of accurate information about new products, then it would still be possible to generate sufficient demand for new products to promote indefinite technological and economic expansion.

There is, however, another, more compelling, argument which is pursued by the consumer society's critics: that is, that technological innovation is capable of restructuring human desire without the intercession of any middle man. Increased production simply creates new desires. Thus Fukuyama observes that 'consumerism and the science of marketing that caters to it refer to desires that have literally been *created* by man himself, and which give way to others in the future. Our present desires are conditioned by our social milieu, which in turn is the product of the entirety of our historical past' (Fukuyama, 1992, p. 63). There are two obvious ways in which increased **production** may condition our present desires. First, the current level of production and the rate of innovation will tend to generate desires for future product development. Thus in present day North America one might reasonably look forward to a time when a high fidelity sound system can be produced that is the size of a matchbox. Recognizing this desire – one which it is difficult to imagine a mediaeval peasant entertaining – firms may invest in developing this product. Second, the mere existence of a product will often create a desire for it. We can imagine, for instance, that someone with no specialist interest in cooking, or in chess, might have had no desire for a food blender, or for a chess computer, until these products became available; but people may well come to want them simply as a consequence of their existing. Anticipating that these goods will prove desirable, firms will invest in developing them. Indefinite economic growth could, therefore, be driven by desires that are created within a definite 'social milieu', but are not the product of manipulation. [2] Furthermore, many (if not most) of the things that are produced in the course of this development are Good Things: washing machines, safer motor cars, chess computers, food blenders, high fidelity sound systems, and so on. Other things being equal, indefinite economic growth is a desirable objective.

Two further arguments remain to be considered: (i) that we would be more satisfied if we had less growth and fewer of the desires that are generated by that growth; and (ii) that the pursuit of increased private consumption involves the sacrifice of other desirable goals: in particular, that of the alleviation of toil.

III

If the points made in the preceding section are conceded, then a society which strives after the constant expansion of production might appear to be less satisfying than one which abandons this goal for some alternative form of life. For a number of reasons, however, this suggestion is profoundly unconvincing. Let me mention three. First, our goal may not be satisfaction. As J.S. Mill famously observed, it is 'better to be a human being dissatisfied than a pig satisfied; better to be Socrates dissatisfied than a fool satisfied' (Mill, 1962, p. 260). For similar reasons, it does not follow from the 'fact' that people don't miss what they've never had, that they would be better off not having it: for example, consider a society that had never had reliable harvests, washing machines, or the Mozart operas. Second, we will have unsatisfied desires for unavailable goods (in the broadest sense) at any level of production. The mediaeval peasant will not desire pesticides, but will want the crops not to fail. It seems odd to suggest that we would be more satisfied in a world where crops failed, than in one which encouraged constant innovations in the field of agricultural products. Finally, it might be objected that we should indeed develop technology to a point at which it secures vital needs (reliable harvests, perhaps) but that we should then either abandon further development, or continue it only on a highly selective basis. We should eliminate scarcity – even at the cost of enduring alienating and grossly inegalitarian modes of production – but once we have conquered scarcity we should sacrifice further growth in order to secure other desirable goals. This is a crucial point.

The argument that, because production promotes dissatisfaction it would be better to inhibit it, has considerably more force when viewed in the context of domestic and global inequalities. The bounties of the post-industrial society are flaunted without discrimination: mass communications ensure that the world's poor are free to entertain desires that would never have occurred to the mediaeval poor. Thus Francis Fukuyama writes that 'the irony is that communist societies come to acquire the ever-expanding horizon of wants generated by Western consumerist societies without acquiring the means of satisfying them' (Fukuyama, 1992, p. 133). This is tragedy, not irony. Moreover, this tragedy is intensified by the relativity of aspirations. In seeking to 'catch up' with Western production levels it should not be forgotten that this target may be capable of indefinite retreat. Domestic and global inequalities mean that the desires created in the process of technological innovation extend to those – an overwhelming majority – who have no realistic chances of satisfying them. Poverty itself becomes a function of productivity, as absolute poverty slowly yields to relative poverty. There might seem to be an argument for inhibiting growth, then, premised on the sheer scale of the dissatisfaction that is created as productivity is enhanced. This is not properly an argument concerned with the intrinsic desirability or otherwise of increasing consumption levels, however, but rather an argument concerned with inegalitarian distribution. This issue has been sidelined in order to focus upon the intrinsic character of mass consumerism. However, three points should be made here. First, the absolute and unqualified claims of vital needs – food, clothing, shelter – are sufficiently obvious to require no defence (unless one were so unfortunate, or so ill-advised, as to find oneself debating the matter with someone like Roger Scruton). Second, it is assumed here that the operation of a market-led system is compatible, in principle, with a considerably more egalitarian distribution of resources than currently obtains in the advanced industrial countries. Finally, the existence of **some** inequality in distribution is not **obviously** undesirable. [3] In so far as continued growth depends upon engaging in intrinsically unrewarding activities, then it must be driven either by a sense of obligation or by the delayed gratification of unsatisfied desires.

IV

The consumer society's critics might argue, however, that, to the extent that mass consumerism increasingly generates frivolous, bizarre, or immoral desires, enhanced levels of private consumption should be sacrificed in pursuit of other desirable ends. Perhaps mass consumerism would be desirable if everything else were equal, but everything else is not equal. The emphasis shifts from manipulative product promotion and engages the whole ideological structure that serves to promote the cult of private consumption. In particular, it is argued that the ceaseless manufacture of dissatisfaction ensures that people continually submit to long hours of laborious toil. [4] And something is seriously wrong with a society in which enslavement to a machine serves only to provide the means for satisfying a craving for fashion accessories, or for computer games or for a brief period of utter inebriation.

In *Karl Marx's Theory of History: A Defence*, G.A. Cohen argues that the systematic promotion of increased productivity at the expense of the alleviation of toil is a distinctive contradiction of advanced capitalism. The capitalist will always resist any reduction in working hours: for the alleviation of toil will lead to a reduction in output, a decline in competitive strength, and, therefore, to a fall in profits. Confronted with conditions of scarcity the output bias of capitalism serves a progressive function; under conditions of abundance it becomes a fetter upon the optimal deployment of the productive forces. Cohen argues that at some level of production the utility to be gained from increments of free time must be greater than that from additional increments of consumption: 'It is undeniable that capitalist relations of production possess an output-expanding bias. So the only way of denying that they are potentially irrational in the stated respect is to assert that labour is so enjoyable (or not so unenjoyable) and resources are so plentiful, and the satisfaction to be had from goods and services is so limitless that no matter how much is being consumed it remains desirable to consume more, instead of expanding freedom from labour: a rather large assertion' (Cohen, 1978, pp. 310–311). But if consumption is increasingly unattractive in comparison with toil reduction, then why are people so strongly committed to the enhancement of private consumption? For example, why do people welcome the opportunity to do overtime in order to purchase 'frivolous' consumer goods? Trades Unions have resisted the inherent tendency of capitalism to force down wages-rates, but why are workers generally unwilling to strike in order to secure more free time? Cohen concedes, for the sake of argument, that the products of the affluent society are genuinely desirable, but argues that his opponents are bound to concede that toil is undesirable. Vast expenditures on advertising must be justified, at the very least, because advertisements draw attention to the independently desirable properties of products. But there are no advertisements promoting the alleviation of toil, or reminding us of the costs of private consumption:

> WHEN YOUR UNION NEGOTIATES, MAKE IT GO FOR SHORTER HOURS, NOT MORE PAY. ELECTRIC CARVING KNIVES ARE FINE BUT NOTHING BEATS FREEDOM. (ibid., p. 318)

Cohen is aware of the hazards of attempting to specify at precisely what level of production increments of consumption should yield to increments of free time: he writes that 'for some value of "very high" and some value of "substantial", capitalism is detrimental when consumption is very high and the working day is substantial' (ibid., p. 310). He shares with all the authors discussed in this article the belief that coerced labour is legitimate so long as the objective is the conquest of scarcity, but that it ceases to be appropriate in the 'affluent society'. The question is, however, who decides whether or not consumption is 'very high'? What criteria are to be adopted in order to distinguish scarcity from abundance? The suggestion that we should satisfy only vital needs and then go all out for toil reduction is highly implausible. But then freezing technology at **any** subsequent level will surely appear arbitrary. The answer offered by Cohen is, essentially, that this is a decision to be made by autonomous individuals themselves; that is, by individuals fully apprised of the alternatives, and no longer prey to the ideological biases supporting capitalism. I agree with Cohen that, in the advanced industrial countries, the sacrifice of private consumption to toil reduction (and the full provision of public goods) is long overdue: but the problems alluded to above cannot be circumvented by appealing to people's actual or prospective desires – at least, not in a way that could enable us to renounce all prescriptions regarding the content of the good life.

Cohen's argument might be interpreted in two rather different ways. First, he might be taken as arguing only that if free time were promoted it would become progressively more attractive as levels of mass consumption increased. Assuming the utility of free time to be constant, and the utility to be gained from further increments in consumption to be diminishing, then at some point increased free time is preferred to increased consumption. This, however, ignores a problem identified by Galbraith (1984, pp. 122–125): the doctrine of diminishing marginal utility applies to incremental consumption of a single good. I will get a great deal of satisfaction from my first bar of chocolate; should I immediately follow it with a second, I may find this bar slightly less satisfying; unless I am eating them for a bet I am unlikely to progress much beyond four chocolate bars; more than ten bars and my digestive system will tend to supervene upon any residual capacity for rational choice. One might, then, be prepared to work a whole day to get one's hands on the first chocolate bar, but also to avoid the sixty fifth. Certainly, it will not be very long before I would prefer more free time to more chocolate. However, diminishing marginal utility does not apply when we turn to incremental consumption of a diversity of goods (or to consumption over an extended time-period). Consider a music enthusiast progressing from a mono record player, through an adequate stereo, to a top of the range high fidelity sound system, and finally adding a slightly better turntable to this system. There is no reason to suppose that his or her satisfaction diminishes during this process. One might be tempted to say that the purchase of a whole system must afford more satisfaction than the addition of a slightly better turntable. But the desire to get hold of the turntable might be far more intense than the desire to get hold of the sound system had been: for example, the hi-fi enthusiast may have developed an obsession with the slightest imperfection in the operation of the original turntable, and might willingly go on overtime for months in order to remedy it. Now, it might be objected that once this turntable is installed the long-term satisfaction it gives cannot equal the long term satisfaction of possessing the hi-fi system minus the turntable. This is an attractive suggestion. However, the imperfections of the original turntable may have so offended the delicate ear of the music enthusiast that he or she simply couldn't bear to listen to music at all: minus the improved turntable, the utility of the sound system would therefore be less than zero. There is, then, no reason why slight technological improvements should not produce massively increased levels of dissatisfaction. The music enthusiast may forego hours of free time for the want of a pocket-sized, remote-controlled CD player, just as readily as for his or her first music system.

Alternatively, Cohen could be interpreted as arguing that if free time were rigorously promoted, then its utility would increase. But in a culture in which most people eagerly anticipate their weekends and annual holidays, there is no obvious need for advertisements reminding them of the pleasures of free time. There are two possible responses to this: (i) that people do need reminding of the labour costs of purchasing any particular commodity; or (ii) that the marketing of free time will educate people in 'the theory and practice of leisure' (Cohen, op. cit., p. 320). In the case of (i) we could imagine that legislation has been introduced forcing advertisers to state the labour expenditure required to purchase the advertised goods at average income levels. One might be more reluctant to buy a new suit if one were reminded that one would have to work thirty hours to pay for it. However, there is no reason simply to assume that this would lead to radically altered consumption patterns. People are often aware of the amount of free time that they are required to sacrifice in order to secure particular goods: consider someone taking on an additional cleaning job to finance Christmas or to keep up with shifting fashions in clothing. But imagine that this policy were successful.

Unless the economy had already been restructured, the resulting shift in consumption patterns would play havoc with it: and the resulting collapse in demand would lead to high levels of unemployment. Similarly, imagine that people were prepared to work long hours to secure washing machines, but that all the workers producing them had opted for free time. The price of washing machines would rise, with the possible consequence that aggregate toil throughout the economy remained constant or even increased. The point is that a new allocative system would have to be already in place to facilitate this change, and such a system could not appeal to the intensity or incidence of wants or desires. Or if it did appeal to the widespread desire for increased leisure it would be appealing to a want that had been actively – even if non-manipulatively – promoted.

This final point becomes clearer if we turn to (ii): education in the 'theory and practice of leisure'. Let us say that if people were more aware of the valuable things that could be done with it, they would be more inclined to opt for more free time. As Cohen observes, 'free time looks empty when the salient available ways of filling it are inane' (ibid.). In this sense, the promoter of free time is in the same position as the entrepreneur: he or she is marketing goods and anticipating that people will come to desire them. This presupposes judgements about what is worth promoting, and it involves a conscious effort to restructure desires. Let us imagine that stamp collecting, fishing, and learning a musical instrument are all promoted. To defend this selection it would be argued that if people thought about these activities they would be more likely to want to take them up, and once they had taken them up they would find them far more satisfying than working overtime to purchase all kinds of frivolous consumption goods. In Cohen's terminology, the crucial distinction here is between the **pursuit schedule** and the **satisfaction schedule** (ibid., p 319–320). The pursuit schedule orders objects of desire according to the relative strength of one's disposition to pursue them; the satisfaction schedule according to the levels of satisfaction one will get if one actually realizes them. The justification for promoting worthwhile leisure activities is that it will lead to the alignment of the two schedules: people will desire what they will in fact find satisfying. But this distinction is not sustainable. What I will in fact find satisfying all depends upon what I am inclined to pursue. Consider a collector of stamps who finally gets hold of a rare stamp. The satisfaction of obtaining the stamp is completely incomprehensible unless reference is made to the collector's pursuit schedule. It might perhaps be replied that this is a misleading example. What is at stake here, perhaps, is the satisfaction to be had from stamp-collecting and not from obtaining a particular stamp: the stamp collector will be more satisfied than someone who spends their free time lounging about in front of the television. But this is simply not true. Taking up stamp-collecting may be more 'dissatisfying', in this sense, than continuing to work long hours to finance frivolous and undemanding consumption patterns: one might work even more overtime in order to finance the purchase of stamps. It would be far better to say that these activities should be promoted because they are worthwhile – there is no reason to think that they are more 'satisfying'. It might be objected here that while being a Socrates involves more dissatisfaction than being a fool, no one would actually **want** to be a fool. But this is misleading. I would not consent to be a fool, because this would represent some impairment of my mental faculties. However, I may nevertheless doubt that all the agonies involved in becoming a Socrates are really worth the candle and consent to spend my time in the pub rather than in the great man's sandals.

If this is unconvincing, then let me concede that people really would choose to undertake these fulfilling activities. Clearly they will need things in order to engage in them: stamp-collectors need stamps; fishermen need fishing equipment; musicians need instruments. The problem of allocating resources simply re-emerges at a deeper level. What will the fisherman want? Her ideal will be to have the best available fishing equipment and the maximum free time in which to deploy it. Moreover, she will want things that do not yet exist (for example, a more flexible rod than any currently available): that is, she will want there to be investment in product innovation. The musician and the stamp-collector will have different schedules. Let us imagine that allocation is determined according to the incidence of desire, but in a system where the distribution of resources is completely equal: for example, that it is settled by a vote. If 51 per cent of the voters have opted for fishing, then – so long as the allocation of resources is to be determined only by private desires – they will always enjoy preferment. Nor is the satisfaction schedule of any help. There is no reason to think that the fisherman will get less satisfaction from a slight improvement in the flexibility of fishing rods than the musician will get from being provided with a new instrument. Indeed, the idea that we might compare the intensity of satisfactions in this way is barely intelligible. To the extent that they are at all distinguishable, the satisfaction schedule offers no more guidance for the allocation of resources than the pursuit schedule does. It might be responded that we are to imagine a society in which scarcity has been overcome, and therefore one in which the allocation of resources has ceased to be a problem. But what does it mean to say that scarcity has yielded to abundance? Understood in terms of the satisfaction of wants, scarcity is capable of indefinite retreat. But this is also true if we understand scarcity in terms of the denial of those goods which would contribute to genuinely satisfying projects. Musicians may be indefinitely dissatisfied with their musical instruments; the available scores; their hi-fi equipment; the standard of tuition available; and the amounts of free time they have to pursue the project. Moreover, if everyone else spends their afternoons fishing, then there will be far less production of the things that will prove satisfying to musicians.

V

Let me summarize the argument so far. (1) It is asserted that the affluent society embodies a cult of mass consumption reliant upon the production of dissatisfaction. (2) Some of the consumer goods that it produces would not be desired if it were not for manipulative marketing campaigns. But, (3), it should be allowed that many of these goods are genuinely desirable. (4) Although these goods are genuinely desirable other things are also desirable, but these options are systematically neglected in the interests of capital accumulation. (5) Were people to be reminded of the desirability of these suppressed options, then they would prefer these other goods (particularly increased free time) to further increments of consumption. (6) It would follow that they would in fact lead more 'satisfying' lives if they forswore increased consumption for relief from toil. (7) This transformation could only occur within a planned economy.

The appeal of this argument is that it implies that the abandonment of frenetic productivity can be accomplished non-coercively. If they are not subjected to manipulation, then individuals will choose to opt out of the consumer society, and they will choose to do so in order to maximize the very thing that had driven consumerism: the satisfaction of private desires. I am broadly in agreement with (1), (2), (3), (4) and (7), but I hope at least to have raised some serious doubts about (5) and (6). Let me conclude by drawing together some of the points that have already been made, and offering some impressionistic remarks which might suggest an alternative approach.

If manipulative marketing were suppressed, and the alternatives to mass consumerism were promoted, then we might reasonably expect: (i) a dramatic change in consumption patterns; and (ii) a shift away from ceaseless toil and towards increased increments of free time. Autonomous individuals would place a greater emphasis upon the pursuit of active self-development, and a weaker emphasis upon the passive consumption of 'frivolous' consumer goods. However, this need not signal the collapse of a growth-orientated economy. Nor does it straightforwardly follow that people would be any less inclined to sacrifice free time to the pursuit of increased consumption. [5] This is because the kinds of project that would occupy autonomous individuals would require that they have access to a range of products: many new products serve to enhance projects, or even to initiate new and valuable ones. Furthermore, 'toil' is more accurately contrasted with 'work', rather than with 'leisure'. If toil is understood as activity undertaken solely for remuneration, then such work can be seen to contribute to active self-development: doctors, teachers and social workers, for instance, do not typically consider their work activity as a mere means to remuneration. Worthwhile individual and collective projects benefit from high levels of production and technological innovation: in this sense, they also benefit from toil. (Notice, also, that the definition of 'toil' adopted above – following Cohen – obscures the realm of domestic labour. Many of the goods that we might work overtime to purchase are actually toil-reducing: for example, washing machines, pre-prepared foods, perhaps even electric carving knives. The question arises of whether the manufacture of these goods has involved more 'toil' than would have been incurred had they not been available for consumption.)

It follows that production will never reach a level at which the allocation of resources ceases to be a significant issue. Any given allocation will benefit some interests at the expense of others. This applies both to (i) the development and distribution of goods; and (ii) the extent and distribution of toil. The apparently radical distinction between scarcity and abundance is not finally sustainable. Autonomous individuals who were committed to 'genuinely satisfying' projects would not obviously be any less inclined to sacrifice free time to remunerative toil. The musician may prefer a high increment of toil plus a new hi-fi system to increased leisure and no hi-fi system. Moreover, so long as the musician is concerned only with her own 'satisfaction', she will favour a system in which she enjoys complete freedom from toil, while others incur long hours in order to produce the goods that forward her project. This problem is not resolved by appeal to diminishing marginal utility: the desire for a new turntable may be every bit as 'urgent' as the desire for the hi-fi had been; equally it may be as 'urgent' as someone else's desire to avoid the toil involved in producing the turntable. Similarly, a doctor could certainly favour endless product development and innovation within the health industry over toil-reduction for labourers within that industry. (Imagine saying that we had reached a point of 'abundance' in the field of health care provision.)

But then how are we to allocate resources? In the free market the satisfaction of private desires – given a particular distribution of purchasing power – determines the content of production. The market is operating 'efficiently' when it is producing those things that people want to buy. Judgements about the value of what is produced are anathema for economic liberalism. As Galbraith observes, 'nothing in economics so quickly marks an individual as incompetently trained as the disposition to remark on the legitimacy of the desire for more food and the frivolity of the desire for a more expensive automobile' (Galbraith, 1984, p. 122). The principal criticism considered here of the market is that it perpetuates itself through the manipulative generation of demand – in particular, through an ideology that promotes passive consumerism, while suppressing the alternative of toil-reduction. Let us then imagine a society in which resources are equally distributed, and individuals are engaged in genuinely worthwhile projects, but in which resource allocation is still aimed at the maximization of 'satisfaction'. For example, let us say that resources are allocated by representative democratic institutions which serve to aggregate the votes cast by individuals solely concerned to maximize their own satisfaction (or for that matter to maximize aggregate satisfaction). To persist with an artificial and somewhat misleading example, this system would give equal weight to the musician's desire for a hi-fi, the same person's subsequent desire for a new turntable, and the fisherman's desire for a more flexible rod and for more free time in which to use it. **Any** system for allocating resources that aims to maximize 'satisfaction' will have nothing to say about the legitimacy or importance of rival claims upon resources. In this particular sense, the attacks upon the consumer society that appeal to the promotion of genuinely satisfying forms of life are not finally successful. Unsurprisingly, we cannot rely upon **any kind of market** to arbitrate concerning the legitimacy of rival claims upon resources. But, if it is accepted that some claims should enjoy priority over others, then who is to arbitrate in disputes over allocation? The answer is that, as far as possible, these issues should be decided democratically. That is not by a representative system which aggregates the private preferences that have been registered on ballot papers, but through participatory forums (at various levels) in which the claims of rival projects are rationally debated. In such forums the strength of personal desires are unlikely to prove persuasive. To the extent that resource allocation is decided publicly it is – to a greater or lesser extent – the subject of reasoned argument; to the extent that it is harnessed to satisfying the desires of atomized individuals it will remain neutral regarding the content of production.

Notes

1. Marcuse fails to clearly distinguish between two senses in which an agent might be said to 'really want' something. The first sense concerns the intrinsic properties of the object: for example, it might be said that 'What X really wants is some food, not another pint of beer', or 'What X really wants is to get down to some work'. This is not a claim concerning the agent's actual or prospective mental states: to say that X really wants Y, in this sense, is to say that X **wants for** Y. The second sense concerns the causal history of preference-formation: having freed people from repressive and manipulative social forces, we can find out what they 'really want' by simply asking them. Marcuse emphasizes this second sense: 'In the last analysis, the question of what are true and false needs must be answered by the individuals themselves, but only in the last analysis;

that is, if and when they are free to give their own answer. As long as they are kept incapable of being autonomous, as long as they are indoctrinated and manipulated ... their answer to this question cannot be taken as their own. By the same token ... no tribunal can justly arrogate to itself the right to decide what needs should be developed and satisfied' (Marcuse, 1964, p. 8).

2. There are clearly problems in deciding what precisely is to qualify as 'manipulation' here. For the purposes of this article it is assumed that the desire for a good is a 'product of manipulation' if it did not arise as a result of the provision of accurate product information: to promote a food processor by saying that it is very good at dicing carrots (if it is) is fine. An example of manipulative demand creation would be the fashion industry's tendency to disguise imperative statements as informative ones. When a fashion house announces that 'Blue will be in fashion this season' it is not predicting this trend, but creating it. If it were providing accurate information it would say, 'If you buy blue, then blue will be in fashion this season'.

3. This might seem to endorse John Rawls's 'difference principle': that social and economic inequalities are justifiable so long as they are to the advantage of the worst off group in society (Rawls, 1972). Certainly, unequal distribution may be required in order to provide the incentives that stimulate economic growth. However, Rawls fails to pay sufficient heed to the distinction between absolute and relative poverty, or fully to recognize the increasing salience of the latter in the advanced industrial economies. Nor does Rawls address the question of whether the indefinite expansion of production frontiers is a desirable objective.

4. J.K. Galbraith also points out that the cult of private consumption relies upon a hostility to public provision which is incomprehensible except in the context of the ideological structure of the 'affluent society'. 'The family which takes its mauve and cerise, air-conditioned, power-steered and power-braked automobile out for a tour passes through cities that are badly paved, made hideous by litter, blighted buildings, billboards and posts for wires that should long since have been put underground ... They picnic on exquisitely packaged food from a portable icebox by a polluted stream and go on to spend the night at a park which is a menace to public health and morals. Just before dozing off on an air mattress, beneath a nylon tent, amid the stench of decaying refuse, they may reflect vaguely on the curious unevenness of their blessings. Is this, indeed, the American genius?' (Galbraith, 1984, p. 192)

5. A distinction needs to be drawn between a society in which there is demand for consumable goods and a consumer society. In particular, if agents consume in order to realize projects, then consumption has ceased to be an end in itself. While this is an important point, I do not

think that it bears upon the arguments that are developed in this final section.

References

Arendt, H. (1951), *The Origins of Totalitarianism*, Harcourt Brace, New York.
Arendt, H. (1958), *The Human Condition*, University of Chicago Press, Chicago.
Arendt, H. (1963), *On Revolution*, Viking, New York.
Bannock, G. et al. (1984), *The Penguin Dictionary of Economics*, Penguin, London.
Begg, D.K.H. et al. (1984), *Economics*, McGraw-Hill, Maidenhead.
Bottomore, T. (ed.) (1991), *A Dictionary of Marxist Thought*, Second Edition, Blackwell, Oxford.
Cohen, G.A. (1978), *Karl Marx's Theory of History: A Defence*, Oxford University Press, Oxford.
Elster, J. (1985), *Making Sense of Marx*, Cambridge University Press, Cambridge.
Elster, J. (1986), *An Introduction to Karl Marx*, Cambridge University Press, Cambridge.
Fukuyama, F. (1989), 'The end of history?', *The National Interest*, 16, pp. 3–18.
Fukuyama, F. (1989), 'A reply to my critics', *The National Interest*, 18, pp. 21–28.
Fukuyama, F. (1992), *The End of History and the Last Man*, Penguin, London.
Galbraith, J.K. (1984), *The Affluent Society*, Fourth Edition, Penguin, London.
Gottlieb, R.S. (ed.) (1989), *An Anthology of Western Marxism*, Oxford University Press, Oxford.
Hirst, I.R.C. and Reekie, W.R. (eds.) (1977), *The Consumer Society*, Tavistock Publications, London.
Kymlicka, W. (1990), *Contemporary Political Philosophy*, Oxford University Press, Oxford.

Leiss, W. (1978), *The Limits of Satisfaction*, Marion Boyers Ltd., London.
Lessnoff, M. (1974), *The Structure of Social Science*, George Allen and Unwin Ltd., Surrey.
Lukes, S. (1973), *Individualism*, Blackwell, Oxford.
MacIntyre, A. (1985), *After Virtue*, Second Edition, Duckworth, London.
Marcuse, H. (1964), *One Dimensional Man*, Beacon Press, Boston.
Marcuse, H. (1969), 'Repressive tolerance', in Wolff, R. et al., *A Critique of Pure Tolerance*, Jonathan Cape, London.
Mason, R. (1981), *Conspicuous Consumption*, Gower Publishing Co., Aldershot.
Menger, C. (1985), *Investigations into the Methods of the Social Sciences*, New York University Press, New York.
Mill, John Stuart (1962), *Utilitarianism, On Liberty and Essay on Bentham*, Warnock, Mary (ed.), Fontana, London.
Miller et al. (1991), *The Blackwell Encyclopedia of Political Thought*, Blackwell, Oxford.
Nozick, R. (1974), *Anarchy, State and Utopia*, Blackwell, Oxford.
Pratt, V. (1978), *The Philosophy of the Social Sciences*, Routledge, London.
Raphael, D.D. (1981), *Moral Philosophy*, Oxford University Press, Oxford.
Rawls, J. (1972), *A Theory of Justice*, Oxford University Press, Oxford.
Shaw, W H. (1978), *Marx's Theory of History*, Hutchinson, London.
Tucker, R.C. (ed.) (1978), *The Marx-Engels Reader*, 2nd ed., Norton and Co., London.

7 Liberalism and welfare: The limits of compensation

Phillip Cole

I Introduction

The theme of this article is the relationship between liberal theory and the capitalist market. Liberal political theory is committed to the moral equality of persons: all persons are of equal moral value and carry equal moral weight. The problem I focus on is how liberal theory attempts to reconcile its commitment to the moral equality of persons with the economic and social inequalities of life-prospects produced and required by the capitalist market system.

One way to deal with this seeming contradiction is to set up a distinction between the political sphere and the economic sphere, and insist that what is required in order to respect our moral equality is equality as 'citizens' within the political sphere, rather than equality in the economic sphere: we are public equals, but in private there can be no enforcement of such an order. However, this distinction does not work: few would seriously argue that equal political citizenship can be maintained in the face of the radical economic inequalities we find in liberal-capitalist states. [1] But even if it could be maintained, this would not solve the problem: for if the commitment to the equal moral worth of persons entails political equality, why does it not entail social and economic equality – the equality of life-prospects? How can we justify drawing a boundary between the comparative moral weight of my life in the political sphere, and the comparative moral weight of my life in the social and economic sphere?

An alternative response is to claim that the capitalist market is the best available regime of equal liberty; that equal liberty is a fundamental value; and that it is not compatible with social or economic equality. However, this response appeals to a definition of liberty as purely negative which few liberal theorists actually hold; [2] or to a contentious distinction between liberty and the worth of liberty. More importantly, it is a distortion of liberal political philosophy: for liberalism is not a single-value ideology, and does not regard individual liberty as supreme over all other values.

Rather, liberal theory does recognize that our moral equality is in fact undermined by economic and social, as well as by political, inequality. Furthermore, it responds to this problem by placing the idea of **compensation** at the centre of the discourse of social justice: the equal value of persons is respected by compensating – by means of redistributive welfare strategies – those whose equality has been undermined through no fault of their own within the capitalist market place. Or, more weakly, the equal moral value of persons is at least **acknowledged** through such compensatory redistribution, in that we recognize that something is owed people for the loss of their equality through capitalism – compensation cannot restore that loss, but is an acknowledgement of it. Whether liberal compensatory redistribution can deliver what is demanded by the stronger thesis, or only that required by the weaker version is, of course, an important question.

II Redistribution as Compensation

This emphasis on the achievement of the demands of social justice through compensatory redistribution recurs throughout contemporary liberal texts. John Gray, for instance, as self-appointed spokesperson for what he calls the classical liberal tradition, insists that '... the moral defence of liberty requires rectification of past injustices...' (Gray, 1986, p. 89). The aim of policy should be to 'compensate for past departures from equal liberty' (ibid., p. 88). Robert Nozick, representing the minimal state position, concedes that even 'past injustices might be so great as to make necessary in the short run a more extensive state in order to rectify them' (Nozick, 1974, p. 231). John Rawls, representing the welfare liberal position, says that his theory of justice is about the 'basic structure' of society, namely 'the institutions that define the social background and includes as well those operations that continually adjust and compensate for the inevitable tendencies away from background fairness ...' (Rawls, 1978, p. 54). Ronald Dworkin generally eschews direct reference to compensation, talking instead in terms of insurance, and suggesting 'a tax scheme constructed as a practical translation of a hypothetical insurance market, which assumes equal initial assets and equal risk ...' (Dworkin, 1981, pp. 326–7). But insurance is of course a compensation scheme, and even Dworkin sometimes uses the language of compensation, especially when discussing the physically disabled (ibid., pp. 296–304).

We should note, though, that there is an important difference between the accounts of compensatory redistribution given by 'classical' or 'libertarian' liberals like Gray and Nozick, and by 'welfare' liberals like

Rawls and Dworkin. For the former, there is a one-off, large scale redistribution to compensate for all the past injustices, and the free market is then left to run on unimpeded from this situation of initial fairness. For the latter, there is the same large scale compensatory redistribution at the start, but it is followed by an ongoing programme of redistribution, on a much smaller scale, in order to maintain fairness. An interesting point to note is that, while for western liberal-capitalist states this stage of initial redistribution is utopian, the former communist states of central and eastern Europe are actually at this stage.

This emphasis upon achieving the demands of social justice through compensation tends to tie liberal theory down to an after-the-event view of social justice, a rather narrow, backward-looking approach. One response is to claim that justice itself is essentially backward-looking, and that therefore any programme of social justice must also be backward-looking. Any programme which aims to secure people's **future** welfare without reference to their past may be all well and good, but it has nothing to do with justice. Genuine theories of social justice – such as Nozick's Entitlement Theory (Nozick, 1974, pp. 149–182) – are therefore essentially backward-looking. According to Antony Flew, this is all that justice amounts to: '... the notion of justice is necessarily backward-looking'; and he contrasts this with the 'ideal of equality of outcome, equality of welfare', which 'is by contrast essentially forward-looking' (Flew, 1985, p. 193). But Nani L. Ranken has pointed out an inherent weakness in such an approach, namely that a forward-looking concern is the necessary corollary of the backward-looking view: 'since the reparation presupposes the **recognition** of the wrong, that very recognition entails a duty to take steps to prevent the repetition of the wrong'; and '... any sincere efforts to compensate for the wrongs caused by such practices must include efforts to change the conditions that perpetuate the practices' (Ranken, 1986, p. 113).

Ideally, social justice will have three directions of concern: for people's past; their present; and their future. We have a backward-looking concern with things that happened in people's pasts which we now consider to have been unfair and which should therefore be redressed; we have a present-looking concern with current conditions which we consider to be unfair; and we have a forward-looking concern with possible future conditions which we consider would be unfair. Our concern with past unfairnesses is restricted to compensation or redress for what happened – we do not have the option to travel back to alter those conditions. But when it comes to present and possible future unfairnesses, we **do** have an option: we can either act to alter present conditions and prevent future possibilities, or we can simply compensate people for their effects.

Liberal theory is usually willing to take all three perspectives, and yet the emphasis is still on compensation. The problem is that even if we allow that compensation can play a rôle in present- or forward-looking concerns, the implication is that we must allow misfortunes to befall people rather than act to alter or prevent them. The only justifications for taking this option are either that the present conditions are unalterable and the future conditions unpreventable or unpredictable; or that the cost of alteration or prevention is too high – it is cheaper to compensate. While the first possibility would impose a genuine constraint on what we can do in the name of social justice, the second possibility creates a much weaker constraint: the most expensive option may also be the most just, and, all things considered, the one we ought to take.

III Models of Welfare

I want to distinguish between three models of welfare:

1. **liberatory**, where the aim is the empowerment of persons to be equal citizens in their society;

2. **power/control**, where the aim is to maintain discipline in the workforce and to maintain social stability; and

3. **compensatory**, where the aim is to compensate people for certain effects of the capitalist market.

Actual theories and practices of welfare are, of course, more complex than this scheme: these are, in a sense, rhetorics or discourses of welfare. The first model lies behind much contemporary socialist thinking, or rethinking, about welfare. The second model is certainly the rhetoric of welfare employed by conservatives throughout the west. The third model is, I am suggesting, the dominant discourse of welfare in liberal theory. It is the weaknesses of this model that I want to examine. I have two complaints against it: (i) it bears little or no resemblance to the political practice of welfare in liberal-capitalist states; and (ii) it is theoretically bankrupt. It is the second of these that I shall investigate here.

Why the emphasis on social justice as compensation in welfare-liberal writing? The answer lies partly in the liberal view of capitalist markets, and why some people do well in them while others do badly. [3] For liberals, people's life-chances should be shaped by their free choices, rather than being determined by the circumstances in which they find themselves. The capitalist market presents a mixture of these factors: an ideal market allows life-chances to be shaped by free choices made by fully rational agents under conditions of full information, and in equal political, social and economic starting positions. But, of course, the real-world market is not like this at all – it allows circumstances to play a significant rôle in determining life-prospects. The differences in circumstances we find between people are largely the product of natural, social and historical accident, and are therefore arbitrary from a moral point of view: people do not deserve them and so do not deserve the social position they determine. It would therefore be unjust to allow arbitrary circumstances to determine the value of life-chances. John Rawls says:

> What the theory of justice must regulate is the inequalities in life-prospects between citizens that arise from social starting-positions, natural advantages and historical contingencies. (Rawls, 1978, p. 56)

These, for Rawls, are the 'fundamental' inequalities: we are morally obliged to prevent them from undermining the value of people's life-chances. However, the best way to deal with these inequalities is not to limit the market freedom of those who have been arbitrarily advantaged: for this would entail heavy-handed state intervention in the market, and interference with individual liberty. Rather, we ensure that there is a system of welfare through which those who do badly because of their arbitrary disadvantages are compensated by those who do well. For example, Rawls argues:

> No one deserves his greater natural capacity nor merits a more favorable starting place in society. But it does not follow that one should eliminate these distinctions. There is another way to deal with them. The basic structure can be arranged so that these contingencies work for the good of the least fortunate. (Rawls, 1972, p. 102)

Of his difference principle strategy, he says that it sets up a

> social system so that no one gains or loses from his arbitrary place in the distribution of natural assets or his initial position in society without giving or receiving compensating advantages in return. (ibid.)

He wants a system

> which treats everyone equally as a moral person, and which does not weight men's share in the benefits and burdens of social cooperation according to their social fortune or their luck in the natural lottery ... (ibid., p. 75)

And so welfare liberal theory takes a distinctly benevolent view of the worst off in capitalist societies: by and large, their position is not their fault – it is a matter of bad luck. And, as people do not **deserve** bad luck (neither do they deserve good luck) it is appropriate to compensate them for their misfortune. Of course, there remains an extent to which people earn their position in capitalist markets and therefore deserve the market outcomes they aim for. Indeed, Dworkin distinguishes between what he calls option luck, 'a matter of how deliberate and calculated gambles turn out ...' (Dworkin, 1981, p. 293) and brute bad luck, which is unpredictable misfortune. What is important, though, is the claim that market outcomes are significantly determined by luck, brutely bad or otherwise, and therefore are not, to that extent, deserved.

I want to contrast this with the Power/Control model of welfare, which takes a much harsher view of the worst off in capitalist markets. On this model their situation is the result of their own shortcomings: they lack the qualities needed to succeed in the competitive market system and this makes them failures in a normative sense. Provided we ensure the freedom to compete for scarce resources in the market, people will deserve what they get, whatever it is. We might say that this position cleaves to a substantive view of the 'virtuous person'; the person who has the qualities needed to succeed in the market. From this perspective the free rider problem is a matter of '... the virtuous citizenry ... robbed by the few who prefer a parasitic life to one of hard work' (Wolin, 1987, p. 475); [4] and the issue of welfare becomes 'a confrontation between parasitism and the work ethic ...' (ibid.). If we take this view of the worst off, then there seems no reason of justice to have a welfare system at all. The worst off have no **claim** to welfare: they deserve what they get – they can have no **rights** against those who have succeeded. Any welfare the successful provide will be a matter of charity. In fact, because, from this perspective, welfare is charity, its provision can be left to charity organizations, and the State need only step in where private charity cannot cope. We can even make our state welfare institutions function like private charities – that is to say, having strictly limited funds, they are forced to make distinctions between deserving and undeserving cases.

There could also be other motives for having a welfare system from this point of view. For example, it could be argued that if people are allowed to fall into the depths of deprivation, then social conditions will be created for unrest and disorder. To avoid these threats to social order, we could provide a welfare system to act as a safety net, specifying a minimum level below which people should not fall; and can calculate that level by reference to the level of poverty which the social system can tolerate before de-stabilizing or losing its legitimacy. This is to see the welfare system as a pay-off to the poorest to ensure that they do not disrupt an economic system which is working in the interests of the more powerful – a pay-off which the former are in no position to turn down.

Another argument for a welfare system could be this: a framework of welfare may usefully serve as a system of discipline, exerting power and control over the worst off. If we make it particularly difficult to obtain welfare payments, either through bureaucracy or through long delays in payment, then people can be forced back into the labour market at lower wages; only the most hopeless and helpless will stick it out. Such a welfare system gives us close economic and social control over people's lives: making them attend particular places at particular times; forcing them to live in certain areas; spying on their private lives on the grounds of fraud detection; constantly updating information about them; keeping them in a constant state of uncertainty and anxiety so that they are rendered powerless to make long term plans or to have long term expectations. This kind of welfare system can operate as a system of power, control and discipline over certain sections of the community. A practical example of this is the way the social security system is used in Britain as a reinforcement of immigration control, such that

> entitlement to education, social security and other benefits and services has become increasingly dependent upon immigration status and in which it has become legitimate for a range of officials to question claimants and others about their status and thus act as agents of immigration control. (Gordon, 1989, pp. 7–8)

Ruth Lister comments:

> Such insidious policies have meant a growth in the indiscriminate passport-checking of black claimants, all of whom are assumed to be a recent immigrant, even if born or long-settled in this country. (Lister, 1990, p. 53)

If we take the less benevolent view of the worst-off which lies behind the Power/Control model of welfare, then the welfare framework emerges as a mixture of a system of charity, a one-sided pay-off for the sake of stability, and a system of discipline. Of course, as we have seen, liberal theory takes a very different and more benevolent view of the situation of the worst off under capitalism: it is, by and large, not their fault, and it is appropriate to compensate such people through a welfare system.

IV The Limits of Compensation

The compensatory approach to social justice might seem a reasonable alternative to the power/control approach. What, then, is so objectionable about it? There are, I think, two particularly formidable problems. First: are the 'fundamental inequalities' Rawls talks of really the result of bad luck? Second: what are the consequences of treating them as though they were?

The immediate difficulty about Rawls' 'fundamental inequalities' is that they arise from natural advantages and historical processes, notions so broad and ill-defined that it is questionable whether their effects on social starting positions can plausibly be seen in terms of **bad luck** at all. For example, one's health is a natural feature that can act as an advantage or disadvantage in the capitalist market. Rawls writes of these natural features as distributed through the 'natural lottery', thus implying that they are distributed throughout the population at random. But the overwhelming evidence is that levels of wealth and levels of health are linked. [5] The problem is, therefore, not simply that one's health can undermine one's ability to compete in the capitalist market, but that the capitalist market undermines the health of certain groups within it. It is not simply that the 'fundamental inequalities' strike at random (although some certainly do): rather, and at least as importantly, industrial capitalism creates such inequalities, and constructs them as problems. Rawls' talk of 'social misfortune' and of people's 'luck in the natural lottery' (Rawls, 1972, p. 75) is, at least, somewhat disingenuous.

However, even if it is obviously wrong to characterize these 'fundamental' inequalities as accidental, it may not be wrong to deal with them as though they were. This, in fact, is the procedure that Rawls himself follows, in common with others, with his device of the original position behind a veil of ignorance (ibid., pp. 136–142): people are placed in a position where they cannot know what their social position or plan of life will be, and must choose the most appropriate principles of justice on that basis. This is, in effect, to treat one's social position and the inequalities attached to it as thought it were a matter of pure brute luck. But there are two difficulties with this approach. First, in characterizing social injustice as misfortune, it places the worst off under capitalism in a highly vulnerable position: people have claims of right against injustice, but have no such claims against misfortune, only claims of insurance or benevolence. Second, it is to treat the conditions of injustice as though they were unalterable, unpreventable, or unpredictable: but this restricts us to just that narrow approach described in Section II, one which leaves the worst off open to the devastation of their life-chances through market forces, and merely seeks to compensate them for this devastation after the event. This is, in effect, to place the worst off outside of the boundaries of social justice altogether.

V The Unfree Rider Problem

We can pose the issue of 'bad luck' in terms of the free rider problem. If certain people are excluded from active participation in the production of social resources, why should they have any access to the rewards of that process? One answer is that since their exclusion is not their fault, there is no reason why they should lose out. But neither is it the fault of those who **do** actively participate, and so why should **they** lose out by having to give some share of their rewards to the non-participants? The non-participants are free riders, and the active contributors could put forward the following complaints.

(i) If the non-participants do not contribute any input to the productive process, on what grounds do they have any entitlement to a share of the output? Any output the active participants grant them is, or is equivalent to, charity; and must, accordingly, depend upon the extent to which these active participants are feeling charitable.

(ii) It might be replied that, (i) not withstanding, these people's **needs** establish a right to some share of social output. But even if this is granted, such a right surely cannot be to the same sized share as that of the active participants. The former should receive sufficient to meet **basic** needs, but no more.

(iii) Even if it is conceded that these people have an equal right to human flourishing, and therefore a right to a share of social resources which goes beyond meeting 'basic' needs, they nevertheless have no right to a say in the **organization** of social production. Surely, only those who actively participate in social production have an entitlement to a democratic share in the decision-making of that enterprise.

These complaints are considerable. The active participants do seem to have prima facie grounds for complaint: non-participants are free riders and the active participants are being treated unfairly if free riders get more than a basic share of the benefits of social cooperation. This treatment of the free rider problem is familiar. [6] Those excluded, however, also have strong grounds for complaint, since they are excluded against their wishes: far from being free riders, they are in fact **un**free riders. Why should they be placed in the precarious position of being dependent on the fickle nature of others' charity? Why, if they have **rights** to resources, should only their 'basic' needs be met, and the extent – and even the chances – of human flourishing be restricted to a 'basic' level? Why should they be denied participation in the negotiation of the rules of cooperation which, without their participation, exclude them? Why should they be rendered silent and powerless? Anthony Skillen comments on the precariousness of the 'situation of one forced to "free-ride" because he or she cannot get a job, cannot **be** an active contributor ... Here we seem to have an injustice that excludes people from the very sphere of reciprocal justice' (Skillen, 1985, p. 11).

The more severe power/control model of welfare clearly confers no bargaining rights upon the worst off; but it is equally difficult to see them as holding any bargaining rights under the compensation model. Raymond Plant, for example, observes that in practice:

> Conferring social rights outside economic performance is not compatible with either the prevailing ideology or, more importantly, the self-understanding of those who are most likely to claim the rights. They are unlikely to see themselves as independent citizens claiming what is theirs by right, rather than essentially recipients of charity, whatever the rhetoric deployed to disguise this. (Plant, 1991, p. 62)

And so, in effect, the compensation strategy of social justice places the worst off outside the boundaries of reciprocal justice. It renders them, as recipients of charity, not only dependent upon benevolence – rather than as rights-holders – but also denies them access to any means of changing such a state of affairs.

VI Conclusion

The compensation strategy thus places the worst off in liberal capitalist states in a very vulnerable position, with little, if any, bargaining power: they must rely on the benevolence of those who have benefited from the system. By treating the situation of the worst off as though it were the result of bad luck, the welfare liberal portrays their position as not an issue of justice at all – because nobody has acted unjustly towards them to place them in this situation, or at least we are going to act as if nobody had acted in that way. One might well conclude from this, with Hayek, that there is no such thing as **social** justice. [7]

What is at stake here is a power relationship in which compensation has a rôle to play. The liberal has acknowledged that the power relationships which make up the capitalist market are harmful for certain groups in society, and has decided either that the harm being caused is not so severe that it ought to be prevented (compensation will do – being worst off under capitalism isn't **so** bad that we ought to consider anything so rash as significantly interfering with capitalism itself); or that the power relationship which is causing the harm to some is so valuable to others that the harm done is outweighed, and so must be preserved – the most we can do is compensate those harmed. Whichever view the liberal takes, the harm suffered by certain groups under capitalism is seen as a price worth paying for its benefits: the damage caused to the life-prospects of such people is written off through compensation. The advantage of the compensation approach is, in the end, that it can be enacted without interfering with existing power relationships: compensation is linked with maintaining or restoring the status quo, or at the very least it does not seek to challenge that status quo. The status of the worst off as equally valued persons cannot be respected if we take the welfare liberal step of regarding their inequality as the result of brute bad luck, rather than as the predictable and preventable outcome of a social and economic system which generates this sort of injustice through its very nature.

An alternative logic to welfare is to see it as the provision of the conditions necessary for autonomous citizenship. This is to move from a discourse of compensation to a discourse of participation: from the 'welfare state', to what Anthony Skillen calls the welfare society (Skillen, 1985) or what Ralf Dahrendorf describes as the social state – 'The social state (as I prefer to call it) is about guaranteeing social citizenship rights for all' (Dahrendorf, 1987). Raymond Plant is perhaps the foremost proponent of such an approach. He argues for a society based on democratic citizenship, a notion which demands 'policies which enable every citizen to lead a full and autonomous life shaped by their own values and purposes,' and a 'framework of education, health care, income and law that underpins such citizenship' (Plant, 1988). This concern for citizenship takes us beyond frameworks of welfare which aim to compensate, towards frameworks of citizenship which aim to enable, empower and liberate – frameworks which aim to provide all with the political, social and economic conditions they need if they are to be equal participators in their own community. Equal participation is the primary signifier of equal moral value. The loss of that participation in the economic, social and political aspects of the community cannot be compensated for in any way that can respect or restore the equal value of persons.

Acknowledgements

An earlier version of this paper was also presented at the 'Critical Legal Conference', Staffordshire University, 11–13 September 1992. I would like in particular to thank Roshi Naidoo, Dr David Gosling, Dr Brian Smart, my colleagues at Staffordshire University, and the students of my 'Philosophy and Public Affairs' course, for their comments and encouragement.

Notes

1. The most effective critique of such claims is Karl Marx's discussion of the distinction between the State and civil society in *On the Jewish Question*, in Bottomore (ed.) (1963).
2. See Flathman (1987), pp. 30–33, where he makes a distinction between pure and impure theories of negative freedom.
3. See Kymlicka (1990), pp. 85–86.
4. I should make it clear that Wolin is simply reporting the prevalence of such rhetoric in Ronald Reagan's America, not endorsing it.
5. See Townsend, Davidson and Whitehead (1988).

6. For example see Hart (1955), p. 185; and Rawls (1972), p. 112.
7. See Hayek (1973–1979), vol. 2, pp. 67–70.

References

Bottomore, Tom, (ed.) (1963), *Karl Marx: Early Writings*, C.A. Watts and Co. Ltd., London.
Dahrendorf, Ralf (1987), 'Perspectives: liberal helpings ...', *Times Higher Education Supplement*, 14 August, p. 9.
Dworkin, Ronald (1981), 'What is equality? Part 2: equality of resources', *Philosophy and Public Affairs,* 10, 4, pp. 283–345.
Flathman, Richard (1987), *The Philosophy and Politics of Freedom*, University of Chicago Press, Chicago.
Flew, Antony (1985), 'The concept, and conceptions of, justice', *Journal of Applied Philosophy,* 2, 2, pp. 191–6.
Gordon, P. (1989), *Citizenship for Some? Race and Government Policy 1979–1989*, Runnymede Trust, London.
Gray, John (1986), *Liberalism*, Open University Press, Milton Keynes.
Hart, H.L.A. (1955), 'Are there any natural rights?', *Philosophical Review,* 64, pp. 175–191.
Hayek, F.A. (1973–1979), *Law, Legislation and Liberty*, Routledge and Kegan Paul, London.
Kymlicka, Will (1990), *Contemporary Political Philosophy: An Introduction*, Clarendon Press, Oxford.
Lister, Ruth (1990), *The Exclusive Society – Citizenship and the Poor*, Child Poverty Action Group, London.
Nozick, Robert (1974), *Anarchy, State, and Utopia*, Blackwell, Oxford.
Plant, Raymond (1988), *Citizenship, Rights and Socialism*, Fabian Tract 531, Fabian Society, London.
Plant, Raymond (1991), 'Social rights and the reconstruction of welfare' in Andrews, Geoff (ed.), *Citizenship*, Lawrence and Wishart, London.
Ranken, Nani L. (1986), 'Compensation vs. fair equality of opportunity', *Journal of Applied Philosophy*, 3, 1, pp. 111–22.

Rawls, John (1972), *A Theory of Justice*, Oxford University Press, Oxford.

Rawls, John (1978), 'The basic structure as subject' in Goldman, A. and Kim, J. (ed.), *Values and Morals*, Reidel, Dordrecht.

Skillen, Anthony (1985), 'Welfare state versus welfare society?', *Journal of Applied Philosophy*, 2, 1. pp. 3–17.

Townsend, Peter, Davidson, Nick and Whitehead, Margaret (1988), *Inequalities in Health*, Penguin, Harmondsworth.

Wolin, Sheldon (1987), 'Democracy and the welfare state: the political and theoretical connections between staatsräson and wohlfahrtsstaatsräson', *Political Theory,* 15, 4, pp. 467–500.

8 Can liberals be feminists?

Pat FitzGerald

I

According to liberal political theory, human beings are essentially rational agents: and rationality consists primarily in individuals' ability to be consistent in the pursuit of their own ends. Liberals regard each individual as alone qualified to identify her or his own interests, which are in principle fulfillable independently of the desires or interests of others. Since, however, the resources necessary to sustain life are limited, individuals are motivated by the desire to secure for themselves as large a share as possible. Liberal political theory therefore sees human beings as essentially egoistic and acquisitive individuals. Its task has thus been to devise social institutions which will protect individuals' rights to a fair share of available resources, while interfering as little as possible with individuals' autonomy and self-fulfilment. John Stuart Mill puts the position succinctly:

> The only freedom which deserves the name, is that of pursuing our own good in our own way, so long as we do not attempt to deprive others of theirs, or impede their efforts to obtain it. (Mill, 1962, p. 18)

For classical (that is, not libertarian) liberal political theorists, the state fulfils the dual function of protecting people and property, while yet guaranteeing individuals the maximum protection from interference. This protection must be against not only 'the tyranny of the magistrate' but also against 'the tyranny of the prevailing opinion and feeling; against the tendency of society to impose, by other means than civil penalties, its own ideas and practices as rules of conduct on those who dissent from them; to fetter the development, and, if possible, prevent the formation, of any individuality not in harmony with its ways, and compel all characters to fashion themselves upon the model of its own' (ibid., p. 9). The province of state intervention is delimited by distinguishing between the private and the public realms.

While the concerns of early liberal political theorists centred primarily on areas of 'civil rights', such as universal enfranchisement and the right to own property, once these civil rights were successfully and 'universally' achieved, the emphasis of liberal concerns shifted. Latterly, liberalism has become increasingly concerned with distributive justice; that is, with the effects of the inequality of wealth on individuals' rights and opportunities. As a result, liberal political theory has developed a theory of the welfare state, one which is perhaps most systematically and influentially expressed by John Rawls.

The development of Anglo-American liberal feminist theory has parallelled these concerns, and is characterized by two 'waves'. Early liberal feminists – Mill, Mary Wollstonecraft (1992), Harriet Taylor Mill (1970) [1] – argued for the extension of liberal notions of rationality and individual autonomy to women; an extension which required a corresponding extension of enfranchisement and property rights. Since its re-emergence in the 1960s – represented by Betty Friedan (1965) and the National Association of Women – Anglo-American liberal feminism has focussed on issues of justice and equality. Liberal feminists argue that the inequality of women in the work place and in education is a social injustice, and not simply an injustice to women. [2] Liberal feminist theory therefore urges the introduction of laws to ensure equality of opportunity in education and in the work place and even argues for the introduction of positive discrimination in favour of women to redress women's under-representation in many areas of employment. But it is clear that such strategies demand increasing state intervention in what liberals would usually regard as the private sphere; particularly in the regulation of family arrangements and of child care.

II

I shall argue that in attempting to retain its feminism, Anglo-American liberal feminism sacrifices its liberalism; and that this demonstrates the inadequacy of liberalism for achieving changes to the social structures which oppress or disadvantage women. Further, I shall argue that liberal feminism's apparent achievements in the area of 'equal opportunities' cannot bring about the kinds of structural change which any feminism must require, and indeed are inimical to such change. Here it should be noted that I do not suggest that feminism has a unified aim which a particular feminist theory embodies. Rather, my point is that all feminisms – whether they acknowledge it or not – embody a central claim about the position of women in society. Depending on the particular theory, women are considered to be oppressed because of their biology or because of the social construction of gender; on one of these grounds, feminist theories maintain that women are either universally oppressed or oppressed as a 'class' in particular types of economic system. Whatever their **explanation** for women's position in societies, feminist theories **describe** that position as being different from that of men: whether it is, for instance, a marxist feminist explanation in terms of industrial capitalism's need for the reproduction and nurturing of its work force; or a radical feminist explanation in terms of men's (ab)use of power as a result of the nature of women's reproductive capacities. For feminists, women are at least disadvantaged and at worst oppressed. The policies which arise from feminist theories are intended to remedy such disadvantage or end the oppression; an end which liberal feminism cannot achieve.

One claim shared by feminisms is that of the centrality of reproduction in creating the conditions for women's oppression; it is because women have been the child bearers, and, in pre-technological societies, have had little choice but to bear children, that men have come to be in a position to oppress or take advantage of them. Most feminisms argue for the necessity of an analysis of the gendered individual: since one sex or another is ascribed to human beings at birth on the basis of their biological characteristics (and sometimes regardless of their biological characteristics) and since it appears that those characteristics have been used to women's disadvantage, an analysis of either gender, biology or both is central to feminist explanations of women's social position. Liberal feminism insists that an individual's sex should be irrelevant; and its policies are thus aimed at providing women with the opportunity to prove their rationality on the same terms as men. Because it must share the liberal understanding of human nature previously adverted to, liberal feminist theory – if it is to remain liberal – has also to retain a belief in the possibility, at least theoretical, of an ungendered individual: it must repudiate any notion of there being a male and female nature, and insist on there being only a human nature. Betty Friedan encapsulates this understanding: '... women are people in the fullest sense of the word, who must be free to move in society with all the privileges and opportunities and responsibilities that are their human ... right' (Friedan, 1977, pp. 316–17).

It is unsurprising that, given its commitment to the ungendered individual, liberal feminist theory has embraced the emphasis of liberal political theory on the rôle of justice in providing equality of opportunity for women. Liberal feminism's analysis of women's position in Western industrialized capitalist society maintains that women have received unequal treatment in social institutions such as the law, education and employment. Initially, liberal feminist theorists such as Wollstonecraft and Mill argued that women's inferior performance in public life and apparent lack of rationality was the result of their virtual exclusion from education. Latterly, liberal feminists have focussed on the discrimination within education whereby boys are apparently encouraged to pursue an education in the 'rational' sciences and girls in the 'emotional' arts. If rationality is an essential human characteristic, then this exclusion and discrimination has in effect denied women full human status, along with the opportunity to discover whether they are, in fact, capable of achieving the same sorts of things as men have achieved. As Janet Radcliffe Richards remarks, '... even if women are less good at reasoning than men that is hardly surprising, since men have always taken very good care that women should never have the opportunity to learn' (Radcliffe Richards, 1980, p. 15). Notice here the twin peaks of liberal feminism: the unchallenged belief that what men do – at least in public life – epitomizes the exercise of rationality; and the unexplained acceptance of the fact that men just happen to have kept women from fulfilling their full human potential.

Since women have been discriminated against in education, they are therefore not only discriminated against by men who occupy positions of power, but, as a result of this educational discrimination, they are also possibly less suited for such positions of power and influence in public life. Liberal feminism maintains that the state must adopt policies to counter such discrimination. Radcliffe Richards, for example, claims that the position in which women now find themselves vis-à-vis their representation in public life is unjust on two counts. First, since women have been denied the opportunity to develop their rational faculties, constraints have been imposed on their individual freedom, which runs contrary to the liberal belief in individual autonomy. Second, the systematic exclusion of women from public life has harmed society in general, and is hence detrimental to the well-being of individuals (ibid., pp. 91–93). To remedy this, she proposes a modification to Rawls' 'difference principle' (Rawls, 1972): in this case to suggest that justice requires that existing social and economic inequalities should be arranged so that they may reasonably be expected to be to everyone's absolute advantage (op. cit., Ch. 3). This represents, for Radcliffe Richards, a Rawlsian appeal to justice: justice here does not consist in total equality, but rather considers every individual equally. She distinguishes between substantial justice and formal justice: substantial justice is to do with having just laws which determine how social goods are distributed; formal justice is to do with applying laws justly. Women's status in society is substantially unjust, as it is embodied in laws which work against women, as do conventions in all other social institutions, since they are governed by men. To eliminate the distinctions at law which differentiate unfairly between men and women, what is required is a reformulation of substantial justice, so that women receive their fair share of social goods. Radcliffe Richards' commitment, just like Rawls', is **not** to absolute equality – whatever that might be – but to equality of consideration. The aim is to make the worst off group of individuals as well off as possible; and this may or may not require equal shares.

It follows that to correct the imbalance – the under-representation of women in public life – the policy which results from such an analysis requires a variety of changes to the legal framework which governs public life. It is not enough to ensure that women be treated equally in education – that, for instance, they be somehow enabled to be equally represented in the sciences. Nor is it enough to promote or legislate for equality of opportunity in the work place. To redress the existing imbalance, Radcliffe Richards argues, there must be positive discrimination in favour of women. Only then will enough women be in positions both to act as rôle models and to ensure that other women are not discriminated against. Positive discrimination – affirmative action in the US – is, for liberal feminists such as Radcliffe Richards, a necessary means of increasing women's representation in public life. Legal changes to achieve this, and thus to facilitate women's entry into public life, are therefore a major element of liberal feminism's proposals, exemplified in the US by the Equal Rights Amendment and to a significantly lesser extent in the UK by sex discrimination legislation (in which positive discrimination plays no part). This difference notwithstanding, the purpose of such legislation is to 'guarantee that each person is treated as an individual rather than as a member of a sex class' (Eisenstein, 1986, p. 233).

A number of questions, however, are raised by such proposals for state intervention and by their actual instantiations: and these questions draw attention to the deficiencies of the liberal notion of the ungendered individual. First, and most important, liberal feminism does not claim that women **are** actually capable of the same sorts of things as men are: the claim is merely that, since nobody has ever had the opportunity to find out, we do not know what women are capable of. In this, liberal feminism adopts Mill's agnostic position:

> Standing on the ground of common sense and the constitution of the human mind, I deny that anyone knows, or can know, the nature of the two sexes, as long as they have only been seen in their present relation to one another ... (Mill, 1975, p. 451)

But it follows that, if we do not know whether women are capable of performing in public life in the same way as men, we are in danger of inflicting damage on society as a whole by allowing them access to public life, and so contravening another liberal principle – that of maximizing individual well being. It is possible that positive discrimination, or even simply allowing women greater access to the work place, could have such an adverse effect on the economic situation that individual well being would be seriously diminished. So it would seem that this sort of discrimination actually **contravenes** both classical liberal principles and welfare liberal principles. Not only does it advocate an increase in state intervention – undermining the position of the state as neutral 'nightwatchman' still adhered to by some contemporary liberals such as Robert Nozick – but it also runs the risk of diminishing social goods. At an individual level, too, such intervention appears unjust; individual well-qualified men would necessarily be displaced in favour of less-qualified or – at least initially – less capable women.

Radcliffe Richards' response to some of these criticisms is to mobilize quite radically the notion of substantial justice. If it were the case, she concedes, that women's place in society was the outcome of liberal political theory's having already been put into practice – in other words, if the world, or this corner of it, had always been run on sound liberal principles – liberal feminists could have no justifiable complaint against their place. Indeed, there could **be** no 'liberal' feminism in such a society. As it is, however, individual autonomy has been interfered with, and

> ... women have, traditionally, been systematically excluded from nearly all interesting and influential activity and most kinds of education, and have been left in a narrowly circumscribed sphere of children, domesticity, and occupations ancillary to men's. Their having been in this sphere has not ... just been an accident ... There have been deliberate rules to exclude them from other activities. (Radcliffe Richards, op. cit., p. 98)

In other words, women have not had the opportunity of a free choice. Men have benefited from these substantial, and not merely formal, injustices. Therefore, any apparent injustice which men might suffer through, for instance, the operation of positive discrimination policies in favour of women, would be as a result of their expectations having been unjustly raised. The claim here is not that **what is proposed** can necessarily be shown to be just, but that **the existing situation** can be shown to be unjust to women: for example, lack of child care facilities keep women out of the work place; discrimination by the largely male selectors keeps them out of influential positions once in the work place. Exclusion and discrimination have affected both public prejudices and women's expectations of themselves. Liberal feminist theory argues that, if women are really unsuited to certain tasks, it is unnecessary to prevent their doing them. In this way, Radcliffe Richards claims to demonstrate that existing conditions constitute an injustice to women. And since women are more than half the population, it seems to follow that society in general will benefit from enabling women to participate fully in public life. Their inclusion will increase the production of social goods, to the benefit of all individuals. Increased state intervention, then, is advocated only to redress an existing injustice: once the imbalance has been corrected, the state can withdraw its active intervention and revert to its rôle of neutral administrator of justice in the public sphere. Both positive discrimination and increased state intervention are seen as necessary for a transitional period only, until women have 'caught up' with men.

III

The reason this position is inadequate, however, is that it employs a neutral notion of justice. To see why this is problematic, it is necessary to say a little about liberalism's wider intellectual commitments. For liberal political theory, the good society consists of freely choosing individuals circumscribed by a notion of justice which, while neutral regarding the content of the good life, is intended to ensure fair distribution of social goods: 'political decisions must be, so far as is possible, independent of any particular conception of the good life ... Since the citizens of a society differ in their conception, the government does not treat them as equals if it prefers one conception to another' (Dworkin, 1978, p. 127). Because of its understanding of what constitutes human nature, liberalism is not in a position to say what constitutes 'the good' – it is, by and large, whatever people want it to be, as my first quotation from Mill suggests (p. 121): it is individuals, after all, who are best qualified to identify their own interests. If a number of people, or indeed only one person, wants something, and if what is wanted will not cause harm to another individual, there are no remaining grounds for denial. Moral grounds which invoke such notions as the common good, God's will, etc., are not open to liberals, since they can deny individual wants only on grounds of their inconsistency with that individual's or group's other wants, or on grounds of their interfering with another individual's or group's wants. [3]

This might not seem to be a problem: the response to the question of whether, without a notion of the good, a notion of justice is possible could simply be, 'It depends what you mean by justice'. If justice is to be defined as some kind of mechanical process of sharing out goods, then, once it had been shown that this is what people wanted and that no harm would come to anyone by such a process, there might indeed be nothing further to be said. [4] However, if justice is to have any kind of **substantial** moral content, then an understanding of what constitutes the good cannot be dispensed with. Here is not the place to enter the details of this debate: but see, for instance, Michael Sandel (1982) for one view, Anthony Flew (1977) for another. Suffice it to say, however, that the liberal notion of justice might allow a society of benign slave holders – as long as the slave holders were happy; the slaves were happy to be owned; and their respective desires did not conflict with other desires or harm other individuals. But feminism – in common with socialism – surely requires some substantive notion of justice; the understanding that, for instance, oppression is an injustice in any context and that it cannot be 'a good', however many people claim to want it. A liberal feminist appeal to a concept of substantial justice along Radcliffe Richards' lines and not based in any claims about its substantive **content**, simply begs the question of the possibility of a context-free justice: what she claims to be substantial justice is in fact a reflection of the liberal understanding of what is needed to achieve the good society, and not substantive at all. Justice as a social construct can be neither value- nor context-free and cannot but reflect the ideology of those formulating it. It is thus liberal feminism's insistence on the ungendered individual which underlies its inadequacies. For liberal feminism, as I have remarked, makes no claims about what women are like – other than that they possess rationality – or what they might be able to achieve. If that is the case, however, how are we to know when the balance has been redressed and 'equality' has been achieved? If liberal feminism claimed that women and men were **equally** rational, it would be straightforward enough: it would simply demand a number-crunching exercise whereby equality would have been achieved when there was the same proportion of women in all areas of public life as in the general population. But this is not the claim, so the solution cannot be that clear cut. If the criterion is not a numerical one, then what could it be – since there is no recourse possible here to an insistence that the outcome would be good for people? If we do not know what women are capable of, how can we know when the transitional period is over and the state can withdraw its active intervention?

Lacking a basis in any notion of the good, an appeal to justice in these terms cannot offer an adequate practical solution to women's oppression and disadvantaged position in society. For the analysis of women's position, if it is to remain liberal, must retain an emphasis on public life, since it is through participation in public life that rationality is evidenced. But in focussing its efforts on enabling women to achieve equality in the public sphere of paid employment, liberal **feminist** theory finds it increasingly difficult to avoid advocating state intervention in those areas which liberal **political** theory has hitherto held to be private – the areas of reproduction and the family. Since the marriage contract, for example, affords differential rights and responsibilities, some American liberal feminists have argued for changes in the law to provide identical and, crucially, legally enforceable rights and responsibilities for both partners (Eisenstein, 1986, Ch. 8). Such a requirement brings an ostensibly private arrangement into the public domain of state regulation, since it would result in marriage contracts' having a similar status to business contracts and, as Jaggar points out, it would thus 'become generally accepted that the details of family life should be regulated by the state' (Jaggar, 1983, p. 198). Other liberal feminists, however, believe that the existence of 'a single form of marriage contract, even if it is written in sex-neutral language, unduly restricts individual choice and constitutes undue state restriction on how individuals may choose to live' (ibid.). The contradiction is unavoidable.

Feminist theories have of course always identified the areas of reproduction and the family as central to women's oppression: and it is hardly surprising that their consideration should throw into sharp focus just why liberal feminism fails. Anglo-American liberal feminist theory – forced perhaps by the insights of the more recently formulated theories of radical and social feminism to recognize that 'the personal is political' – comes increasingly close to requiring state intervention in every aspect of reproductive and family life, intervention which is necessary to ensure that women are allowed equal opportunity with men to enter the paid work force. Abortion, for instance, is a central issue for liberal feminism (as it is for other feminisms): its position is that anti-abortion laws interfere with a woman's individual autonomy, which the state has a duty to protect. Similarly, child-care provision should be available to all women; to allow them freedom to enter the paid work force. But, unlike other feminist theories, liberal feminist demands simply assume that it is **women,** and women alone, who are disadvantaged by the lack of childcare provision. The (social) context of childcare provision and its associated practices and assumptions is not even noticed, let alone challenged: and this just because no substantive notion of the good can be brought in at least to question what is, or appears to be, wanted and thus the relevant institution itself, rather than just the distribution as between women and men of its practices and requirements. Since liberal feminism fails to offer an adequate analysis of how women came to be relegated to the private sphere, and since it aims to end oppression through equality of opportunity in the public sphere, it can seek to effect change only by a gradual erosion of the private and a consequent enlargement of what constitutes the public in order to justify state intervention. This position is the inevitable consequence of a 'feminist' theory's attempting to retain a notion of the ungendered individual; turning a gender-blind eye to the meanings and values that have (historically) supervened upon the biological has led inexorably to this inability either to explain or effectively to counter the social and political realities that are inscribed in those meanings and values.

Liberalism notwithstanding, little, if anything, can actually remain 'private' for liberal feminist theory, if 'justice' is to be pursued through legislation that would grant women equality of opportunity. Indeed, to be consistent, such a notion of justice can and should be employed even in those areas which liberal feminists themselves might still want to retain as private – but then, of course liberal feminism's (political) liberalism goes by the board. For instance, the justification for positive discrimination in the work place can surely be applied to pornography. Would the pornography industry have developed in the way it has, had women always been afforded equality of opportunity in public life? It is at least possible that it would not, since many women believe that pornography interferes with their individual autonomy in that it promotes sexist attitudes. In line with Radcliffe Richards' argument in favour of positive discrimination, then, should pornography not be banned until a state of equality – whatever that turns out to be – has been achieved? A similar argument can be applied to sexuality. Would women have freely entered into heterosexual relationships if they had always played a rôle in shaping the prevailing ideology of sexuality – perhaps then the great god Phallus would not have achieved his current status? If Freud is even partly right in his description of the development of sexuality (Freud, 1977, pp. 142–44) for instance, it is at least possible that women – given the ability freely to choose – might prefer to remain in the active, clitoral stage of development rather than pass into the passive, vaginal stage. They have never been given the opportunity to make that choice: does this not require some sort of state intervention to redress the injustice that this interference with their individual autonomy represents?

As well as illustrating the inadequacies of the appeal to justice previously adumbrated, such questions point up the inadequacies of a liberal feminist explanation of women's status. Unless they are to resort to biologist claims – a route denied them by virtue of the liberal understanding of human nature – how can liberal feminists explain the grounds on which women **came to be** in the position of having been denied access to the public sphere? Because of its liberal understanding of human nature already noted, liberal feminist theory cannot offer any adequate explanation for women's existing social position: neither can it suggest any explanation for men's apparent desire or willingness to maintain that position.

Yet one cannot deny that Anglo-American liberal feminism can claim a degree of success in achieving equal opportunities legislation in education and in paid employment. Particularly in America – and increasingly in the UK – women are becoming prominent in business and the media; although not – with a few notable exceptions, who have had little, if any, effect on the structures and institutions of their respective nations – in political life. A number of legislative 'victories' have been won: married women are no longer regarded as chattels of their husbands; the legal system in the UK now recognizes rape in marriage. Such legislation is surely having an effect: there are more rôle models for women and women's increased participation in public life is engendering at least some change in attitude towards women. Is the feminist cause, then, not well on the way to being won, and won by liberal feminist strategies? Both so-called post-feminists, such as the American academic Camille Paglia (see, for instance, Paglia, (1992) on date rape and sexual harassment) and anti-feminists, such as the British writers Neil Lyndon (1993) and David

Thomas (1993) would go further: feminism – like Fukuyamian liberalism – has won. Discrimination is illegal: women are in fact in a privileged position, allowed when at work to make the sorts of jokes and comments about men which, when made by men about women, are deemed sexist and degrading.

This sort of argument represents an impeccably liberal belief in individual autonomy and the ungendered individual: if women, in general, have been enabled to achieve equal status with men in public life, then any subsequent failure must be their own, as individuals. Such neglect, both intellectual and practical, of the **structures** which continue to oppress and disadvantage women follows ineluctably from the adoption of liberal feminist policies by a male-dominated capitalist system. By selecting those demands which are most public, and which can best be accommodated within such a system, the underlying structure – the systematic use and abuse of women which serves both men and capitalism – is obfuscated. A grateful state and its still male-dominated institutions – such as the Church of England – can thus be seen to be supporting women by allowing them access to power as individuals – women priests, for instance – while retaining supposedly neutral but actually patriarchal structures, and shunting those feminists who still see grounds for complaint onto the sidelines of extremism.

And yet grounds for complaint proliferate: the average working woman's wage in the UK and the US in 1991 was just over two thirds of a man's wage for the same work; not only do child-care facilities remain limited and under-funded, but the premise that child care is the woman's responsibility remains unchallenged. Seldom has this been made so apparent as it was during President Clinton's attempts shortly after his inauguration to appoint a woman to the post of Attorney General. On both occasions, it was the women who were held responsible for the illegal arrangements they **and their husbands** had made for child care. In both cases, the women not only lost the opportunity to hold office, but their honesty and morality were subjected to minute scrutiny by the media. Their husbands' positions and status remain untouched. To take another example, legislative changes have failed to alter the fact that women are disproportionately the victims of violence, particularly in their own homes; or that their bodies, and parts of their bodies, are still used to sell consumer goods and even safety precautions. (A British Safety Council poster in 1992 depicting Madonna wearing the now-familiar Jean Paul Gaultier funnel-shaped construction across her chest, and little else, urged the – male – construction workers to wear hard hats 'to protect their assets'.) The point is, of course, as I suggested earlier in saying that the question of childcare provision was not one for women alone, that changing women's lot – as opposed to making sure that (some) individual women get a better deal – entails structural change. Just as the poor of the world cannot become significantly less poor without radically affecting the life of the rich, so any feminism must imply radical change affecting us all. It is in **this** sense, of course, that feminism may properly be said to be in everyone's interest.

IV

Thus the result of liberal feminism's 'successful' policies has simply been increasingly to integrate women into an existing capitalist economy, without asking how that system could ever be maintained in the absence of oppression of some kind – not, of course, a question which **has** to concern feminists – or, more importantly, adequately questioning whether equality of opportunity in the public sphere could possibly be sufficient to remove the causes of women's oppression. It assumes that women in positions of power and influence will necessarily be in sympathy, if not with feminist aims, then at least with women's needs in general. The former assumption is patently not the case: in fact, it is equally plausible to argue that in order to achieve in male-dominated public life, women have largely to subscribe to male-dictated norms of performance – they may therefore be less sympathetic towards women who suffer discrimination. The latter subsumes a further assumption – which liberal feminism must make, since it cannot offer an analysis in terms of, for instance, class or race – that there is a constituency, 'women', with common needs which can be met in this way.

By helping to make good the claim that women are now equal at law, Anglo-American liberal feminism has impeded an adequate analysis of women's continuing subordination and oppression in both public and private realms, and therefore also impeded the possible formulation of policies which could adequately address their subordination and oppression. Liberal feminism's achievements cannot effect any **structural** change in women's position in society: a fact implicitly recognized by those liberal feminists who demand increasing state intervention in 'private' life, and a recognition which displays the contradictions of the term 'liberal feminism'. Since the basis for women's subordination lies in what liberalism deems to be the private sphere and since – as I have briefly suggested – feminism demands a notion of the good, feminism cannot be liberal. On the other hand, unless we are to believe that individuals are indeed 'pre-social' and not born into pre-existing social structures which give meaning and value to their biological attributes, liberals cannot be feminists.

Notes

1. I recognize that the ascription 'feminist' to these authors is contentious within the feminist movement. This article is not the place to enter into that debate: I make the ascription on the grounds of their description of women's position in society and their belief that that position should be changed.
2. A case forcefully put by Janet Radcliffe Richards, to whom I shall return later.
3. For further, more detailed, discussion, see the preceding articles by Carol Jones and Bob Brecher.
4. The question of what constitutes harm is, of course, far from straightforward, but for reasons of space will not be pursued here.

References

Dworkin, R. (1978), 'Liberalism' in Hampshire, S. (ed.), *Public and Private Morality*, Cambridge University Press, Cambridge.

Eisenstein, Z. (1986), *The Radical Future of Liberal Feminism*, Northeastern University Press, Boston.

Flew, A. (1977), 'Wants or needs, choices or commands', in Fitzgerald, R. (ed.), *Human Needs and Politics*, Pergamon, Rushcutters Bay, NSW.

Freud, S. (1977), 'Three essays on the theory of sexuality', in Richards, A. and Dickson, A. (eds.), *On Sexuality*, Penguin, Harmondsworth.

Friedan, B. (1965), *The Feminine Mystique*, Penguin, Harmondsworth.

Friedan, B. (1977), *It Changed My Life*, Dell, New York.

Jaggar, A. (1983), *Feminist Politics and Human Nature*, Rowman and Littlefield, New Jersey.

Lyndon, N. (1993), *No More Sex War*, Mandarin, London.

Mill, J.S. (1962), *On Liberty* in *Utilitarianism, On Liberty and Essay on Bentham*, Warnock, M. (ed.), Fontana, London.

Mill, J.S. (1975), 'The subjection of women' in idem, *Three Essays*, Oxford University Press, Oxford.

Mill, J.S. and Mill, H.T. (1970), *Essays on Sex Equality*, Rossi, A.S. (ed.), University of Chicago Press, Chicago.

Paglia, C. (1992), *Sex, Art and American Culture*, Viking, London.

Radcliffe Richards, J. (1980), *The Sceptical Feminist*, Routledge and Kegan Paul, London.

Rawls, J. (1972), *A Theory of Justice*, Harvard University Press, Cambridge, Mass.

Sandel, M.J. (1982), *Liberalism and the Limits of Justice*, Cambridge University Press, Cambridge.

Thomas, D, (1993), *Not Guilty: in defence of the Modern Man*, Weidenfeld and Nicholson, London.

Wollstonecraft, M. (1992), *A Vindication of the Rights of Woman*, Brody, M. (ed.), Penguin, Harmondsworth.

9 Liberalism on the bolshevik model: The status of women in Lithuania

Alina Zvinkliene

I

Before suggesting that all is far from rosy for women under the presently developing liberalism of eastern Europe, and of Lithuania in particular, it will be necessary to outline something of the historical context within which these developments are occurring. For my argument that the economic liberalism being grafted on to a civil society still largely rooted in its immediate Soviet past is no friend of feminism requires at least a gesture in that direction. There is of course a large and interesting set of questions around that of the extent to which current developments build on Lithuania's pre-communist past, and the extent to which its incorporation into the Soviet Union was itself at least eased by a similar use of tradition. They require, however, far more detailed treatment than is possible here, where my concern is largely with one particular aspect of the perhaps more obvious question: to what extent do current liberalizing policies have their roots – actual as well as ideological – in the communist experience?

Liberal ideas and ideals are by no means foreign to Lithuania: indeed, Rousseau long ago idealized the Federal State of the Great Lithuanian Principality and the Polish Kingdom as an example of the sort of republicanism he wished to advocate. Furthermore, the 1791 constitution – the result of a reforming alliance between the emergent bourgeoisie and elements of the nobility – while it neither abolished serfdom nor recognized peasants' rights, nevertheless laid the foundations of the liberalizing tendencies of the nineteenth century. It is interesting to note, for instance, that from 1810 onwards, Smith and Ricardo were both taught at the University of Wilna. The main features of the development of liberal attitudes were: a recognition of the need to abolish serfdom (achieved in 1861); attempts to institute a system of universal education; an increasing religious tolerance; and the eventual emergence, towards the end of the nineteenth century, of a social democratic movement. It was only after the First World War, in the wake of which Lithuania gained its independence, that such developments came to an end – for with independence came an anti-democratic nationalism, culminating in the authoritarian putsch of 1926. It is maintained by some historians (e.g. Junevissius, 1992) that it was this deeply nationalistic regime of Smetona which, with the support of the Church, opened the door to the annexation of Lithuania by the USSR in 1940: and that this is the case largely because of the promise of greater liberty, however ultimately illusory, which was held out by the Lithuanian Communist Party and the USSR. In particular, this was what attracted to it both many liberals and a large section of the Jewish population, the latter having been excluded by the Lithuanian state from their traditional professions, and forced during the 1930s to become ordinary workers.

Under the Stalinist-Brezhnevite totalitarianism which ensued after annexation in 1940, the individual was regarded as a citizen whose status depended entirely on the state: the sorts of rights and liberties which constitute liberalism were entirely denied, both theoretically and in practice. The corporate state presided over an ideology which stressed collective and state interests over and against those of the individual – and in doing so encouraged, however paradoxically, an extreme individualism which disregarded both moral standards and the law. In short, as Krivorotov (1990) persuasively argues, communist Lithuania, in common with the rest of the USSR, is best understood as a hybrid of oriental despotism and a late capitalism based within a framework of state monopoly. The perestroika [1] to which this had inevitably to give rise, however, has had an outcome which is as unexpected for Marxists as it is for liberals: the renaissance of nationalism. And yet this development should not surprise us, even if its implications, as I shall argue, are hardly to be welcomed: for nationalism is nurtured in the womb of liberalism. [2] Its commitment to the right of national self-determination, after all, is historically modelled on its notion of the autonomy of the individual: 'nationalism is generally conceptualized in psychological categories, and the fact that it is an ideological movement is often overlooked' (Valentejus, 1991, p. 91; cf. Kohn, 1946). And in Lithuania, that ideology has long been intertwined with a liberal tradition, both to some extent in imitation of the west and yet also wary of 'westernization' – hence the ambiguities of the 1920s and 30s to which I referred earlier (Kavolis, 1992). Thus, to put it briefly, although Lithuania has formally adopted a liberal democratic constitution, as of the referendum of 25 October 1992, the – so to speak – cultural norms of western liberalism are largely absent: the nationalism with which it is associated, although to a lesser degree than in Estonia and Latvia, in conjunction with the legacy and impact of fifty years of soviet domination, takes the form of an inward-looking provincialism combined with a bolshevik-style imposition of economic liberalism.

II

It is the implications of this set of contradictions which largely determine the present status of women in Lithuania.

Now, Marx had already noted in his *Critique of the Gotha Programme* that simply to confer equal rights upon all individuals, regardless of the differences between them in terms of power, capacities, needs etc., is essentially to maintain inequality. Lenin and his followers, however, considered that any attempt to fight for specific rights for women instead of struggling directly for the transformation of the whole of society was a purely bourgeois and diversionary undertaking. Since discrimination against women was to be understood as a particular case of the general oppression of people in a society divided against itself, the problem would be solved automatically with the victory of socialism. The chief means in practice of realizing the equality of men and women under soviet communism was thus taken – to an extent as a matter of course – to consist not only in greater representation in the labour market, and in social and political life, but also in a balance between these and the daily round. The actual continuing inequality of women during the entire period of soviet power was then duly explained away by reference to just that daily round; and it is the problems to which this gives rise which remain unsolved to this day. Despite the undoubted achievement of socialism in constitutionally establishing the social equality of women and men, the refusal to recognize domestic work as socially useful labour meant that, under the general compulsion to undertake such labour, women were forced to do paid work in addition to fulfilling their traditional domestic rôle.

Under Stalinism, therefore, Lithuanian women came to be 'liberated' in the same way as other women elsewhere in the USSR. In reality, and despite the propaganda of 'socialism', they suffered a dual deprivation of civil and economic rights. For the principle of equal rights was used – in a society anyway deprived of actual everyday rights – to impose the duty to go out to work on top of the duty of motherhood: and both these duties were, of course, officially represented as instantiations of rights.

The banning of abortion in 1936; the virtual prohibition of divorce; the introduction of civil proceedings for ascertaining paternity and recovering allowances due to children from their father on separation; and the tax on childlessness introduced in 1944: all these measures were directed at increasing the birth-rate in the USSR. Although much new legislation under Stalin was somewhat more liberal in respect of the position of women and questions of the family than laws enacted during the period of Lithuania's independence, it nevertheless continued, for all its communist provenance, in the traditions laid down by Catholic canon law.

After Stalin's death, the solution to 'the woman question' was considered to be a function of the successful economic and social development of the USSR. The immediate question was, in the view of most people, how women should combine their professional rôle with family duties; and this was widely assumed to be a question which – in common with other social questions – would be solved in the fullness of time by those who knew best, namely the Party and the government. Interestingly, the only officially mentionable crisis in the USSR during the sixties, when sociological research was once more permitted, was the crisis of the family; and one of the main reasons for this turn-around in propaganda was the decreasing birth-rate. Slogans appealing to women to go out to work and participate in social labour were replaced by slogans appealing to women to pay more attention to their families. And yet, in spite of such appeals, nobody was actually disposed to help women achieve this. The patriarchal stereotype of woman's predestination for motherhood and its duties was now continually stressed, but without any concomitant attempt to make it economically possible for a family to survive with only one person, the husband/father, as breadwinner. Two wages were essential to make ends meet. The result was that, at work, women – as also mothers – were relegated to secondary rôles; while, at home, they were still usually expected to take sole domestic charge. To succeed in a professional career, women had to display purely masculine qualities; but on advertising hoardings they had to demonstrate all the qualities of a housewife. Under these conditions, the standing of the few women who did not work outside the home was extremely low – and people's attitude towards mothers who had a large number of children remained similarly negative. Here, then, is an example of the way in which soviet ideology was characterized by contradictions between declared rights and the real conditions of their realization. One of the many paradoxes of the communist system was that women, while ostensibly having equal rights, were in fact exploited even more than before. For the so-called interests of society required – and still require – from women that they be active in the sphere of social production, even though such a demand went hand in hand with an equal insistence on their primary participation in family life. This legacy of double standards remains: and the hidden discrimination against women in the former USSR continues in independent Lithuania. [3]

III

The ways in which the double standard remains is particularly evident in the areas of employment, education and, of course, the family itself.

First, employment. The USSR was characterized by a great imbalance between women's numerical representation in the workforce and their proportionately professional representation. In 1989 the percentage of women making up the total number of workers and salaried persons was 52 per cent in Lithuania; 54 per cent in Latvia and Estonia; and 51 per cent in the USSR overall. Nevertheless, although 61 per cent of the total number of specialists having a higher and secondary education were women, their percentage among leaders of the first rank accounted for only 5.5 per cent in Lithuania; 5.7 per cent in Latvia; 2.9 per cent in Estonia; and 5.6 per cent in the USSR (All-Union Research on Women's Work and Family Life Conditions 1990, 1991). Women were expected to go out to work – but clearly, to some sorts of work rather than others.

Second, higher education, which has a particularly important and prestigious place in Lithuania. Well-educated people achieve higher positions and better pay, they feel they have more control over their own lives, and continue their education later on in life. This picture, however, is less accurate in the case of women than men: in particular, although women appear to have equal, or even better, access to education, they obtain fewer benefits from their educational achievements. Furthermore, the educational attainment of a substantial portion of the population is – as elsewhere – considerably affected by family background, so that education may be seen in this way to play a crucial rôle in the reproduction of inequality, sexual as well as economic, from one generation to another. Although people in the higher social strata have children who tend to do well in school, and these children's attainments in turn tend to secure them relatively well-paid positions, once working women obtain such a job they are generally little interested in improving their professional skills (Hernes and Knudsen, 1991, p. 151–2). This is hardly surprising, of course: for women are comparatively unlikely to gain promotion. Thus an average of only 20 per cent of women who were interviewed in 1990 obtained higher wages as a result of further professional training. Moreover, managers are less interested in the development of women's professional skills than are women themselves (All-Union Research, op. cit.). No wonder, then, that women are under-represented at the higher professional levels. Nor is it surprising that, as unemployment (formerly hidden) increases, so some 70 per cent of those registered as unemployed should be comparatively highly educated women with young children: and as one might expect, further differentials are now appearing as between Lithuanian and non-indigenous women. This all has clear implications for everyday life and the conditions under which women experience it: and, in particular, for family life.

The problems which beset the family in contemporary Lithuania generally conform to the typical state of affairs in the West. There is a high incidence of marriage which is duly matched by a high level of divorce. At the same time, the average life-span of a marriage is falling; and the average number of children decreasing. The attitude of most Lithuanian women towards women's and men's rôles in the family, however, is perhaps more in keeping with the traditional asymmetrical model: the woman should ideally be a housewife and the man support the family. The majority remains unconvinced that a working mother can establish just as warm and secure a relationship with her children as a mother who does not go out to work, or that having a job is the best way for women to secure independent status. There is only one indicator that does not correspond with this traditional model: most women think that both women and men should contribute to the household income. This is a result of the state of affairs under socialism, where working husbands were unable adequately to support their families.

The financial position of families, especially of young families, has as a rule long depended directly on both the financial help given by the 'senior' family and on state assistance (Zvinkliene, 1991). What is of particular significance is that the latter was increased during the 1970s and 80s owing to the real threat of depopulation in the European part of the USSR, a threat which produced an immediate response from the State. The position was as follows. For society simply to reproduce itself, each woman has to bear an average of 2.1 children in the course of her fertile life. In the USSR, however, the fertility rate in 1975–76 was 2.4 and by 1980–81 had fallen to 2.2. For a country committed to extensive economic development, this reduction in the potential labour force was clearly a serious problem. In 1981–83, therefore, supplementary family assistance measures were instituted: special grants in connection with the birth of a child were established; the period of partially state-paid post-partum maternity leave was extended; and various other measures taken to stimulate the birth-rate. By the later 1980s, the fertility rate had increased to 2.3–2.5 (Demographical Year Book of the USSR 1990, 1990, p. 639). This was one of the rare cases in the history of the USSR, then, when state and personal interests coincided: for, as suggested earlier, the majority of Lithuanian women, as well as men, prefer a traditional family rôle to going out to work, a preference attributable in part, perhaps – but only in part – to the continuing influence of the Catholic Church.

Nevertheless, despite both such increased incentives for women to produce more children, and despite also the general attitude towards familial rôles, the Lithuanian family of the last ten years has generally remained one in which both parents go out to work; and although lip-service is paid to the principle of equality in respect of the relations of members of a family, the distribution of men's and women's rôles remains in reality traditional. It should not come as a surprise, therefore, that an increasing level of conflict is being noted in the interrelations both between husband and wife and between parents and children. This state of affairs has recently come to be exacerbated by the economic policies of the newly independent Lithuania; for one of the central elements of state policy in respect of the family is that assistance has been dramatically reduced. State subsidies for children's meals and clothes have been abolished; spending on nursery schools and related institutions is being reduced, and even abandoned altogether; and welfare provision in general is being drastically cut. All of this is at least in part the result of economic pressures, but may also be attributed to the political demands of a nascent market system and the historical values upon which it rests.

The Lithuanian family then, and its women in particular, is being subjected to a variety of often contradictory pressures: that of the Catholic church, with its traditionalist values, partly interwoven with a deliberate rejection of the legacy of the soviet-inspired exhortation to women to play an active part in the labour market (itself anyway already contradicted by Stalinism's early re-assertion of traditional 'family values'); the at least partial reversal during the later 1970s and 80s of the latter policy, in response to fears of depopulation; the economic exigencies of the soviet period which made it very difficult for one person to support a family, exigencies which are currently being exacerbated; the lack of adequate housing and of those consumer durables which render housework and its associated activities less onerous; and the State's need to keep (male) unemployment in check. Thus the contemporary Lithuanian family, just as much as its former soviet incarnation, continues to exhibit a classic double discrimination against women: a notional equality defined in the traditional male-determined terms of the workforce, and both undermined and rendered psychologically threatening by the lack of change in the patriarchal system; and a (partly self-imposed) reluctance to challenge that system.

IV

The struggle around abortion and contraception is one which clearly illustrates these paradoxes, in the post-communist Baltics as elsewhere. Opposition to abortion (whatever one takes to be the moral rights and wrongs of the matter) is historically rooted in the desire to maintain the traditional rôles of women and men; and it is therefore incumbent upon a progressive state to legislate for the provision of abortion even if for no other reason than as a means of vesting reproductive responsibility in women. And yet any state is likely also to have its particular demographic interests, interests which would seem at least arguably more important than those of any particular individuals. The tension to which these two considerations can give rise may be seen in the history of the development of family planning in the former USSR, including Lithuania and the other Baltics.

The USSR was one of the first countries to recognize the right to abortion. In 1920 abortion was legalized and made available free of charge, partly on the basis of its being considered a human right, and partly on practical grounds, in order to protect the life and health of women – especially against exploitation by back-street abortionists. By 1936, however, the situation had changed: and it was the discrepancy between avowed political commitment and demographic statistics which served as one of the main reasons for its prohibition. There had been a sharp deceleration in the growth-rate of the population as a result of repression, hunger and the increasing number of abortions itself (despite the actual limitation of access to abortion) a state of affairs which its prohibition was expected, on Malthusian grounds, to remedy. Less than twenty years later, the situation changed again. In 1955 – after the death of Stalin – the 1936 act banning abortion was annulled. The new preamble justifying abortion referred to protecting women's health against the effects of illegal abortion and to the need for social assistance and information. Furthermore, the act also emphasized the need to create conditions in which women could make independent decisions about motherhood, quoting the United Nations' declaration of 'the right of parents to decide freely and responsibly on the number and spacing of their children, and have access to the information, education and means to enable them to exercise these rights'. Despite the new legal situation which enshrined the existence of a formal right to abortion throughout the USSR, however, the publication of statistical and other data on the actual situation regarding family planning remained under prohibition. When this ban was rescinded in the mid–1980s, the reason for its enactment became clear. For a very interesting fact immediately came to light, showing how family planning in the former USSR was connected with unique features of the social, cultural and demographic development of the country: the Soviet Union was the only economically developed country in the world to witness a diminishing birth-rate. Furthermore, this demographic trend appeared to be directly related to the incidence of abortion; and that, in turn, to the fact that the great majority of women in the European republics did not use contraception. [4] What seems to follow from this is that the State in fact had an interest in not making contraceptive advice widely available; and in ensuring that abortion was used as a contraceptive method of last resort precisely because of its comparatively lesser impact on the birth-rate. However unofficially, abortion was encouraged as **the** means of contraception – precisely so as to disadvantage the latter. For women who did not wish to bear children were practically forced to resort to abortion, with all the disincentives that are built into it – which, however increasingly residual, remained nevertheless very considerable, and especially so as it came in effect to serve as a means of contraception. The result of this was that, annually, some ten per cent of women of reproductive age had an abortion: and yet family planning and abortion itself – and indeed the whole gamut of issues around human sexual experience – went largely undiscussed in the public domain. Ambivalence and confusion around these issues, then, is precisely what is to be expected.

In Lithuania in particular – the most conservative and Catholic of the Baltics – such ambivalence towards abortion was fed by traditional attitudes, most especially, of course, those of the Catholic tradition. [5] This view is corroborated by the findings of the 1990 Value Survey in respect of Lithuanian women's attitudes towards divorce and unfaithfulness, as well as towards abortion (Purvaneckiene, 1991, p. 10 ff.): indeed, family planning itself is rejected by many socio-political groupings, with the result that abortion is presented – for all its obvious disadvantages – as the sole alternative. This in turn is adjudged to undermine a growing national self-consciousness based on the revival of a traditionalistic culture in which Catholicism plays a leading rôle. What we are now faced with, then, is a curious alliance between a conservative traditionalism on the one hand, and what might be termed as the soviet tradition on the other: abortion is presented as undesirable, even harmful, within both, albeit for (arguably) different reasons. The result is, again unsurprisingly, that public opinion towards abortion is largely hostile; and that, as of mid-1993, the Seim (Parliament) has carefully avoided any debate of the issue. Where women were until recently subordinated to the (demographic) interests of the State, they are now subordinated to the (patriarchal) interests of a nationalistic Catholic-inspired traditionalism. Most importantly of all, the fact that abortion was legally permitted and, however inadvertently, practically encouraged by the soviet system, makes it all the more difficult now to resist opposition to it, the more especially as the 'actually existing socialism' of the recent past and the nationalism of the present are equally antithetical to open discussion of contraception and of sexuality in general. The latter regards the western liberal ideology within which an enlightened attitude to these matters might readily find a home as a sort of bolshevism, while the former's principles were belied by its practice. No wonder, then, that the situation of Lithuanian women continues to deteriorate.

History shows that the position of women tends to improve as crises emerge in the course of social and political struggle. As soon as the situation stabilizes, however, men re-emerge to create and then fill new hierarchical structures which once again exclude women – as the brief career of the first prime minister of independent Lithuania, Ms Prunskiena, shows all too clearly. As the democratic movements which gave birth to a women's movement in Lithuania begin to show the features of a totalitarian revival, the prospects of an active feminist movement cannot but recede. Where then does this leave Lithuanian women?

The recent history of Lithuania illustrates how the same sort of disparity between the stated aims of policy and the actual state of affairs it underpins and/or furthers – often for 'reasons of state' which go hand in hand with traditional interests – can nevertheless continue across ideological systems and structures which are in many ways antithetical. In particular, the imposition of policy from above, in the present case the imposition of economic liberalism in the absence of the preconditions of a liberal civil society – liberalism on the bolshevik model – shows how history repeats itself; that it is doing so in more humane form should not disguise the fact that it leaves women very much where they were. New rights bring with them additional duties; and the rôle of women in society remains a minor one. In Lithuania, this process is at least clearly visible: whereas in the West, it sometimes seems that elements of the feminist movement overlook this continuing disparity, with the result that a spurious post-feminism can claim that the victory has already been won.

Notes

1. A perestroika foreshadowed by Kruschev's famous claim that the Soviet Union would overtake the USA as an economic power: for its failure to keep up with the West is what lies behind the Soviet Union's eventual collapse. Brezhnev's 'period of stagnation' consisted in an unavailing effort to avoid the inevitable by insulating the Soviet Union from the West, largely by setting up an 'alternative reality' for internal consumption.
2. See Ross Poole (1991), Ch. 5, for an account of the way in which nationalism arises from liberalism.
3. It is interesting to see how a male researcher interprets sociological data regarding sex-discrimination:

    > Lithuanian men believe that sex discrimination seldom occurs, while women say it happens often. This finding provides a good illustration of the sociological assumption that where one stands determines one's reactions. Women tend to be less rewarded for their efforts than men. This is also how many of them feel. Thus, they say they are discriminated against quite often, while men appear to be less sensitive to this question. (Hernes and Knudsen, 1991, p. 151–152)

4. According to data collected by the Medical Institution of the Soviet Public Health Ministry in 1989, Russia had the highest number of abortions per thousand women aged 15–24 (117.5); the USSR overall 95.6; Latvia 75; Estonia 74.5; and Lithuania the lowest, 54.3. The vast majority of women in the European part of the USSR were reported as not using contraception. The percentage of women doing so was: 18.7 per cent in the USSR; 26.4 per cent in Estonia; 18.6 per

cent in Latvia; and, significantly, only 12.1 per cent in Lithuania, by far the lowest percentage of all the European republics.
5. The rights and wrongs of abortion is not something than can be discussed here. Suffice it to say that the influence on Lithuanian opinion of the Roman Catholic church is extremely powerful; that there are internal problems within Catholic doctrine (not least the difference between the view developed by Aquinas and recognized at the Vjenn Council of 1314 and that of the *Apostolicae Sedis* of 1869); and that Catholic teaching on contraception is of course a further aspect of the tradition which largely informs Lithuanian attitudes.

References

All-Union Research on Problems of the Family, Maternity and Childhood Protection 1989 (1991), no. 8, Vestnik Statistiki, Moscow, pp. 55–64.
All-Union Research on Women's Work and Family Life Conditions 1990 (1991), no. 2, Vestnik Statistiki, Moscow, pp. 53–60.
Baltic Surveys 1992 (1993), no. 3, Rytu ir Centrines Europos Eurobaramoetras Lietuvos rytas, 26 March.
Dahrendorf, R. (1990), *Reflections on the Revolution in Europe*; Lithuanian translation, Periodika, Vilnius.
Davidson, M. (1987), 'You've got a long way to go, baby: a conversation about the women's movement with Ruth Hubbard' in Finsterbusch, K. (ed.), *Sociology 88/89,* University of Maryland, College Park, pp. 70–73.
Davydov, A.A. (1990), 'Optimum of unemployment in the USSR', *Sociologiczeskije Issledovanija*, 12, pp. 37–41.
Demographical Yearbook of the USSR 1990, (1990), Finansy i Statistika, Moscow.
Gaidys, V., Turekyte, D., Sutiniene, I. (1991), 'The historical memory of Lithuanians (empirical characteristics)', *Filosofija, Sociologija,* 1, pp. 77–86.
Gray, J. (1986), *Liberalism,* Open University Press, Milton Keynes; Lithuanian translation (1992), Atviros Lietuvos Fondas, Vilnius.
Hayek, F.A. von (1944), *The Road to Serfdom,* University of Chicago Press, Chicago; Lithuanian translation (1991), Mintis, Vilnius.
Hernes, G. and Knudsen, K. (1991), *Lithuanian Living Conditions. A Sociological Study*, FAFO–SOTECO Report, Norwegian Trade Union Centre for Social Science and Research, Aurskog.
Human Rights (1986), Moscow University Press, Moscow.
Hurst, J. (1989), *The History of Abortion in the Catholic Church*, Catholics for a Free Choice, Washington.
Junevissius, A. (1992), 'Liberalizmo doctrinos samprata', *Politologijos*

studijos, II dalis, Technologija, Kaunas, pp. 142–155.
Kavolis, Vytautas (1992), 'Liberalaus galvojimo erdveje', *Metmenys*, 63, pp. 33-45.
Kohn, H. (1946), *The Idea of Nationalism*, The Macmillan Company, New York; Lithuanian summary translation (1991), *Filosofija, Sociologija*, 3, pp. 99–117.
Krivorotov, Viktor (1990), 'The Russian way', *Znamia*, 8, pp. 140–165.
'Lietuvos statistikos departamento tyrimai' (1993), *Respublika*, 9 February, p. 5.
Lithuanian Social Development in 1990, (1991), Lietuvos Statistikos departamentas, Vilnius.
Lithuanian Women and The Family (1992), Lietuvos Statistikos departamentas, Vilnius.
Marx, K. (1969), 'Critique of the Gotha Programme', in Feuer, L.S. (ed.), *Marx and Engels: Basic Writings on Politics and Philosophy*, Fontana, London.
Minogue, K.R. (1991), 'Liberalism', *Encyclopedia Americana*, International edition, Grolier Incorporated, vol. 17, pp. 294–297.
Nekrasov, S.N. & Vozilkin, I.V. (1991), *Womens' Life–Scenarios and Sexuality*, Ural University Press, Sverdlovsk.
Official Lithuanian Statistics (1990, 1991, 1992), Lietuvos Statistikos departamentas, Vilnius.
Poole, R. (1991), *Morality and Modernity*, Routledge, London.
Popov, A & Zvinkliene, A., (1992), 'Interview with Sovereign Chrisostom, Archbishop of Vilnius and Lithuania, on the problems of abortion and contraception', *Pravoslavnaja Obschina*, 1, pp. 60–67.
Purvaneckiene, G. (1991), 'The family in social context: a women's view', paper presented at the 3rd World Family Therapy Congress, 2–6 June, Jyvaskyla, Finland.
Sapoka, A. (ed.) (1936), *Lietuvos Istorija*, Svietimo ministerijos Knygu, leidimo komisijos leidinys, Kaunas.
Sperling, U. (1988), 'Marxismus und Feminismus – Frauen, Reform und Revolution', *Marxistische Blätter*, 12, pp. 73–74.
Topornin, B (1990), 'The Human Rights Declaration: the new approach', in Lukasheva, E. (ed.), *Human Rights: Problems and Perspectives*, AN SSSR, Institut gosudarstva i prava, Moscow, pp. 5–27.
The Baltic States. A Reference Book (1991), Estonian Encyclopaedia Publishers, Latvian Encyclopaedia Publishers, Lithuanian Encyclopaedia Publishers, Tallinn, Riga, Vilnius.
Vaitkevissius, B. (ed.) (1978), *A History of the Lithuanian SSR*, Mokslas, Vilnius.
Valentejus, A. (1991), 'Sociological aspects of nationalism', *Filosofija, Sociologija*, 3, pp. 75–91.
Voronina, O. (1990), 'The woman question', in Mukomel, V.B. (ed.), *USSR: Demographical Diagnosis*, Progress, Moscow, pp. 351–373.

Zvinkliene, A. (1991), 'The young Lithuanian family in the mid–1990s', *Filosofija, Sociologija,* 3, pp. 52–67.

Zvinkliene, A. & Popov, A. (1990), 'Perspectives on family planning in the Baltic republics', *Sociological Research in the Baltic States,* Institute of Philosophy, Sociology and Law of the Lithuanian Academy of Sciences, Vilnius, pp. 114–120.

10 Liberalism, Europe and the environment

Avner de-Shalit

In recent years a new issue has come on to the political agenda: the state of the environment. Scientists and ecologists have argued that the damage to the environment caused by human activities is often irreversible: and, only three hundred years after abandoning the theocentric for the anthropocentric attitude, men and women are being urged to abandon both for the biocentric or the ecocentric – namely the views, respectively, that all individual objects in Nature have intrinsic value, or that moral value resides in ecosystems rather than in their individual members, that all life on earth is interdependent. Our quality of life is linked not only to the contamination of water, but also to the pollution of the soil, the damage to the ozone layer, the dangers arising from radioactive waste management, the extinction of certain animal species, misguided urban development, and many other phenomena, all of which constitute the 'environmental problem'.

Liberal society and liberal philosophy have both offered a fertile ground for the promotion of ecological attitudes, the evolution of 'green' ideas and an environmental philosophy. But as these have migrated from the academy to the realm of politics, liberalism has found itself in difficulties: while it has encouraged debate on environmental issues, traditional assumptions prevent its own advocates of environmental policies from actually implementing them.

Environmental philosophy is helpful to Greens and other ecological interest groups in expressing their demands, suggestions and proposals as 'inputs' into the political system. But a government responds with policies, regulations, legislation, propaganda, and allocations (all of which can be called 'outputs'): and it is here that a liberal government may find itself in deep water. Explaining to a government office why a certain conservation project is important is somewhat easier than the ministry's task of confronting the developers. No wonder, then, that many liberals have voiced anxieties regarding the future of democracy. They fear that lack of resources on the one hand, and selfish behaviour on the other, can have only one possible result: an environmental crisis necessitating the imposition of state regulation. William Ophuls, for example, predicts that a return of scarcity 'portends the revival of age-old political evils' (Ophuls, 1977, p. 145). But this prophecy need not become the case: Ophuls' appeal for strong leadership is only one of the alternatives open to humankind. Nevertheless, while any environmental policy should be congruent with democratic values, the present environmental crisis may be such as to require active state intervention, intervention which may and should be predicated on a democratically agreed notion of the public good.

It is sometimes claimed that such issues are not political, but rather economic, or even 'just' technical. Such thoughts are especially common among right wing politicians, [1] but also abound among those scientists who have claimed either that the solution to all environmental problems is simply technical, or that there are technical solutions to all environmental problems. But although most environmental problems have, in principle, scientific or technological solutions, in practice these solutions are unavailable on account of economic considerations; in part, of course, because here too scarcity is central. Thus, for instance, we could invest huge sums of money in improving the technology for generating solar energy, and then subsidize the manufacture of solar energy systems; but someone would have to pay for all this. Environmental policies involve political decisions mainly about the allocation of financial resources and the distribution of money and power. Several 'Green' authors have therefore insisted that political considerations ought to play a larger and more explicit rôle in the ecological debate (Paehlke, 1989, Spretnak, 1990, Goodin, 1992a).

Many economists have taken the scientists' common standpoint on technology, adopting the radical liberal position that the market is the best arena for solving environmental problems (see Eckersley, 1992). Here is not the place for detailed debate about the rôle of the market: nevertheless, it is worth asking if market solutions **can** be finally satisfactory. The market clearly can find solutions to immediate environmental problems: when the quality of the water is bad, someone may manufacture and market mineral water; when there is too much noise, we are offered cheaper double glazing. But do we want to pay more for drinking water than we do for petrol, instead of simply drinking decent tap water? Do we wish to travel ten miles to find somewhere green to sit and relax? Can we all afford these things? Even if we accept the market as a system relevant to the 'environmental era' and congruent with liberalism, we are very likely eventually to realize that no economy sensitive to environmental concerns can be a **purely** market one: there is thus always a need for politics, in environmental as in other arenas (Moberg, 1991, van der Straaten, 1992). But then, the pro-market economists fail not so much in their economic as in their political theory: rather than the question being whether or not we are best served by a 'market' or 'non-market' economy, the important question is that of a more appropriate politics.

At this point a distinction should be made between two conceptions of politics, each at least congruent with, if not perhaps simply representing, two rival interpretations of liberalism. One, which generally speaking is the contemporary mainstream American variety, and which may be termed the dominant view, at least in respect of contemporary influence, is based on the values of neutrality, minimal state intervention, an opposition to regulations and a conception of politics in which the public sphere serves as a mechanism for the aggregation of the autonomous decisions of sovereign individuals – all of which are antithetical to environmental policies. The other, European, interpretation is, by contrast, far from hostile to advancing certain ideas of the good (e.g. conservation) or to state intervention: here, the public sphere plays a more pro-active rôle in relation to individuals' decisions.

Let us consider the former variety first. Although controversial, neutrality is, in the eyes of many liberals, the core of contemporary liberalism. According to this attitude the state should stay out of the debate on the nature of the good. Official policies should not promote any particular conception of the good life: on the contrary, the state should remain neutral. The distribution of resources should never be governed by any substantive conception of what is good, either for the individual or for society (Ackerman, 1980, Rawls, 1985, Gauthier, 1986, Dworkin, 1986, Kymlicka, 1989; but see Raz, 1980). But, thinking again of governmental outputs, can one remain neutral here? For a neutral argument in favour of conservation is also an argument for a fair political procedure governing the selection of a particular output: but a fair (i.e. neutral) procedure cannot guarantee conservation (de-Shalit, 1993c). Yet contemporary liberal governments acknowledge the need for environment-friendly policies, while remaining committed to neutrality. It seems that they want to have their cake and eat it.

To see this more clearly, let us examine what conservation implies. First, it is more than a simple preference for one alternative over another. By deciding to preserve a picturesque house, an historic monument, or a beautiful landscape, the government declares that although there are powerful forces backing the development projects that would destroy these things, their demands should be rejected. The developers put forward strong social arguments: development would bring about prosperity, improve the welfare of the needy, create more jobs, create conditions for a more egalitarian distribution of wealth, and so forth (see Attfield and Dell, 1989). If, in spite of all these considerations, the government decides to conserve, there must be a very strong reason for doing so, namely that those in government believe that this house, street, church, town, landscape etc. is part of what is good in this world. This is precisely the difference between a certain village or a work of art on the one hand, and a nuclear bomb on the other. One is part of the good in this world; the other is part of the evil. We do not want to conserve – indeed we sometimes destroy – nuclear weapons; and we do not put energy into conserving what we think is valueless. In short, an argument in favour of the conservation of a certain object must be based on the claim that this object is part of some good, or, indeed, is in itself good – and this especially when to conserve it goes against the present interests of certain parties.

At this point one may answer that while this may be broadly right, nevertheless the dominant liberal view is much more democratic, inasmuch as, according to its doctrines, political decisions should reflect nothing other than the aggregate of people's preferences, respecting absolutely their choices. Indeed, choice and autonomy are basic to this version of liberalism (Beiner, 1992). In America, belief in the importance of autonomous individuals' exercise of their right to choose is so strong that private preferences and economic measures, backed by the legitimacy of 'rational behaviour', have supplanted debate on political ideals, collective goods, and the image of the good life. [2] This philosophy holds that society is an instrument for the aggregation of the preferences of individuals: everything is reduced to private interests, which are held in the balance by a market or exchange (Elster, 1986). All the more, therefore, should nature be subjugated by human beings, who through its progressive transformation satisfy their individual desires (Taylor, 1975).

But it is repeatedly argued and widely accepted that what is now needed in environmental politics is something more sophisticated: not merely policies which are responsive to individual preferences and neutral regarding outcome; but policies which, while responsive, also take into account the good of the community as a whole, offering solutions to problems which are rarely considered – and still less resolved – by purely individualistic, self-centred or short-term interests. [3] Moreover, it is always likely that, in the environmental context, individual and private preferences will contradict the general good. Thus, for example, economic and self-interested individualistic preferences could easily lead to the continuing depletion of scarce resources, whether oil, clean air, or scenic landscape. The question of how to reduce, say, pollution on the roads, is a good illustration. When in 1974 the Israeli government issued a regulation according to which each car could be on the road for a maximum of six days a week, everyone realized that Israel was short of petrol and that the cities were too polluted: nevertheless, many people simply bought a second car, hoping that it would be others who would play their part in the national effort to save energy and reduce pollution. Garret Hardin's well-known 'Tragedy of the Commons' makes clear why this must always be a likely outcome of pure non-interventionism. The state of the environment resembles a pasture open to all. Each person is interested only in his or her own position, however, and therefore he or she tries to keep as many cattle on the common, or pasture, as possible. But, of course, the capacity of the land is insufficient. Now, suppose that each person receives all the proceeds from the sale of an additional animal; the utility of adding one more animal to one's herd will be +1, whereas the disadvantage will be only **a fraction** of -1, because the effects of overgrazing are shared by all the other people concerned. The problem is that everyone reaches the same conclusion; they all add one more animal; and the pasture disappears. Hardin's conclusion, that 'the laws of our society follow the pattern of ancient ethics, and therefore are poorly suited to governing a complex, crowded, changeable world' (Hardin, 1968, p. 1245) in which 'freedom to breed is intolerable' (ibid., p. 1246) is somewhat drastic. But a much less drastic conclusion could be drawn from this example – namely that the state is necessary to enforce environmental policies on the basis of the general good.

It might therefore be possible to develop policies which are neither totalitarian nor overly authoritarian, and which may be justified explicitly on moral grounds rather than those of neutrality. Environmental policies would then be regarded as matters of principle that could not be bargained away in an economic fashion (Ophuls, 1977, p. 186) and members of society would not be primarily consumers, but rather citizens (Sagoff, 1988, p. 27). As citizens we would identify our own good with the good of the community rather than with narrowly defined personal interests; and as citizens we would have **obligations** which would not always be compatible with our private **preferences**. These obligations would have to receive priority if we were to achieve 'a certain kind of self-determination ... [and to decide] who we are, not just what we are' (Sagoff, 1984, pp. 172–3). There are substantial rights and wrongs involved in environmental policies; and these are moral rather than financial or economic. Our proper relation to the environment constitutes a moral question, and the answers to moral questions do not necessarily tie in with the private interests of individuals. To deny this, as some thorough-going liberals of the 'dominant' persuasion do, is to deny the very **possibility** of specifically **moral** issues.

These issues of self-determination and of the proper moral relations with the environment also inform the beliefs of many Greens: that to live in rural areas, for instance, is 'living more in harmony with nature' (Goodin, 1992a, p. 51) than living in an urban jungle of cars and industries. These Greens may be understood as arguing that there is less alienation in village life, or none at all, or in other words that one sort of life is better than another because it constitutes the good life or at least a way of life closer to it. But even if one subscribes to their view, it is important to remember that it is politically contestable and controversial:

something which its being presented as simply an empirical psychological fact tends all too easily to obscure is that, after all, there have been times in which just this type of harmony was regarded as impoverishing, even as degenerate and degrading. The legitimacy of a debate on whether this sort of life is indeed a, let alone the, good life in fact demonstrates that debate about the idea of the good is not only intelligible, but necessary. For any Green, **o r counter-Green**, contention must make some assumption about the good: any theory, even a preference-based one – and, thus purportedly substantially neutral about the good – is **a** theory of the good.

The state of the environment, then, calls for a politics of the common good; and thus for a debate about the good. At this point two further objections might be raised. Firstly, a contractor's wish that a certain valley should be inhabited and developed – whether or not the matter is put in terms of the common good or of private preference – is in no way less deserving of serious attention than the environmentalist's demand that all work should stop and the valley be preserved. We are simply faced with contrary views, neither of them inferior to the other. But this begs just that question; for the issue is not a matter of inferior or superior 'standpoints': both developers and environmentalists express ideas of the good life, images of how this world should be and how people should live, regardless of the terms of their, or others', metaethics. They sometimes even use similar reasoning: for instance, developers put forward the psychological argument that if there are more roads and more jobs, people will be less anxious; while environmentalists argue that, since tension is caused by noise, traffic, and the rushing rhythm of our lives, reducing it depends upon limiting growth, constructing fewer roads, etc. The central point is that this is not simply a case of conflicting preferences that can be bargained over until a compromise is reached. The two sides cannot but represent different conceptions of a good world, of what is and what is not desirable. Second, it may be argued that, metaethical considerations apart, the Greens' environmental concern just does not represent a collective good at all, but rather no more than just an individual's, or a set of individuals', preferences. The Greens' claim that the world will be destroyed if their suggestions are not implemented is similar to the warnings issued by many religious fanatics, who demand that we should all attend churches, synagogues, mosques, etc., for the cynical, even if unacknowledged, reason that they themselves want us to – because (although not necessarily, of course) they would gain more power. This challenge, however, is easily met: environmentalism is based on **rational** evaluations and upon scientific, empirical knowledge, whereas religious fanaticism is not. The system of religious fanatics is irrational in essence, because it is not based on any empirical or even quasi-empirical grounds; environmentalists, on the other hand, base their call for change on scientific grounds and empirical – although controversial – evidence (de-Shalit, 1993b). So environmentalists do not simply express preferences, but put forward arguments based on scientific knowledge in terms of which their ideas of the good may be tested, discussed, amended, etc.

But if the state of the environment calls for a debate on the good and a politics arising from such debate, then there is a price to be paid for the liberal's insistence on regarding politics as a matter of autonomous individual decisions, especially if these impose limits on our consideration of the good of the community, welfare policies, etc. What is needed if politics is to provide the framework in which the general interest is discussed and protected, let alone perhaps promoted, is state intervention. Now some liberals would nevertheless argue that you do not have to debate the nature of the good in order to justify state intervention. The Rawlsian theory of justice is neutral, it is argued, but is nevertheless in favour of state intervention. This debate, however, is beyond the scope of this paper. [4] For our purpose it is sufficient to claim that, even if Rawls' (or any other liberal) appeal to the idea of neutrality does justify a certain kind of interventionism, then it cannot be the one which suits the case of the environment. As we have seen, where the latter is concerned, interventionism must be based on and justified by considerations of the good. Any less weighty reason for intervention would not justify the **dramatic** policies necessary to deal with the ecological disasters with which we are faced and the political difficulties which accompany them. Indeed, the state is the only institution with the necessary financial and human resources to provide environmental outputs. If such drastic outputs were to be implemented other than on the basis of a genuine debate on the good, they would turn out to be nothing more than what Ophuls feared they would be: namely regulations imposed on a large section of the population who did not understand their necessity, and which would therefore endanger the very democracy and liberty which liberalism champions.

I have so far argued that in terms of a public environmental policy and its justification the neutral liberalism of the American tradition is quite futile: to the extent that liberals adhere to neutrality, and regard liberal-democratic politics primarily as a matter concerning the wills of individuals, they are unable to deal adequately with environmental issues. For these require a politics of the common good and consequently must imply a degree of interventionism.

It does not follow, however, that no liberal government can tackle the environmental challenge. For a liberal political tradition which takes seriously the common good can be found in Europe, a tradition of liberalism which, while recognizing the demand of liberty, nevertheless incorporates a considerably interventionist welfare state. In the last section of this paper, then, I shall elaborate this theme, arguing – very briefly – that this European conception of liberalism both embodies a real alternative tradition to the dominant variety of liberalism and that it is better suited to the environmental era. Europeans simply have to dig a little into their recent past to uncover this tradition and to blow away the dust which has obscured this conception of liberalism. Such an interpretation of liberalism has been supported by European political theory and philosophy since the late nineteenth and early twentieth centuries. In the works of Hobhouse, Hobson, T.H. Green, John Keynes, Ralf Dahrendorf, and Guido de Ruggiero the state has played a positive rôle: to provide welfare; to encourage participatory citizenship; and to ensure that everyone can enjoy the advantages of the liberty that the state sustains.

In contrast to America, possessive individualism has not been the most important pillar of European liberal societies: although European liberalism started as a defender of the individual against the church and the state, it did not stop there. Thus the economist and philosopher John Keynes regarded individualism as 'a scientific study of the consequences of rational self-love' which conduces to a 'liberalism accorded with the practical notions of conservatism' (Keynes, 1971, pp. 285–6). This version of liberalism is based on a conception of persons as having a social character: thus, for example, for Thomas Paine, among others, people have a natural tendency towards a social life because they need society.

At the same time, European liberals have challenged the idea of 'the miracle of a divine harmony' between private advantage and the public good, which Keynes defined as 'the retirement of the political philosopher in favour of the businessman':

> The world is *not* so governed from above that private and social interest always coincide. It is *not* so managed here below that in practice they coincide. It is *not* a correct deduction from the Principles of Economics that enlightened self-interest always operates in the public interest. (Keynes, ibid., p. 286)

Or again, de Ruggiero, a leading Italian liberal between the two World Wars, argued that the concept of freedom which had developed in Europe was a realization of the social nature of humanity, a reflection of political maturity, or the replacement of atomistic individualism by politics and social life:

> To be free ... is to be independent of others in the sense that all natural and coercive dependence is abolished and replaced by dependence spontaneously affirmed in the consciousness of duty towards oneself and others. (de Ruggiero, 1959, pp. 351–2)

Men and women were considered as by nature political animals, and therefore as living in a political realm constituted by their community. On the basis of an atomistic conception of society, rights were attached to responsibilities rather than to self-interest. But if individuals are social, 'interwoven in significant ways with groups and communities' (Freeden, 1991, p. 63); if citizenship implies 'playing an active rôle in determining (one's) society's future, and taking responsibility for the collective decisions' (Miller, 1989, p. 247); if ideas of the good are to be discussed in political terms; and if the public sphere is the arena for all these activities: then it follows that the state should intervene to guarantee and serve social and collective ends, as a reflection and fulfilment of our social obligations. [5]

The distribution of liberty was itself such a collective end. de Ruggiero, for instance, asking what liberalism was, drew a distinction between two concepts of freedom. His definition was significantly different from Berlin's better known distinction: while negative freedom, he said, is freedom **from** the state, positive freedom is freedom **through** the state (op. cit., p. 350). This conception reflects a respect for the state and a desire to see it intervene to guarantee and promote liberties; and, as time went on, it came to underpin the expectation that the state promote not only liberties but also welfare. Liberalism was reinterpreted as requiring that we help raise closer to our own level those living on a lower one. It is therefore not surprising that the state was urged not only to remove all obstacles to personal development, but also to embark upon new and more complex legislation and related governmental activities – including intervention in moral debates – to further such an end. The European liberal state was more than the individualistic state, and freedom was seen not merely as a right but as a 'task':

> The end to which these liberal means are directed is nothing but freedom. ... Liberty arouses energy, trust, and consent, and creates a spontaneous spirit of association and co-operation. (ibid., p. 359)

European liberalism, then, was clearly influenced by socialist thought and the philosophy of the welfare state. Some liberals even argued that individualism and laissez-faire favoured the interests of the ruling class, or 'the great men of affairs'. The recognition that liberty should not be restricted to some individuals or to one or two classes, but rather must be enjoyed by **all** in order for there to be a better society, and that personality could not develop without the flourishing of society, implied certain centralistic policies. Hence Keynes, as a professor at Cambridge and later as director of the Bank of England, advocated deeper state intervention in the post-First World War economy. He thought that the task for liberal philosophy and economics was to find the golden mean between what the state ought to take upon itself on the one hand, and what ought to be left to private initiative on the other.

The general suspicion of the state characteristic of early liberalism thus diminished in Europe during the earlier 20th century. For some, the state came itself to constitute a moral entity: and these became the first fascists. But for others, who clung to liberalism, the state became an ethical framework (Freeden, 1978, pp. 52–70, 195f.) in the sense that, although not constituting the good per se, its task was nevertheless to promote the good. At first this good was quite narrowly defined in terms of liberty and autonomy only; later, however, the definition was widened to include an egalitarian dimension.

Such a conception of liberalism underlies such contemporary views as those of Brian Barry, who suggests that liberalism should point 'towards a more active rôle for the state ... fostered by positive state action' (Barry 1989). While in the mainstream American liberalism that has come to dominate and obscure this other, European, conception, the emphasis is on the right of individuals to demand that the state should not interfere in their private spheres of life, in European liberalism one of the individual's crucial rights is precisely that the state **will intervene** to promote, sustain and defend liberty for all. Such a principle, unlike the individualism of the American model, can usefully apply to environmental policies: European liberalism can certainly accept not only that people have the right to a cleaner and healthier environment, but also that such an environment is part of their common good and of the good life. It is, however, a right which imposes duties on the state, as the only institution with the necessary resources to provide such an environment. According to this tradition, the current political imperative to improve the state of the environment without recourse to totalitarian methods arises on the twin bases of individual rights and the common good.

No doubt liberty must be respected: but the current state of the environment demands comprehensive state intervention, justified by a consideration of the common good. Neutrality, the politics of the aggregate of autonomous decisions, and an economics of individual preferences, are of no avail here. While a 'neutralist' liberalism might, as in the USA, encourage the environmental discourse, it does not permit its conclusions to be put into practice. However, the interpretation of liberalism which is more common in Europe could allow for a justification of environmental policies in terms of liberal convictions and, indeed, institutions. Europe would therefore be well advised to pay heed to its own tradition of liberalism if it is to develop the environmental policies which are crucial for its future.

Notes

1. Mrs Thatcher, in a speech to the Royal Society on 27 September 1988, in which she declared that she had a commitment to the environment; and during which the Tories declared that they were the greatest friends of the Earth and its trustees for future generations.
2. For two examples, see Arrow (1962) and Dahl (1970).
3. See David Miller's account (1992) of environmental (energy) policies and social choice according to the two models of politics; and also Jonathon Porritt (1984, p. 116).
4. I subscribe to the view that in fact Rawls cannot put forward the idea of interventionism without being committed to some positive idea of the good: see de-Shalit (1992a); and cf. Nagel (1975).
5. For a discussion of the link between rights and individualism on the one hand, and rights and community on the other, see Freeden (1991, pp. 63–82).

References

Ackerman, B. (1980), *Social Justice in the Liberal State*, Yale University Press, New Haven.
Arrow, K. (1962), *Social Choice and Individual Values*, Wiley, N.Y.
Attfield, R. and Dell, K. (eds.) (1989), *Values, Conflict and the Environment*, Ian Ramsey Centre, Oxford.
Barry, B. (1989), 'How not to defend liberal institutions', *British Journal of Political Science*, 20, pp. 1–14.
Beiner, R. (1992), *What's the Matter with Liberalism?*, University of California Press, Berkeley.
Dahl, R. (1970), 'Political man' in idem, *Modern Political Analysis*, Prentice-Hall, Englewood Cliffs, N.J.
de Ruggiero, G. (1959 (1927)), *The History of European Liberalism*, Collingwood, R.C. (trans.), Beacon Press, Boston.
de-Shalit, A. (1992a), 'Community and the rights of future generations', *Journal of Applied Philosophy*, 9, 1, pp. 105–116.
de-Shalit, A. (1992b), 'Environmental policies and justice between generations', *European Journal of Political Research*, 21, pp. 307–316.
de-Shalit, A. (1993a), 'Liberalism and the environment', (unpublished).
de-Shalit, A. (1993b), 'Ruralism or environmentalism?', (unpublished).
de-Shalit, A. (1993c), 'Urban preservation and the judgement of King Solomon', *Journal of Applied Philosophy*, (forthcoming).
Dworkin, R. (1986), 'Can a liberal state support art?', in idem, *A Matter of Principle*, Clarendon Press, Oxford.
Eckersley, R. (1992), 'Green vs. ecosocialist economic programmes: the market rules O.K?', *Political Studies*, 40, pp. 315–333.
Elster, J. (1986), 'The market and the forum: three varieties of political theory', in Elster and Hylland, A. (eds.), *The Foundations of Social Choice Theory*, Cambridge University Press, Cambridge.
Freeden, M. (1978), *The New Liberalism*, Clarendon Press, Oxford.
Freeden, M. (1991), *Rights*, Open University Press, Milton Keynes.

Gauthier, D. (1986), *Morals by Agreement*, Clarendon Press, Oxford.
Goodin, R. (1992a), *Green Political Theory*, Polity Press, Oxford.
Goodin, R. (1992b), 'The high road is green', *Environmental Politics*, 1, 4, pp. 1–8.
Hardin, G (1968), 'The tragedy of the commons', *Science*, 162, pp. 1243–8.
Keynes, J. (1971), 'The end of laissez-faire', in Sidorsky, D. (ed.), *The Liberal Tradition in European Thought*, Capricorn Books, N.Y.
Kymlicka, W. (1989), 'Liberal individualism and liberal neutrality', *Ethics*, 99, pp. 883–905.
Miller, D. (1989), *Market, State and Community*, Clarendon Press, Oxford.
Miller, D. (1992), 'Deliberative democracy and social choice', *Political Studies*, 40, pp. 54–66.
Moberg, D. (1991), 'Environment and the market', *Dissent*, 38, pp. 511–519.
Nagel, T. (1975), 'Rawls on justice' in Daniels, N. (ed.), *Reading Rawls*, Blackwell, Oxford.
Ophuls, W. (1977), *Ecology and the Politics of Scarcity*, W.H. Freeman, San Francisco.
Paehlke, R. (1989), *Environmentalism and the Future of Progressive Politics*, Yale University Press, New Haven.
Porritt, J. (1984), *Seeing Green*, Fontana, London.
Rawls, J. (1985), 'Justice as fairness: political, not metaphysical', *Philosophy and Public Affairs*, 14, pp. 223–239.
Raz, J. (1980), 'Liberalism, autonomy and the politics of neutral concern', *Midwest Studies in Philosophy*, 7, pp. 89–120.
Sagoff, M. (1984), 'Ethics and economics in environmental law' in Regan, T. (ed.), *Earthbound*, Waveland Press, Prospect Heights, Ill.
Sagoff, M. (1988), *The Economy of the Earth*, Cambridge University Press, Cambridge.
Spretnak, C. and Fritjof, C. (1990), *Green Politics*, Paladin, London.
Taylor, C. (1975), *Hegel*, Cambridge University Press, Cambridge.
van der Straaten, J. (1992), 'A sound European environmental policy: challenges, possibilities and barriers', *Environmental Politics*, 1, 4, pp. 65–83.

11 Maoist liberalism? Higher education in contemporary Britain

Jo Halliday

I

From his revolutionary 'think tank' base at Yenan in 1942, Mao Zedong wrote:

> A man studies through from grade school to university, graduates, and is then considered learned. Yet, in the first place, he cannot till the land; second, he has no trade; third, he cannot fight; fourth, he cannot manage a job ... What he possesses is only book knowledge. Books cannot walk, and you can open and close a book at will; this is the easiest thing in the world to do, a great deal easier than it is for the cook to prepare a meal, and much easier than it is for him to slaughter a pig. (Chen, 1981, p. 88)

Nineteen years later, and after twelve years of Communist Party power, Mao commented when visiting a 'spare time' university set up in a factory:

> What you have been doing has my full support. A school run on the basis of part work and part study, self supporting through hard work, without having to ask the State for a single cent, a school embracing primary school, middle school, and college courses ... I hope that other provinces will set up this kind of school. (ibid., p. 72)

At the height of the Cultural Revolution, when both education itself and intellectuals in general were coming under intense scrutiny and being held responsible for the slow pace of economic, social and political change, Mao insisted:

> While their main task is to study, [students] should also learn other things, that is to say, they should not only learn book knowledge, they should also learn industrial production, agricultural production, and military affairs. They should also criticize and repudiate the bourgeoisie. The length of schooling should be shortened, education should be revolutionized, and the domination of our schools and colleges by bourgeois intellectuals should not be tolerated any longer. (Kerr, 1978, p. 111)

About a hundred years earlier, in the very different context of nineteenth century Britain, John Stuart Mill had said:

> That the whole or any large part of the education of the people should be in State hands, I go as far as any one in deprecating ... A general State education is a mere contrivance for moulding people to be exactly like one another: and as the mould in which it casts them is that which pleases the predominant power in the government, whether this be a monarch, a priesthood, an aristocracy, or the majority of the existing generation; in proportion as it is efficient and successful, it establishes a despotism over the mind, leading by natural tendency to one over the body. (Mill, 1859, p. 98)

Furthermore:

> [The University] is not a place of professional education. Universities are not intended to teach the knowledge required to fit men for some special mode of gaining their livelihood. Their object is not to make skilful lawyers, or physicians, or engineers, but capable and cultivated human beings. It is very right that there should be public facilities for the study of the professions. It is well that there should be Schools of Law, and of Medicine, and it would be well if there were schools of engineering, and the industrial arts ... and there is something to be said for having them in the same localities, and under the same general superintendence, as the establishments devoted to education properly so called. But these things are no part of what every generation owes to the next, as that on which its civilization and worth will principally depend ... Men are men before they are lawyers, or physicians, or merchants, or manufacturers; and if you make them capable and sensible men, they will make themselves capable and sensible lawyers or physicians. What professional men should carry away with them from an University, is not professional knowledge, but that which should direct the use of their professional knowledge, and bring the light of general culture to illuminate the technicalities of a special pursuit. (Mill, 1867, pp. 4–5)

And in the same vein, John Henry (Cardinal) Newman had earlier insisted in one of his most influential writings on education that he was

> prepared to maintain that there is a knowledge worth possessing for what it is, and not merely for what it does. (1852, p. 157)

These pronouncements illustrate two completely different theories of higher education. Mao's position, designed to serve specific political purposes, is clearly both ideological and revolutionary. Mill's and Newman's, however, articulate an open-ended liberal position, valuing education 'for its own sake' as essential for the cultivation of the individual human being.

What is immediately striking is that even the most casual observer of contemporary British society can see that the kind of liberal statements made by Mill and Newman about education are entirely at odds with contemporary policy. The autonomy and freedom traditionally enjoyed by British universities have been challenged, ideologically, in the latter part of the twentieth century. As higher education has been brought under increasing state control, it has become subject to national government funding and other systems of accountability; has increasingly been distanced from local democratic control; and has consequently been increasingly vulnerable to party political direction. At the same time, universities – like all other British 'service industries' – are increasingly being encouraged to 'stand on their own two feet' and to operate in the 'free market', just like corporate business enterprises, competing with one another to persuade their 'customers' to buy their 'quality products'. There are now more explicit interventions than ever before at national level in both the form and content of the higher education curriculum, a curriculum increasingly steered towards the promotion and adoption of narrowly occupational demands – largely through funding incentives. Centralized managerialism at both government and institutional levels is encroaching on traditional notions of academic freedom, collegiality and pluralism. How is it, then, that British higher education has moved so dramatically from its earlier liberal position and undergone such an explicitly ideological revolution?

II

One way of exploring this shift is to investigate the history of vocationalism in British tertiary education. Apart from the elite professions (such as medicine or law) vocational education and training had its beginnings in further education. It could be argued that, from its working class roots, vocational further education originally posed a challenge to the exclusivity of liberal higher education, in that it provided an alternative route to the acquisition of the benefits of educational status and social mobility. Yet precisely because it enjoyed less power and prestige, vocational further education was susceptible to structural, curricular and financial control by the dominant ideology it may have attempted to challenge. In short, it has always been a way of offering the working classes limited access to some education and training 'on the cheap'. This, combined with the fact that, traditionally, only very few people have been allowed to participate in Britain's elitist higher education system, has served as a basis for the State's exercising greater control over higher education as a whole. The vocational alternative, presented as both anti-elitist and economically necessary, and accepted both by liberal members of the academic profession and by the general public as a challenge to elitism, has been used as a pragmatic means of achieving the ideological goal of taking greater control over the structure and process of higher education.

It is the former polytechnic sector, [1] with its roots in the vocationalism of further education, which has served as a significant means of achieving the 'vocationalization' of British higher education. It is therefore necessary to chart at least briefly the history of the parallel system of universities and polytechnics in Britain from the 1960s to the 1990s: for one obvious and influential interpretation of such a history is that elitist higher education has been successfully and beneficially challenged by the impact and development of vocationalism. Was not the culmination of this success of the polytechnics their elevation in 1992 to university status?

In 1964, Harold Wilson's Labour Government needed to respond to political and social pressures to expand the national higher education system, but was faced with the problem of how to do so when public expenditure was coming under increasing strain. That Government rejected, therefore, the Robbins' Committee's (1963) proposals to expand and enhance the existing autonomous university sector and instead encouraged, at far lower cost, the growth of advanced level work in public sector colleges. [2] In 1966, these colleges were upgraded to higher education status through the organization of a polytechnic sector and the burgeoning of degree level work, much of it in new vocational areas, through the powers of the Council for National Academic Awards (CNAA). The effect of these changes was to bring within national – albeit locally devolved – administrative and financial control the approximately forty per cent of higher education outside the universities. An explicit decision was made to promote a separate polytechnic sector, rather than to extend the number of universities, partly for pragmatically economic reasons and partly as a means of establishing state control:

> There is an ever-increasing need and demand for vocational, professional and industrially-based courses in higher education – at

full-time degree level, at full-time just below degree level, at part-time advanced level, and so on. This demand cannot be fully met by the Universities. It must be fully met if we are to progress as a nation in the modern technological world. In our view it therefore requires a separate sector, with a separate tradition and outlook within the higher education system ... it is desirable in itself that a substantial part of the higher education system should be under social control, and directly responsive to social needs ... (Crosland, 1965, p. 204)

Mill's objections to state control were being overridden. The resulting upward academic drift of the vocational curriculum in higher education is very often explained in pragmatic terms, using the justification of existing structures and perceived political, social and economic demands. But this is to conflate the well-meaning intentions of some with the hidden agenda of others: for recent Tory governments have been able to build quite explicitly on these historical opportunities – and in particular on the discomfort of the mainstream liberal tradition with elitist higher education – in order to subvert the traditional values of higher education in favour of an ideological commitment to work-related training. Thus, however unwittingly, the Labour Government's moves in the 1960s to challenge the elitism and traditionalism of the universities through the creation of public sector polytechnics were to lay the foundations for the later expression of the Tory Party's ideological agenda.

The ex-public sector of higher education – while receiving praise for its expansion both in terms of student numbers and range of curriculum development, particularly in directly occupational areas, such as business studies, accountancy, nursing, midwifery, hotel and catering studies – has both challenged and been used to neutralize and subvert the original liberal-humanist values of higher education. Now that the line between universities and polytechnics has fallen, new lines are being formed – or reformed – between higher education and occupationally-driven training. The success of this ideological conversion of education to training can be gauged by the widely-believed rumour that the Department for Education and the Department of Employment are to have ever-closer links and might eventually amalgamate. Such moves are of course assisted by a coincidentally high level of unemployment. Institutions have fast become prey to a carefully engineered 'market' need to attract 'extra' funding by, for example, increasing student numbers in specific vocational subjects to the detriment of others; adopting 'enterprise' initiatives; offering 'fast track' two year degrees and diplomas; and welcoming students who gear their studies to a system of national vocational qualifications. The Chair of the Business and Technology Education Council (BTEC) has recently pointed out that there is a danger that the Government-funded body charged with aligning educational and vocational qualifications – the National Council for Vocational Qualifications (NCVQ) – will become 'a prescriptive regulator, saying that this is what must be taught', rather than an accrediting body for existing educational qualifications designed and offered by universities. He went on to describe current Government policy in these terms:

> It is as if some heavy handed government laid down the minimum specification for a particular size of car but also forbade any manufacturer from offering a higher specification. You can sell a Lada to anyone who will buy it, but you may not add to its market appeal by adding power steering and halogen lights because it will then not meet government specification. That attitude is daft in any circumstances; how much dafter it is when done in the name of a government which is dedicated to market forces. (BTEC, 1992)

The notion of vocationalism might have served as a catalyst to enable higher education to expand from an elitist system to one which allowed many more people to undertake full-time and financially supported higher education. Instead, however, it has been used to enable governments at once to promote higher education 'on the cheap' (an aim both of the Labour Party in the 1960s and subsequently, and of later Tory administrations) and – more importantly – to infiltrate and subvert those of its values and practices which challenge the status quo (a priority of successive Tory administrations since 1979). The promotion of cheap, short and vocationally 'relevant' higher education courses is a deliberate means of redirecting the sector's liberal democratic traditions towards a system requiring a high level of State control. Liberal ideals – such as accountability, flexibility of access to higher education, personal freedom, student choice, control over one's own learning – have been turned round and used against just those liberal educationalists most highly committed to expanding higher education. For example, the development of credit accumulation and modular systems, whilst originally – and in many cases still, and whether naively or not – promoted by liberal educationalists as a way of affording wider access to those traditionally excluded from higher education, is allowing time for study in universities to be reduced through giving substantial educational 'credit' to students for their employment and other 'experiential learning'. [3] This process, combined with the fact that student poverty is putting the supposedly 'free' full time higher education system out of the reach of many who do not have access to private means, is resulting in some parts of higher education reverting to the fragmented evening class or 'day release' model originally used by their precursors in further education. Students' curricular 'choice' is thus being manipulated by what is constrained to be on offer. Career promotion in some vocational areas, such as nursing, is increasingly dependent on the acquisition of a university qualification in that specific field rather than in another less specifically vocational, more academic, area. Demand is thus in fact being created, rather than occurring 'naturally' in a 'free market'. Its autonomy thus weakened, higher education has become a central instrument of social and political change.

The ideological function of the process of the vocationalization of higher education needs to be exposed for what it is: a means of increasing central government control rather than simply some 'natural' and/or pragmatic response to the development of economic and social needs. Higher education policy and everyday practice now demand a high level of commitment to a specific, politically dominated, and increasingly narrow view of vocationalism and work-related concerns. The Government set the scene in 1987 when it stated the sector's aims and purposes as follows:

> Higher education should:
> * serve the economy more effectively
> * pursue basic scientific research and scholarship in the arts and humanities
> * have closer links with industry and commerce, and promote enterprise.
>
> (Secretary of State for Education and Science, 1987, p. iv)

Higher education has now become one of the key items on the political agenda in Britain and has assumed an explicitly ideological function in promoting the state's policies:

> There has been an encouraging willingness on the part of higher education to take account of the needs of industry and commerce as evinced by ... the positive response to the Department of Employment's Enterprise in Higher Education initiative which, through partnerships between higher education institutions and employers, aims to develop more enterprising graduates with a knowledge of the world of work. (Department of Education and Science, 1991, p. 9)

Ministers and others have sought to explain and justify their policy decisions on higher education in terms of economic pragmatism – in some cases naively, in others as a means of obfuscating with rhetoric a clear ideological purpose. In spite of the fact that British liberal ideology was originally supportive of the concept of higher education for its own sake, higher education in Britain has in a comparatively short space of time been realigned with a government's ideological concerns. Laissez faire economics and the free enterprise of the stock market have not been accompanied by a policy of laissez faire for those who study and work in the current British higher education system. Clearly a government's power to dictate these directions – or any other – is a long way from

Mill's liberal insistence on the cultivation of the individual human being.

III

A number of liberal-minded commentators themselves have recently remarked on these developments. John Passmore, for instance, points out the irony of a high level of state control over teaching and learning prevailing in democratic, rather than totalitarian, states. Educational institutions in Britain and Australia, he says, are becoming 'enterprises designed to turn out a particular kind of product', namely a '"good citizen" ... [who is] law-abiding, amenable, no kind of troublemaker, never asking inopportune questions, accepting such of the "traditional values" as are not inconsistent with the maximization of wealth. Governments will find it profitable to subsidize teaching institutions which turn out such products' (Passmore, 1989, p. 567). This is echoed in observations made by Michael Prowse, writing on the National Curriculum. Describing a visit to the People's Republic of China (PRC) a few years previously by Willie Lamont, he comments on how the Chinese were nonplussed when Lamont explained that there was no official history textbook in British schools:

> If Professor Lamont were to return to China today he would have to admit that the British system is being remodelled along Chinese lines. Mrs Thatcher's Government is creating a national curriculum which will ensure that all children are taught the same things in the same way ... A national curriculum, whatever its other advantages, is going to crush experimentation and reduce choice and diversity. It also threatens to make education a political football. Those who cheered Mr MacGregor's intervention should wonder how they would feel if a Labour Education Secretary were to demand extra courses on the rise of working class solidarity in the late 19th century. (Prowse, 1989)

How is it, then, that liberals have come to permit a shift to such strong state control? Two explanations suggest themselves. One is that the liberal tradition has simply been replaced by another more powerful ideology; another that liberalism is itself inherently contradictory, because, in claiming to be 'neutral', it is in fact adopting a position which is infinitely malleable and thus open to attack by the very forces, mechanisms and interference which it claims to seek to minimize. Laissez faire permits anything; and in doing so, cannot but be open to ideological manipulation. While a conclusive assessment is beyond the scope of an article such as this, or even a book such as this, I am inclined to think that it is the latter view which both enables us to make sense of what is happening in British higher education and which is in turn supported by the evidence it offers – at least to the extent that such matters may be susceptible to empirical evidence at all. [4]

A consideration of the epitome of the British liberal university tradition – Oxford and Cambridge – demonstrates how liberal individualism has given rise to greater State control. The laissez faire model par excellence of the pursuit of higher learning is to be found in the traditional Oxbridge model of one-to-one tutorials, a practice which encapsulates the paramount importance ascribed to the individual. At the feet of the great masters, a small and limited number of individuals strove to acquire the canon of knowledge as ordained by the experts. Under that model, academics were entitled to pursue research and were funded to do so, without having to declare in any great detail outside the university either their expected research outcomes or their relevance to politically defined social and economic needs. For the few students able to afford access to the benefits of this privately funded and elitist system, there was no need for the curriculum to be governed by considerations of being a means towards a practical and specific end. As Mill had professed in 1867, university education was for the cultivation of individual human beings, and ought not to be concerned directly with enabling them to earn a living, or with the state's interest in the manner in which they did so.

This model of higher education is expensive, elitist and – to a contemporary liberal educationalist – unacceptably exclusive. The contemporary liberal response has therefore been to welcome moves to widen access to higher education, while failing, however, to recognize the politically motivated forces behind their encouragement. The following are examples of some of the changes which have thus occurred: shorter and more fragmented modular degree courses, a challenge to the concept of uninterrupted, continuous and developmental study; the alignment of courses to more 'relevant' vocational areas to meet the 'needs' of industry; the incorporation of direct work experience into purportedly academic courses (something doubtless familiar to central and eastern European readers from the Stalin-Brezhnev days); distrust of theory and a celebration of the overriding value of practice; concentration on the short term training needs of the economy; promotion of the benefits of technological subjects over others; moves towards the standardization of the curriculum (through a national credit rating system); encouragement of 'distance learning' through standardized 'learning packages'; and encouraging students to attend local universities and live at home. These moves have helped the Government to manipulate higher education, by limiting the democratic scope of governing and academic bodies; forcing educational institutions to compete with one another; cutting the real value of grants and valuing instead students' economic self-sufficiency; masking unemployment figures and regional difficulties; fostering anti-intellectualism and distrusting experts and professionals; and, perhaps worst of all, winning over and using intellectuals as tools of its ideological ends.

Although some school teachers, educationalists and trade unionists are exposing the scenario in schools for what it is, the situation in British universities is on the whole less well understood – either by participants or the general public. [5] The Government is engineering the availability of the higher education curriculum to meet its political ends by overtly manipulating 'market forces' and 'student choice'. The 'Band 1' fee which universities receive for teaching each student enrolled on classroom-based subjects – predominantly humanities and social sciences – has recently been cut by thirty per cent to £1,300, while laboratory-based 'Band 2' subjects – mainly science and engineering – attract about £2,700. Since many universities will not be able to afford to expand in 'Band 1' areas, this of course constitutes direct intervention in a university's curriculum and is contrary to the Government's previously promoted notions of student access and choice. Similarly, the Government is directly promoting – through financial incentives – access to certain subjects rather than others [6], and giving substantial backing to the National Council for Vocational Qualifications (NCVQ), [7] in an effort to drive all universities to align their curricula with vocational qualifications. A 'velvet revolution' has occurred in British universities. Will it be much longer before we have an explicitly Government-imposed national curriculum in higher education – before, that is, the liberal model of higher education implodes?

IV

One way of exposing the situation in British universities is by looking at rhetoric. As I suggested at the beginning of this article, the relationships advocated between higher education and the State in the PRC and in the British tradition seem quite different. And yet some recent Government pronouncements are very much reminiscent of Mao Zedong's language in his comments on intellectuals and universities.

In 1958, Mao's Directive on Educational Work encompassed three cardinal principles: education was to serve politics, include productive labour, and be under Party leadership (*Renmin Ribao*, 1958). Existing education was criticized for its neglect of these, for perpetuating education for its own sake, for continuing to separate mental from physical labour and for concentrating educational authority in the hands of experts. As the Cultural Revolution intensified, teachers were evaluated and appointed for their correct political and ideological commitment as much as on professional qualification. A student's progress was also judged according to the level of political consciousness. Work-study schools and universities were favoured as the best revolutionary model of education. Although policy did not go so far as to suggest the abolition of all regular schools, direct Party control was ensured throughout education via Party leadership and membership of governing bodies. Educational reform was in fact one of the major driving forces of the Cultural Revolution. Mao insisted that

> Education must serve proletarian politics and be combined with productive labour. Working people should master intellectual work and intellectuals should integrate themselves with the working people. (Kerr, 1978, p. 111)

Colleges and higher education institutions were closed to allow time to work out reform measures. Students were encouraged to form revolutionary Red Guards. Higher education and its cadres were attacked – and attacked each other – for maintaining three major differences: the separation of mental from manual work; of industry from agriculture; and of town from countryside. When institutions re-opened, the study of Mao Zedong Thought formed an important part of the daily curriculum. Admission to university was no longer through the highly competitive and elitist examination system but on the recommendation of the prospective student's production unit. Courses were reduced to two or three years, during which time the curriculum was based on production work and its ideological and political context. Mao thus turned his original distrust of higher education to revolutionary purposes. In the words of his 1968 directive:

> It is still necessary to have universities; here I refer mainly to colleges of science and engineering. However, it is essential to shorten the length of schooling, revolutionise education, put proletarian politics in command and take the road of the Shanghai Machine Tools Plant in training technicians from among the workers. Students should be selected from among workers and peasants with practical experience, and they should return to production after a few years' study. (ibid.)

The school or college was no longer perceived as the only, or most important, seat of learning and teaching. Teachers and officials were 'sent down' to the countryside to be re-educated in order to administer the revolutionary system. Higher learning and universities were taken out of the control of the bourgeoisie. Students and teachers – referred to by the Gang of Four as 'the stinking ninth category' (a phrase perhaps reminiscent of our own Government's dislike of 'the chattering classes') – could be trained directly to serve the State.

V

These very brief examples from the history and development of Maoist ideology in relation to higher education demonstrate the use of rhetoric and ideology to serve the needs of political power. Now, although it would of course be facile to draw detailed comparisons between Maoist China and the Tory Britain of the 1990s, some similarities in ideological method and revolutionary fervour are evident in two cultures seeking to undermine the power and autonomy of education. It is important to draw attention to this similarity of political method, notwithstanding the differences in political context, in order to persuade British liberal higher educationalists that their culture has radically changed, having been undermined and attacked from within and without. It is striking that one of the basic tenets of Maoism – that of constant radical revolution – has been used to great effect by recent Tory governments to mask the reality of this political process. Peter Scott (1988) has criticized exactly this constant upheaval and drawn attention to the 'reformers'' hidden agenda:

> The formal position of ministers, of course, is that they are simply encouraging, and innocently participating in, a wide-ranging debate about the future pattern of higher education. There is an open agenda; no options are foreclosed; thinking the unthinkable is not forbidden. But this is a disingenuous exercise – however convenient a fiction it may be to soothe the worries of ministers about talking choice and decentralization and practising planning and centralization, and in fending off far-right critics who want to tear down all established institutions.

The editorial goes on to argue:

> If government is seen largely as an arena for cultural counter-revolution rather than as an exercise in rational public administration, sensible policies are difficult to sustain. As they are implemented, they become established and immediately lose their ideological zing. So they are pushed aside by apparently more radical policies. Then the danger arises of a collapse into silliness and so ineffectiveness. Something like this seems to be happening to the Government's policies for higher education ...

Recent British governments have been able to capitalize on the contradictions of liberalism to promote an ideology which relies on strong state control: higher education has been made 'to serve politics, include productive labour, and be under Party leadership'. British liberals have found themselves in the ambivalent position of not wanting to block attempts to raise the level of expertise in the workforce or to widen access, even if at the expense of higher education per se. The state has been increasingly enabled to dictate what it wants from higher education, both in relation to short-term economic requirements and in terms of ideological purpose, whether that be the creation of polytechnics under a Labour government; their transmutation to cheap and local universities threatened with greater control of the curriculum under the Tories; moves towards the evaluation of teachers to check their political commitment to the values of the dominant ideology; or the construction of students' 'choices', and the monitoring ('profiling') of their progress in both the university and the workplace.

At first sight, the development of higher education from liberal individualism to state control appears to be contradictory in both historical and conceptual terms: but such a view underestimates the significance of an ideological agenda. In order to challenge unsubstantiated but nevertheless politically powerful claims about the rôle and purpose of higher education presented pragmatically in terms of 'common sense', 'natural development' and greater freedom from regulation, it must be recognized that education is serving as a central means to persuade people to believe and accept – as a matter of course – whatever the state says it needs. What appears as a paradox in a liberal higher education tradition – namely Passmore's description of a high level of central state control in a liberal democracy – is better understood when it is seen as a consistent outcome of an ideological process. Of course, Mill's original liberal model is not itself some 'natural' state of affairs: it embodies, for instance, a particular set of elitist values which are untenable. Indeed, it is the very elitism of British liberal higher education which has made it vulnerable to explicitly ideological conversion by the New Right.

What I have sought to demonstrate, then, is that what has been presented in the recent history of higher education as both a utilitarian economic need for a more 'relevant' curriculum and as a liberal-humanist response by educationalists to social demands to develop high level vocational competence in a wider section of the population, is in fact the agent of a general ideological thrust. Liberalism has served as a cover, a Trojan horse, for what is in fact an antithetical ideological purpose: in Passmore's words, 'greater State control over teaching and research' (op. cit., 1989).

Notes

1. The further education system in Britain traditionally offered vocational and leisure courses below degree level for school-leavers and for adults who could attend for a day or half a day a week (released from work) or in the evenings. By the mid 1960s, some of

the larger and more prestigious colleges were offering degrees externally validated by the universities. In 1966, the then Labour Government legislated for some of these colleges (to be called polytechnics) to expand their degree work, and to be validated by a national degree awarding body called the Council for National Academic Awards (CNAA). This created a 'binary system' of higher education: the universities offered their own degrees; the polytechnics and colleges of higher education offered degrees of the CNAA. On 1 April 1992, this binary line was abolished. All previous polytechnics have acquired university status: that is, they have adopted university titles and are entitled to award their own degrees.

2. Robbins had proposed, inter alia, the establishment of six further new universities, a few special university institutions (SISTERS) devoted to high level undergraduate and postgraduate teaching and research in science and technology, and the eventual and gradual promotion to university status of the twenty five Regional Colleges and Scottish Central Institutes. This would have resulted in the incorporation and promotion of vocationally-oriented institutions as part of the university sector, instead of what I claim occurred, namely an incipient vocationalization of higher education as a whole.

3. For a criticism of the political and educational dangers of modularization – in terms of uniformity, central control, and the accompanying rhetoric of the marketplace and the production line – see The Critical Lawyers Group of the University of Kent at Canterbury (1992).

4. This description of the issue assumes, of course, far too simple a model of 'theory' and 'practice'. What counts as evidence and how it is interpreted is at least to some extent a matter of the context within which one approaches it. Charles Taylor's 'best account principle' at least offers a way forward :

> How can we ever know that humans can be explained by any scientific theory *until* we actually explain how they live their lives in its terms? This establishes what it means to 'make sense' of our lives ... The result of this search for clairvoyance yields the best account we can give at any given time, and no epistemological or metaphysical considerations of a more general kind about science or nature can justify setting this aside. The best account in the above sense is trumps. (1989, p. 58)

5. The successful challenge to liberal education can be seen much more clearly in the schools sector. Against the will of the profession – although initiated and originally promoted by it – the Government has introduced a National Curriculum. In addition, it is promoting the testing of children's progress at the ages of 7, 11 and 14, and the

publication of league tables of 'standards' and of the 'quality' of schools as allegedly demonstrated by their examination results. These are radical challenges to school teachers' professional expertise. What were once considered to be solely the concerns of teachers have been, to put it bluntly, hijacked. The professional debate has been manipulated and incorporated into a Government-led campaign, backed up by an ever increasing array of Government-sponsored reports and statistics to support and promote the imposition of politically driven educational policies, which are propagated by the media under such slogans as 'parent power', 'choice' and 'access to information'.

6. For example, through funding students who have arts or social sciences 'A'-levels to undertake a financially supported foundation year as an integral part of an extended degree in science or engineering (Department for Employment, 1992).

7. In its 1991 Budget, the Government announced that students on training courses leading to NVQs could deduct standard rate tax when paying fees to their college. The college then claims the difference from the Government. Educational courses popular with adults – such as evening classes and Open University courses – do not qualify for the concession; neither do adult 'returners' who choose to study for academic qualifications such as GCSEs.

References

BTEC (1992), Annual Report Launch, Press Release of Chair's Speech, 27 May.

Chen, T. Hsi-en (1981), *Chinese Education since 1949: Academic and Revolutionary Models*, Pergamon, New York.

Committee on Higher Education (Robbins) (1963), *Higher Education: Report of the Committee appointed by the Prime Minister under the Chairmanship of Lord Robbins 1961–3*, HMSO Cmnd 2154, London.

The Critical Lawyers Group of the University of Kent at Canterbury (1992), 'Education changes: the hidden agenda', *Radical Philosophy*, 60, p. 64.

Crosland, A. (1965), Speech by the Secretary of State for Education and Science at Woolwich Polytechnic on 27 April 1965, in Pratt, J. and Burgess, T. (1974), *Polytechnics: A Report*, Pitman, London, pp. 203–207.

Department of Education and Science (1966), *A Plan for Polytechnics and Other Colleges: Higher Education in the Further Education System*, HMSO Cmnd 3006, London.

Department of Education and Science (1991), *Higher Education: A New Framework*, HMSO Cm 1541, London.

Department for Employment Circular (1992), ACL 9/92, London.

Drucker, H.M. (1977), *The Political Uses of Ideology*, Macmillan, London.

Eagleton, T. (1991), *Ideology: An Introduction*, Verso, London.

Hickox, M. and Moore, R. (1990), 'TVEI, vocationalism and the crisis of liberal education' in Flude, M. and Hammer, M. (eds), *The Education Reform Act: 1988,* Falmer Press, London, pp. 133–152.

Hinton, W. (1972), *Hundred Day War: The Cultural Revolution at Tsinghua University*, Monthly Review Press, New York.

Kerr, C. (1978), *Observations on the Relations Between Education and Work in the People's Republic of China: Report of a Study Group*,

Carnegie Council on Policy Studies in Higher Education, Berkeley, California.

Lal, D. (1989), *Nationalised Universities: Paradox of the Privatisation Age*, Centre for Policy Studies, London.

Mill, J.S. (1859), *On Liberty*, in Spitz, D. (ed.) (1975), *On Liberty: Annotated Text, Sources and Background Criticism*, Norton, New York, pp. 3–106.

Mill, J.S. (1867), *Inaugural Address Delivered to the University of St. Andrews, February 1st. 1867*, Longmans, Green, Reader and Dyer, London.

Newman, J.H. (1852), *On the Scope and Nature of University Education*, Everyman (1943 edn.), London.

Passmore, J. (1989), 'Hearing voices', *The Times Literary Supplement*, 26 May – 1 June, pp. 567–568.

Price, R.F. (1977), *Marx and Education in Russia and China*, Croom Helm, London.

Prowse, M. (1989), 'Teaching British history the Chinese way', *The Financial Times*, 26 August, p. 7.

Renmin Ribao (The People's Daily) (1958), 20 September, p. 1.

Scott, P. (1988), 'On the silly side', editorial in *The Times Higher Education Supplement*, 11 November, p. 40.

Secretary of State for Education and Science, Secretary of State for Wales, Secretary of State for Northern Ireland, and Secretary of State for Scotland (1987), *Higher Education: Meeting the Challenge*, HMSO Cm 114, London.

Silver, H. and Brennan, J. (1988), *A Liberal Vocationalism*, Methuen, London.

Taylor, C. (1989), *Sources of the Self: The Making of the Modern Identity*, Cambridge University Press, Cambridge.

Williams, G. (1985), 'Graduate employment and vocationalism in higher education', *European Journal of Education*, 20, 2–3, pp. 181–192.

12 Liberalism after communism: The Czech civil service

Ludek Kolman

The words 'liberal' and 'liberalism' denote multifaceted concepts: they mean considerably different things to different people at various times and in different places – a state of affairs to which the current Czech political scene bears witness. Liberal ideas and ideals are professed, or at least mouthed, by various political factions who readily accuse one another, now of being, now of not being, 'liberals'. [1] Because of these confusions and ambiguities, it is difficult to locate these concepts in a clear-cut way in the central or eastern European context. Notwithstanding this, however, it is clear that liberal ideas played an important rôle in the overthrow of communism at the end of 1989; and that these ideas, for all the differences that they cover, nonetheless denote at the very least a certain set of convictions about individuals and their rôle in society, convictions which may perhaps be characterized as permissive as opposed to authoritarian; and individualistic as opposed to totalitarian. It is thus that Václav Havel, then the hero of the revolution, and now President, may be understood as both expressing and embodying liberal ideals – the right of the individual to perceive the world in his or her own way and, crucially, to act upon that perception in the pursuit of his or her own freely chosen ends (Havel, 1989, 1990). What this amounts to in political practice, and across the differences to which I have adverted, is primarily a commitment to a certain way of doing things, a certain sort of practice – in short, to **rational** procedures and practices. For the openness which is a necessary condition of individuals' functioning vis-à-vis society in the way I have indicated has to be explicitly created and protected, as Hobbes suggested in a more general context (1968): [2] and this is a requirement which cannot be met in the absence of such procedures and practices. Not surprisingly, then, as other contributors to this volume have noted, liberalism is predicated on a characterization of human beings as essentially rational.

I

The Czech civil service, in common with other areas of political life in the Czech Republic, finds itself peopled by many whose broad commitment to liberalism is similar to that of Havel. It is not at all surprising, then, that the civil service might be expected to function along rational lines, however imperfectly. And yet, as was evident to me from my two years at the Czechoslovak Federal Ministry of the Environment, the changeover from totalitarian to more rational patterns of thought and action is far from complete or successful: the clashing views, outlooks and attitudes in evidence there belie any easily liberal characterization. Far from adopting rational procedures in order to fulfil professed aims, in fact, this particular institution (one which there is no reason to think significantly different in this respect from other organs of state) seems prey to a variety of internal pressures which dramatically hinder any such transformation. Furthermore, these appear to be such as to constitute more than the inevitable imperfections or teething-troubles one might reasonably expect in such circumstances.

Three possible explanations suggest themselves: the liberal commitment of those involved is not at all what they profess it to be, and, indeed, may be thought of as something of a sham; or the proportion of committed liberals in the Czech civil service is simply insufficient to win out against opposing forces; or liberalism (as I have minimally described it) is not equal to its self-imposed task of rational planning and activity. What I want to suggest here is that, tempting though some of these hypotheses may be, they are, whether singly or even collectively, inadequate. It is certainly the case, of course, that today's civil service retains to some considerable extent the approach of the communist period, when there existed a strict hierarchy of command, obedience, rules and procedures, all dedicated to the pursuit of unrealizable ends, a hierarchy which gave rise to slack management and bureaucratic rites rather than producing any concrete achievements. It is equally the case that most of the entrants to the Czech(oslovak) civil service since 1990 are highly educated, of considerable professional reputation in their respective fields and generally committed to liberal ideals of individual achievement, respect for the views of others, and so on. And yet it is also the case that many of these new people are so individualistic as to make it difficult for them to cooperate with others. Nor have they fully understood the practical purpose of routine; and, as professionals, often prefer dealing with discrete problems in the isolation of the viewpoints of their specific expertise rather than attempting realistically or coherently to plan for the future. Moreover, both these groups seem to suffer from a common weakness, even if it is one which has different roots in each case – namely the sheer difficulty of actually taking the decisive action required, however urgent it might be. Furthermore, along with this defensively passive attitude, there is a considerable amount to be found in common between these two kinds of civil servant, despite their many differences. Even on an informal and partial basis of observation, it is clear that they share quite specific patterns of thought, as manifested in their behaviour, day-to-day actions and speech – and that these patterns appear superficially to be irrational.

It is these apparently irrational patterns, however, which afford a clue to understanding what is actually going on; why the three explanations suggested earlier are inadequate; and the sense in which liberalism might – for all its differences and confusions – in fact serve as an antidote to the cause of such patterns' prevalence. What I have in mind is the idea of **myth**: the supposition that if myth and its attendant irrationality were as powerful and immovable as at first glance they might appear to be, then the values of liberalism would be of no practical use; but that, since this need not be the case, these values remain not only conceptually intact – precisely as antidote to myth – but of practical value in the everyday organization of a post-totalitarian state.

These suggestions raise questions too large to answer in an article such as this, of course. But, if the following analysis of myth and its rôle serves at least to stimulate consideration of the issues to which it points, and particularly that of liberalism's arguably emancipatory rôle in relation to mythologized practice, then I will have accomplished my aim.

II

Myth is not some ancient and/or culturally unsophisticated narrative. There are myths which proliferate here today: and they impact directly on people's thought and practice. Myth, it may be claimed, is in part constitutive of the development – whether for better or worse – of nations and societies. [3]

The myths of the ancients which we learned about at high school are primarily grand narratives: and it might at first appear to be a large step to compare these with so-called 'primitive' myths, such as those of the Amazonian Indians. For not only are such myths historically and culturally more foreign to us – since it is, after all, the former which have to an extent formed and informed our own culture – but, more importantly, the grand narrative which the latter constitute is usually unwritten, a matter of oral tradition only. Furthermore, as such cultures become influenced by that of the west, so these narrative fragments are lost from everyday life. And yet it is precisely in this respect that such 'primitive' myths afford a clue to those operating in our own culture. In the case of contemporary myths, too, the narrative is largely missing, so that the evidence of their very existence is incomplete and fragmentary. If a contemporary myth is to be brought to the surface, it has to be searched for; detected by clues and cues; and, finally, reconstructed. There is a danger in such a procedure, of course, that the researcher might easily fall into the trap of confusing or even conflating such a reconstruction with his or her own inventions. Not even the purest ethnomethodology is wholly immune from such danger, however sophisticated – or innocent – the researcher concerned. Nevertheless, once entered, such a caveat may best be transposed into a version of one more prevalent still: let the reader beware. My own tool, then, is Lévi-Strauss's notion of a structure of polar opposites which underlies all myths: and I shall simply take it – since here is neither the place nor the space to enter that debate – that the possibility of the presence of such a structure might serve as a test of the validity of any reconstruction.

The particular contemporary myths I am going to deal with, then, are mostly the heritage of the bygone era of communism, although not without accretions from recent political and social changes. How far and how deep their roots stretch into the past is, again, beyond my scope here. Suffice it to say, however, that, even if there actually never was any complete grand narrative, any all-encompassing tale, then the possibility that such a tale may nonetheless be reconstructed from the fragments – yet again a task for which this is but a prolegomenon – may be justification enough of the direction and form of my attempted analysis. [4] It should be noted also that, although discussion of my four main myths takes place in the context of the Czech civil service, these myths as they are manifested in that institution are instances of a much wider phenomenon, encompassing the whole of society, and, indeed, of societies.

The myth of mystic information is, perhaps, the most conspicuous case of a myth at work in the Czech administration. To explain its operations it is necessary to digress a little into recent history, and to show what was meant by 'information' and what rôle it played under the communist regime.

Information may generally be viewed as a set of facts or data. But – however concrete – a set of facts or data serves no purpose in its own right: taken alone, such a set is devoid of meaning. To serve as information, facts or data have to be incorporated into a conceptual whole, often called by philosophers a **model of the world**, and by psychologists an **image**. People generally develop an image or model by learning, correcting errors and clearing up uncertainties; and it is in this way that new information becomes possible, let alone usable, since it is thus that (a set of) facts or data become(s) information. Under the communist regime, however, there was no such development, for it held fast just to one firm and unchangeable image, or model, of the world – one set by the Party committees' decrees and directions. Consequently, facts played only a secondary rôle in the public administration of communist Czechoslovakia. They were thought of as relevant and accurately (re)presented only insofar as they conformed to the officially accepted model of the world. Acceptable facts served, so to speak, as decoration for administrative acts; unacceptable ones were suppressed. This practice became so widespread that it was accepted even by the general public as an easy and automatic response to everyday facts. Most importantly, even the exceptions – for not everyone accepted the Party view of the world, of course – accepted without knowing it the underlying structure of 'fact' or 'data' as something given. Their image of the world was quite often simply a negation of the Party model. What was broadcast by the Party was just assumed to be simply the opposite of what was actually the case: western European unemployment statistics, for example. The myth of information as 'mystic', as divorced from the realities of the world, was accepted: by some consciously, and even cynically; by many others inadvertently.

This process was, of course, both long drawn out and uncompleted. Nevertheless, it led to a significant loss of capacity to learn from facts, a loss which continues to take its toll in politics, administration, everyday life and human relations in the Czech Republic to this day. The field of public administration is perhaps the clearest exemplification of this process. The fall of communism in 1989 left administrators without any means of forming and adjusting a functional model of the world, with the result that the image used remains under-determined and the administrators uncertain and confused. Even now, one might come across some older civil servants who try to substitute President Havel's speeches for the Party decrees of the past, and the slogans of a market economy for those of a socialist society. But even these civil servants tend to feel that there is something wrong, even if they do not know why.

In October 1990, then, I conducted a small survey in the Office of the Prime Minister in which I asked people what they took to be the rôle of an expert adviser. The answers were almost uniformly of the following stereotype:

> Here, in the Government Office, we need really top experts, people knowledgeable in their respective fields, who know where to gain relevant information. A good adviser is a person who, in their field, can hear the grass growing.

This answer correlates in a rather peculiar way with established practice. The only information with which an adviser to the Office is supplied is reports of cabinet proceedings; reports and other communications put before the cabinet; and details of laws passed. This all represents output information: input information, however, seems to be nonexistent. It is apparently assumed that 'an adviser' simply happens to have all the input information required, as if he or she were personally an information source, or as if he or she were able to gain the relevant information from some special, commonly inaccessible source. At the same time, and not surprisingly, there are hardly any information services in the Office. The library is small, smaller in fact than many technical libraries at the head offices of Czech industrial enterprises: in particular, for example, there are hardly any technical journals, and certainly none from abroad.

The key phrase in the answer seems to be 'hear the grass growing'. In Czech it means exactly the same as in English: 'to be of preternatural acuteness', as the Oxford Dictionary puts it. [5] The Office apparently requests the services of people with quite special capabilities, people who are able to gain access to hidden truths, to a reality unapproachable to someone who lacks peculiar gifts of empathy, intuition or some such – people, as it were, almost out of this world. Such information, which is treated as appertaining to hidden truths, is **mystic information**: as such, it may be construed as having hardly anything at all to do with facts or data. And this is because mystic information – although never, of course, called such – is held to reveal some sort of fundamental essence, of which facts and data appear to be merely accidental and often misleading manifestations. This is precisely the standard view of the nature and rôle of facts which used to be taken by communist ideology in its practice. The most important consideration for political commissars and their bureaucratic equivalents was the same: to ensure the correct exposition of reality. What that reality might actually be like was always of secondary importance, if of any importance at all. The access to hidden truths predicated on some generally unknown image or model of the world demanded of today's government adviser seems just the same as that claimed, disingenuously or otherwise, by his or her communist predecessor. The problem is that both the process of generating mystic information and the model of 'information' on which it is based have outlived their source – i.e., the commissar, the ideology, the Party. Even if such a model were desirable, however – and assuming it to be conceptually at least not more obviously inconsistent or otherwise unworkable than alternatives – there is now, *mirabile dictu*, simply no-one who might be able to plan and coordinate practice predicated upon it: for disingenuousness at **some** level would be required for this to be possible in a wider world **not** controlled by such a myth.

The myth of special expertise is hardly anything new, nor something specific to Czech administration: but it is intimately connected in this country with the myth of mystic information. Whereas facts or data are open to everyone, access to mystic information is available only to those of a very special stamp, initiates possessed of extraordinary sensitivity. To be thus initiated might be thought to require taking part in prescribed rites and ceremonies: but sometimes, it seems, time itself is sufficient. It is just conceivable, in fact, that an administrator might perhaps mature to the appropriate state of initiation just by sitting all alone at his or her office desk: and it is generally agreed that, in the case of Czech civil servants, such maturation takes at least four years.

There are, of course, costs as well as benefits attendant upon waiting for a civil servant thus to mature: and the main benefit is a certain stability within the civil services, coupled with feelings of security among individual civil servants. This latter benefit is so important a phenomenon that it will be useful to digress somewhat at this point to explain its workings. A myth, once accepted, repeatedly reasserts and reconfirms itself, much as does a self-fulfilling prophecy. Through such reassertion are gained feelings of certainty and mental security; and these in turn help to strengthen the myth in question. The world of myth is thus stable and predictable; and a believer can perceive such a world as a whole, without lacunae, contradictions or other such unwelcome features. In contrast, the world of those of us who care about facts is one characterized by limitation, incoherence and fragmentation: it is a mosaic with only the merest hint of a pattern here and there. It is extremely hard to accept the latter sort of view, that is to say, a realistic view of the world – and this most especially in times of great change, when we have most need of certainty, and when at the same time the one thing we can know for certain is that we know almost nothing at all. Refusal to adopt a myth in such circumstances seems a wilful concession to chaos, a chaos which constitutes a danger to one's very integrity. It is quite understandable, therefore, that a believer's response if asked to abandon such belief for the uncertainties of the real world is often withdrawal, negativism or aggression. Far safer to sit still, to learn by experience, to defer to the initiate with special access to mystic information – and to await what might, with luck, be one's own maturation to similar status.

The myth of a world exactly as I believe it to be is another example of a cognitive construct common to many eras. We might readily admit that our ideas and beliefs rarely correspond with how things really are in the external world. Yet some self-assurance and trust in one's own mental processes is a prerequisite of any normal mental functioning at all. What is required, then, is a substantial degree of agreement between what one thinks and what actually exists, and one which has to be attained, moreover, on the basis of some accord with the ideas and beliefs of other people: for without this interpersonal agreement the very possibility of knowing anything would break down. Some such agreement may, of course, be gained by investigation of what other people think, by observation, and by experimentation. But to do this a person has to be open to surprise, paradox and disharmony, something which is hardly to be expected in the practice of people considerably unsure of their own grounds. And yet it is precisely to the extent that one is unsure of oneself, of one's ideas and of their relation to how the world actually is, that one's uncertainty needs to be accepted and affirmed, if one is not to fall into the sort of mistaken certainty outlined above. Given this paradoxical state of affairs, it is hardly surprising that what actually tends to happen is that civil servants, like everyone else, play safe – but in their case with the particular consequences which arise from the fact that theirs is a profession whose immediate object is, in an important sense, information. The result is that the profession is beset by conflict between 'different worlds', a conflict with obvious implications and ramifications for the real world with which it deals: action tends often to be ineffective because it is premissed upon mistaken notions of what is actually the case in the world.

The myth of the one right way is one which perhaps derives directly from our immediate past, a heritage of marxist-leninist totalitarianism, a totalitarianism with which even those opposed to the Communist regime were imbued. It is of course all the more insidious for that, making positive change – as opposed to the substitution of one orthodoxy by another – even more difficult that it might otherwise be. The fallacy in which the myth results is one of over-systematization, based on the supposition that all cases must in principle be amenable to some one overall hypothesis, interpretation, explanation, etc., and thus susceptible of some one grand solution. But what holds in one case need not necessarily hold in another: to suppose otherwise is to demand just that certainty which is the object of the previous myth, for it is to insist on a holism rooted in some one fixed image of the world. Neither, however, need be the case. As with the myths of a world exactly as I believe it to be and that of special expertise, the myth of one right way is intimately bound up with, and ultimately, I would argue, a function of, the myth of mystic information; although it must of course be conceded that such questions of logical and anthropological priority are both complex and controversial, demanding more detailed treatment than is possible here.

Having dealt, albeit only in outline, largely with myths at work in the post-communist Czech bureaucracy, let me outline four myths which find broader application, and which seem to me to require analysis, understanding and, ultimately, extirpation, if democracy is to flourish where communism once reigned. They are – in, I think, ascending order of importance – the following: the myth that 'I can manage all alone'; the myth of 'Silly John'; the myth of success as theft; and the myth of advent. The first two are relatively well known. They are based in a conviction about the exclusiveness of the acting subject, but otherwise they differ substantially: the first is manifest in the behaviour of certain post-revolutionary politicians and administrators; the second is firmly embedded in the Czech national culture. The third and fourth are, I think, more deep-rooted – and thus less well-known. As such, they seem to me to be all the more dangerous, especially as they are also particularly inimical to the development of a democratic process. For this very reason, they demand especially detailed research and analysis, beyond the scope of the present article; I shall here only refer to them very briefly, therefore.

The myth of success as theft represents the commonly held conviction, in the Czech Republic at least, that to be successful is one and the same thing as denying success to another: in a word, *schadenfreude*. **The myth of advent**, which might explain the dissatisfaction currently felt by so many, refers to the expectation that the overthrow of communism would lead to a succession of miracles whereby all the problems created and/or left unsolved under the old regime would vanish. As no miracles have occurred – or at least, not miracles of the kind expected – people feel betrayed, or even deceived. And therein lie great dangers for the future: for the prevalence of feelings, let alone convictions, such as these invites not democracy but authoritarianism.

The first myth, **the myth that 'I can manage all alone'** was clearly manifested in the actions of a considerable number of politicians shortly after the overthrow of the old regime. Believers in this myth typically indulge in massive displays of activity, often haphazard and uncoordinated; they make little effort to communicate with others; cooperation and negotiation are replaced by the frantic efforts of those convinced of their own indispensability. Again, this is not, I think, simply a psychological observation about particular individuals, although it is of course also that. Rather, it is a logical corollary of that 'large scale', society-wide myth of mystic information to which I referred earlier together with that, again generalized, of special expertise: for if there were such a thing as knowledge available only to the initiate; and if I were one of the initiated; then naturally I would be of the first importance.

Turning to the second, arguably particularly national, myth, the most popular hero of Czech fairy tales is a character named Silly John, a young peasant who succeeds against all odds and marries the young queen. The fairy tale and its underlying thesis – special powers may be gained through local birth and knowledge, and/or by remaining local, naive, uneducated, inexperienced and uncorrupted by the sophistication of the metropolis – seems to serve as a model for many Czechs. Believers in **the myth of Silly John** do not put their trust in the industry and forbearance of the protestant ethic; instead, they have faith in themselves as having some 'special nature' through which they will eventually win through and inherit the world. In consequence, they have no interest in learning anything new, lest it blemish the purity of their parochialism and transform them into just those sophisticates they despise. [6]

III

Václav Havel (1985) characterized the period of communist rule as a peculiarly timeless era: and this with good reason. For there really is nothing like linear physical time to be found in the world of myths, whether communist, Amazonian or any other. Rather, mythic time resembles the sort of time experienced in dreams, a time which is characterized by changes of speed, scale and direction: an unfocussed dream-time where past, present and future coexist in some fuzzy whole. In much this fashion, time under communism – that is to say, the sort of time that communist mythology dealt in – consisted in the rhythms of the progression of its guiding ideas; a non-material time, then, unconfined by human-related parameters of place or space. It is thus hardly surprising that the thinking and behaviour of people living under the conditions of such a myth should have been characterized by a certain detachment and abstraction from the real world.

Now, if one follows through Lévi-Strauss's structuralist theory of polar opposites in relation to myth, then what one would expect also to be broadly affective – if nevertheless in absentia – under the domination of such a mythology are connection and concreteness. Recalling the salient features of the myths outlines earlier, then, one might thus posit the following table of polar opposites in relation to ex-Czechoslovakia's immediate past and thus to the present state of affairs in the Czech Republic:

Inner experience	Information derived from the outside world
The gifts of an initiate	Skills gained by learning
Conservatism	Openness to change
Detachment	Connectedness
Abstraction	Concreteness

This table suggests an underlying structure to what I have so far been describing: the left-hand column contains characteristics and attitudes, together with their epistemological and ontological conditions, which are regarded as good; the right-hand column their polar opposites which are regarded as bad. Efforts to promote the latter thus produce psychological and conceptual stress – stress which is the consequence of the changes the people of this country are living through, a response both psychologically acquired and conceptually formed during the decades of the communist regime.

At this point I need to say more about the idea of polar opposites. Lévi-Strauss's ideas were based on those originally developed by linguists concerned with analysing human speech. The act of understanding a spoken word, they argued, may be construed as the differentiation of binary distinctions such as vowel–consonant or voiced–unvoiced. For example, it is the second distinction which enables us to know whether it is 'fan' or 'van' which is being said. This idea was first generalized in application to other linguistic categories, and then to the study of human culture and social systems, conceived by structuralists as structures of meaning. Lévi-Strauss, then, uses such polar opposites to analyse the myths of Amazonian Indians and others:

> ... If we compare two matrilinear tribes such as the Iroquois and the Manda of North America, whose modes of life include both agriculture and hunting, we are at first surprised to discover that, in spite of the features they have in common, their respective mythological systems link the high and the low with opposite sexual rôles ... (1986, p. 331)

This exemplifies the way in which Lévi-Strauss sifts through ethnographic and anthropological material, picking out pairs such as sky–earth, young–old, fire–water, or human–animal and weaves them into an impeccably logical pattern. Once such a pattern is woven, one perceives quite clearly that it was there all along; but that it had been hitherto obscured by its own detail.

Or again, take his explanation of an old custom in La Vendée which prescribes a special procedure respecting the marriage of the youngest child of a family. A bladder full of water is placed at the top of a young tree decorated with flowers, and surrounded by bundles of sticks and faggots. On her return from the religious ceremony, the young bride is asked to light the fire and the husband has to shoot at the bladder to burst it. Now the rite, Lévi-Strauss tells us, links this desirable social conjunction with a conjunction between the elements, water and fire, to which might be attributed cosmological significance (ibid., p. 330): the mythic mediates between opposites and contradictions in the world as ordinarily perceived. Myths, for Lévi-Strauss, are the means whereby harmony and peace are built out of the chaos of contrary and opposing forces which threaten the human existence. We may expect an analysis of myths, therefore, to teach us more about ourselves.

Myth, however, always assumes some kind of external intelligible force, existing independently of any individual human mind. But liberalism **denies precisely any such force**, whether it be that which structuralists insist is common to all myths, or some other allegedly external force such as the class struggle of Marx, the archetypes of Jungian psychology or even the universal linguistic structures of Chomsky. Thus to the extent that myth plays a rôle in the thinking and practice of a society, to that extent such a society is influenced by the notion of some 'external' force, or at the very least, constraint, acting upon it; and, specifically, following Lévi-Strauss, the polar structure of such a force or constraint. Liberalism, however, with its insistence on reason – as against any 'external' determination, whether Marxist, Jungian or anything else – stands against such mythic practice, even though it might be said to seek to achieve ends similar to those otherwise pursued through myth. What is important is that liberalism is not some alternative myth, however, but rather not a myth at all: and that is precisely what distinguishes it from other political theories. Thus, for example, liberalism claims not to have a substantive notion of the good, so that, in relation to justice, it could be said to constitute a procedure. It might be added that it is in this respect too that it is to be distinguished from any political theory or practice reliant upon myth: for a myth is always a set of contexts and not a way of doing things. If liberalism has any mythic element at all, then it is one which consists in its perhaps naive belief that peace and harmony are realizable social ideas. But that, I would argue, is very far from constituting the sort of full-scale myth which I have been describing; and this just to that extent that it is not marked by structural polar opposites. Its commitment to rationality and to 'raw' facts as, so to speak, mirrors of the world, mark it off from **any** mythical system. It is because liberalism is fundamentally anti-mythical that the transition to it is proving so difficult and so beset by contradiction and paradox. For the adoption of liberal attitudes and systems involves the rejection of myth tout court rather than the substitution of one (set of) myth(s) by another. No wonder, then, that people in post-communist central and eastern Europe, even while advocating liberal ideas, nevertheless perceive the world and believe in it in ways quite incompatible with their stated ideals.

Addendum

The first draft of this article was written in the spring of 1991, on the basis of the author's personal experiences as an adviser in the Czech Government Office (i.e. the office of the Czech Prime Minister). A year later, elections in Czechoslovakia resulted in a stark polarization of the nation: and both Czech–Slovak and right–left distinctions and disagreements were so strong that they were cited as the two reasons for splitting the country. The above analysis of myth, however embryonic, makes it possible to explain these unhappy events rather as workings of defence mechanisms in response to the stresses and anxieties of post-communist times. New, post-communist myths have replaced the old ones; one set of rigidities has been replaced by another; and quite a number of erstwhile believers settle for another kind of totalitarianism which they find more comfortable than the uncertainties of the world as it actually is. To understand the myths of post-communism and the set of a post-communist mind, then, might be of practical help in supporting the development of democracy in central and eastern Europe. If this is to be achieved, however, still more myths will have to be analysed, understood and dissipated.

Notes

1. Cf. 'conservative' in today's Russia.
2. *Leviathan*, Pt. 1, especially Ch. 13: 'where men live without other security, than what their own strength, and their own invention shall furnish them withall ... the life of man [is] solitary, poore, nasty, brutish, and short' (1968, p. 168, para. 62).
3. Compare Barthes' characterization of myth as cited by Tom Hickey in 'They are not tigers ...', p. 61 of this volume.
4. This is, of course, a large and interesting problem, and one which calls into question the very distinction between myth and reality. How far should we go with postmodernism?
5. Translator's note: the recent history of the traditional saying, 'There's someone who can hear the grass growing' – used to refer to those who have their ear so close to the ground that no nuance of a situation escapes them – is instructive. In the immediate aftermath of 1989, the new prime minister, Petr Pithart, was in the habit of using the phrase to remind people that there were more important things to do than raking over the details of people's pro-, non- or anti-communist credentials. As things have been turning out, however, more attention to just these considerations might well have repaid the effort: for the grass was in fact growing all along, so to speak. Partly consonant with this is its common current usage: people attempting to conceal their own limitations and/or pasts or attempting to deny the reality of a state of affairs, will often seek to deflect analysis or interrogation by referring to their interlocutor's 'overemphasis' on detail, as an insistence of over-fussy people trying to hear the grass growing. The phrase may also be used to 'explain away' one's own lack of knowledge: 'I've no patience with listening to the grass grow'. More subtly, it may be used positively as a cover to avoid taking action – despite one's clear understanding of what is needed – because one is unsure of an opponent's response.
6. Deeply rooted though this myth is in Czech culture, it is by no means unique to it, as students of societies marked by a nostalgia for variously lost golden ages will know very well.

References

Havel, V. (1985), 'The power of the powerless', in Keane, J. (ed.), *The Power of the Powerless: Citizens against the State in central-eastern Europe*, Hutchinson, London.
Havel, V. (1989), *Living in Truth*, Faber, London.
Havel, V. (1990), *Disturbing the Peace: A Conversation with Karel Hvíždálka*, Hvíždálka, K. (ed.), Faber, London.
Hobbes, T. (1968), *Leviathan*, Macpherson, C.B. (ed.), Pelican, Harmondsworth.
Lévi-Strauss, C. (1986), *The Raw and the Cooked*, Penguin, Harmondsworth.

Contributors

Richard Bellamy is Professor of Politics in the School of Economic and Social Studies at the University of East Anglia. His many publications include *Modern Italian Social Theory* (1987), *Liberalism and Modern Society* (1992) and, with Darrow Schecter, *Gramsci and the Italian State* (1993) as well as numerous articles in journals and collections. His main interests include political philosophy, especially liberalism, and Italian politics.

Bob Brecher is Principal Lecturer in Philosophy in the School of Historical and Critical Studies at the University of Brighton. His publications include *Anselm's Argument: the Logic of Divine Existence* (1984) and articles in the *Journal of Medical Ethics*, *Radical Philosophy*, *Philosophy*, etc. and in various collections. His main interests are in moral philosophy and he is currently working on a critique of liberal morality.

Phillip Cole is Lecturer in Applied Philosophy in the Department of Philosophy and Religion at Middlesex University. His publications include 'Social liberty and the physically disabled', *Journal of Applied Philosophy* (1987) and his main interest is in political theory; he is currently working on issues of citizenship and cultural identity.

Avner de-Shalit is Lecturer in Political Philosophy and Environmental Ethics and Politics in the Department of Political Science at the Hebrew University, Jerusalem. His publications include several articles on environmental ethics and on Rawls; and a book on obligations to future generations, entitled *Why Posterity Matters* (forthcoming).

Pat FitzGerald is working on a doctorate on analytical feminism in the Department of Philosophy at the University of Kent, and is a visiting lecturer in the School of Historical and Critical Studies at the University of Brighton. Her main research interests are in biological essentialism in feminist theories and in the relationship between feminist theory and political practice.

Otakar Fleischmann is Lecturer in Psychology in the Faculty of Education at J.E. Purkyně University, Ústí nad Labem. His publications include, with Stanislav Navrátil and Karel Klimeš, *Komunikace v Pedagogických Situacích* (*Communication in Educational Contexts*) (1993) and his main interests are in communication theory and in psychological issues surrounding immigration.

Jo Halliday is Head of Academic Standards and Audit at Anglia Polytechnic University. Her publications include another article on the ideological function of vocationalizing the higher education curriculum, entitled 'Maoist Britain?', in *Curriculum Studies* (forthcoming). Her main research interest is in an analysis of how liberal ideology comes to permit public policy to be defined in particular party political terms; and in the rôle of rhetoric in this process.

Tom Hickey is Principal Lecturer in Political Economy in the School of Historical and Critical Studies at the University of Brighton. His publications include, with Bob Brecher, 'In defence of bias' in *Studies in Higher Education* (1991). His main research interests are in social theory and in the philosophy and economics of liberalism.

Carol Jones is an MA student in the Department of Philosophy at the University of Warwick. She has published 'Reason without emotion' in *Radical Philosophy* (1992) and her main research interest is in a Kantian approach, with radical feminist modifications, to problems of the self and of rationality; and in the political, ethical and economic implications arising from particular philosophical models.

Ludek Kolman is Head of the Department of Social Resources at J.E. Purkyně University, Ústí nad Labem. His publications include *Pamět a Rozpoznávání* (*Memory and Recognition*) (1976), *Rukověť Vedení Lidí* (*Manual of Leadership*) (1987) and *Psychologie Pro Mladého Managera* (*Psychology for the Young Manager*) (1989). His research interests include management psychology and architectural theory.

Miroslav Kryl is Lecturer in History and Political Science in the Education Faculty of J.E. Purkyně University, Ústí nad Labem. His publications include 'Deportacje wezniow terezinskiego getto do obozm koncetracyjego na majdankw' ('The deportation of prisoners from the prison in the Terezin ghetto to Majdanek concentration camp'), *Zeszyty*

Majdanka (1983) and 'Karel Hermann's collection, 1942–45: a significant source of information about prisoners' activities in Terezin concentration camp', *Pragno Jedota Bohemia* (1986). His research interests include anti-semitism and theories of history.

Marcus Roberts is working on a doctorate on the origins and development of analytical marxism in the School of Historical and Critical Studies at the University of Brighton, and has reviewed for *Radical Philosophy*. His other research interests include personal identity, themes in social and political philosophy and Hannah Arendt.

Alina Zvinkliene is a Sociologist in the Institute of Philosophy, Sociology and Law of the Lithuanian Academy of Sciences. Her numerous publications include 'The character of changes in attitude to marriage' in Matulionis, A (ed.), *Sociological Research into the Way of Life of Youth* (1988); with Popov, A, 'The necessity of family planning in Lithuania', *Filosofija, Socioloija* (1991); and 'Reproductive freedom in the former USSR', *Journal of Psychosomatic Obstetrics and Gynaecology* (1992). Her main research interests include issues concerning the family and the status of women. She is currently working on wider questions of contemporary society and politics.